P9-AFA-984

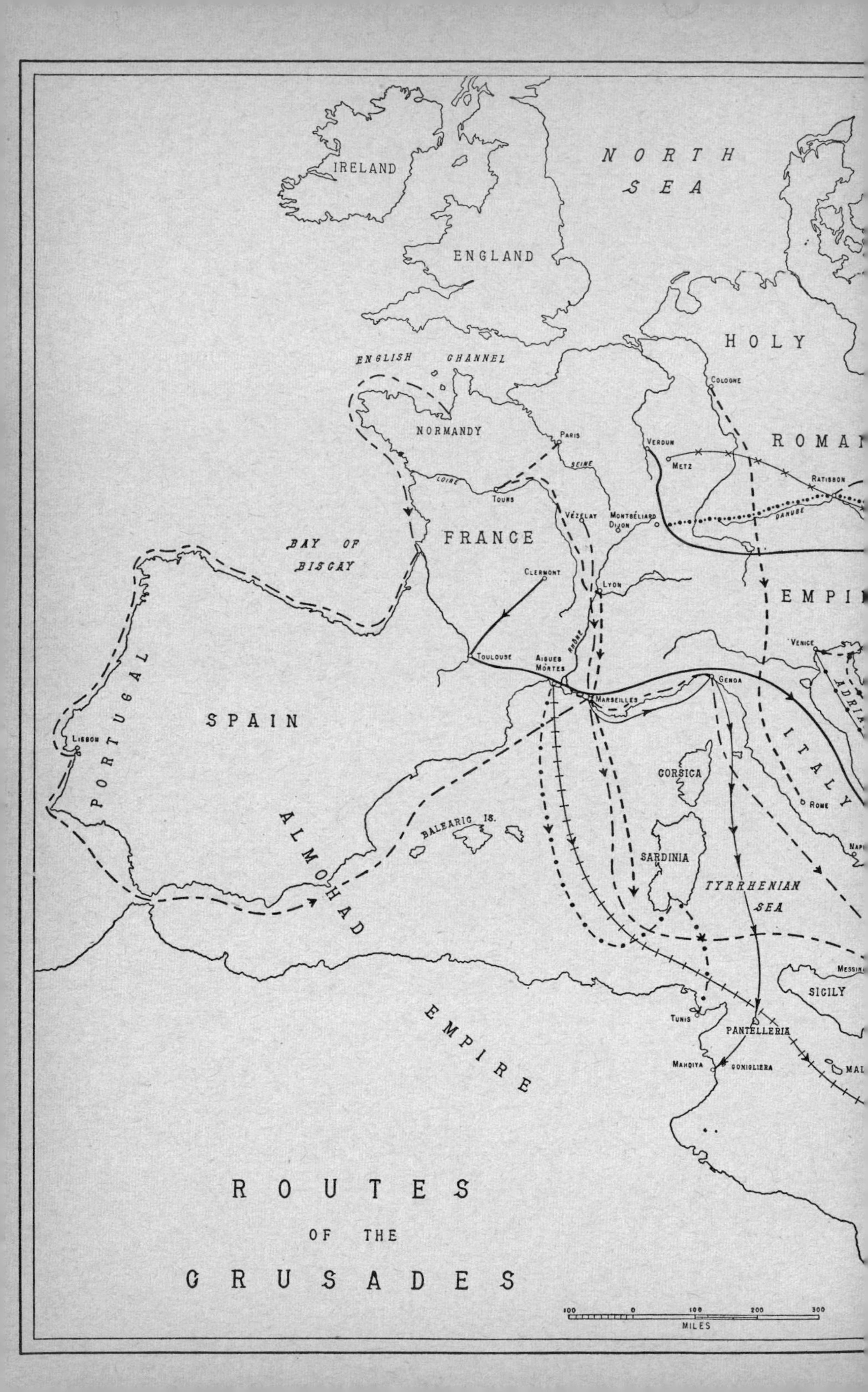

ROUTES OF THE CRUSADES

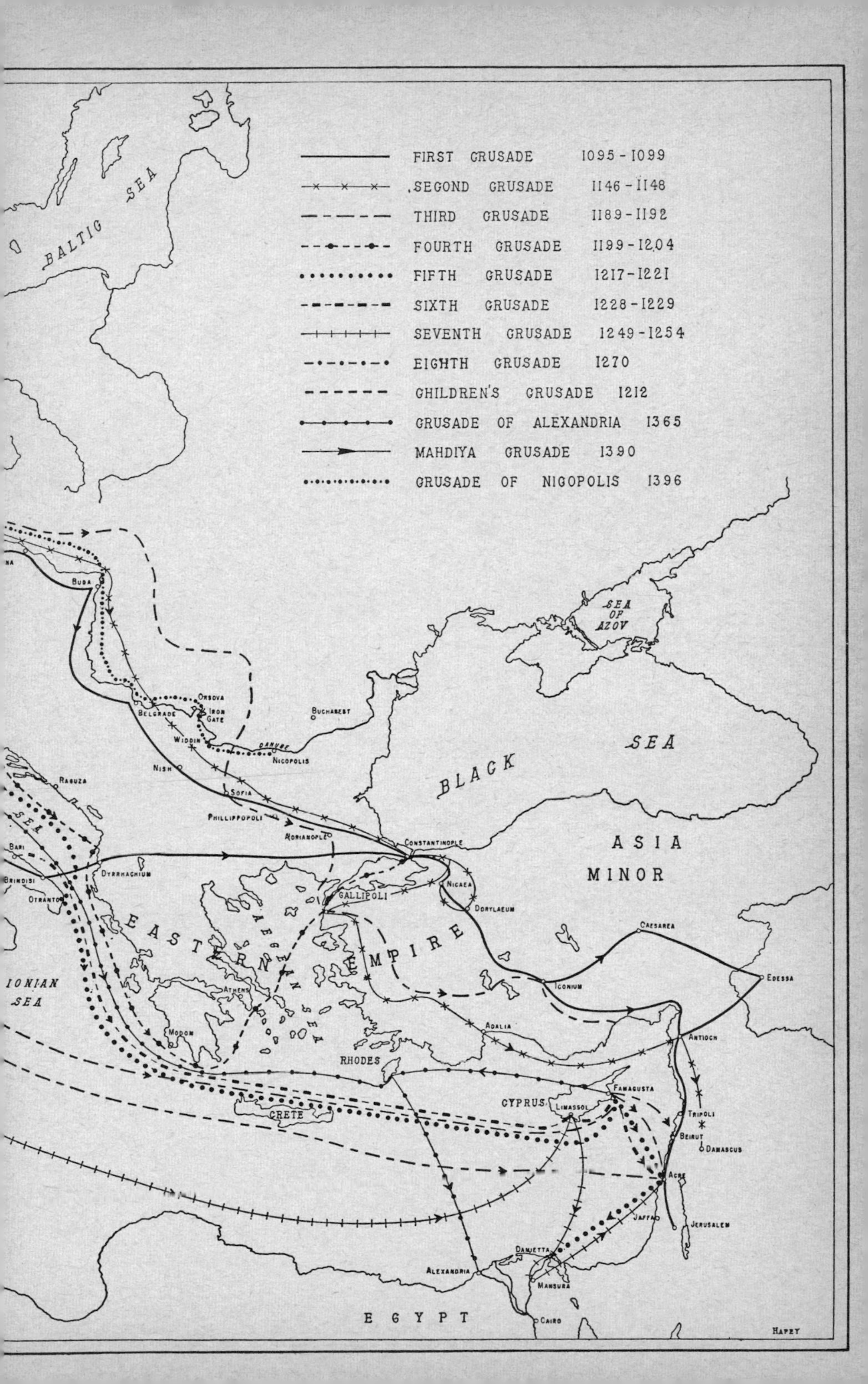
FIRST CRUSADE 1095-1099
SECOND CRUSADE 1146-1148
THIRD CRUSADE 1189-1192
FOURTH CRUSADE 1199-1204
FIFTH CRUSADE 1217-1221
SIXTH CRUSADE 1228-1229
SEVENTH CRUSADE 1249-1254
EIGHTH CRUSADE 1270
CHILDREN'S CRUSADE 1212
CRUSADE OF ALEXANDRIA 1365
MAHDIYA CRUSADE 1390
CRUSADE OF NICOPOLIS 1396
BALTIC SEA
SEA OF AZOV
BLACK SEA
ASIA MINOR
EASTERN EMPIRE
AEGEAN SEA
IONIAN SEA
Buda
Belgrade
Orsova
Iron Gate
Widdin
Danube
Nicopolis
Bucharest
Nish
Sofia
Ragusa
Phillippopoli
Adrianople
Constantinople
Bari
Brindisi
Otranto
Dyrrhachium
Gallipoli
Nicaea
Dorylaeum
Caesarea
Edessa
Iconium
Athens
Modon
Adalia
Antioch
Rhodes
Crete
Cyprus
Limassol
Famagusta
Tripoli
Beirut
Damascus
Acre
Jaffa
Jerusalem
Damietta
Mansura
Alexandria
Cairo
EGYPT
Hapzy

Crusade, Commerce and Culture

Crusade, Commerce and Culture

AZIZ S. ATIYA

SCIENCE EDITIONS®
John Wiley & Sons, Inc., New York

THIS BOOK HAS BEEN PUBLISHED WITH THE
ASSISTANCE OF A GRANT FROM THE FORD FOUNDATION

PUBLICATION AS A SCIENCE EDITIONS PAPERBACK
AUTHORIZED BY INDIANA UNIVERSITY PRESS

FIRST SCIENCE EDITIONS PRINTING 1966
SCIENCE EDITIONS TRADEMARK REG. U.S. PAT. OFF.

LIBRARY OF CONGRESS CATALOG CARD NUMBER: 62–8980
MANUFACTURED IN THE UNITED STATES OF AMERICA

THE PATTEN FOUNDATION

Mr. Will Patten of Indianapolis (A.B., Indiana University, 1893) made, in 1931, a gift for the establishment of the Patten Foundation at his Alma Mater. Under the terms of this gift, which became available upon the death of Mr. Patten (May 3, 1936), there is to be chosen each year a Visiting Professor who is to be in residence several weeks during the year. The purpose of this prescription is to provide an opportunity for members and friends of the University to enjoy the privilege and advantage of personal acquaintance with the Visiting Professor. The Visiting Professor for the Patten Foundation in 1957 was

PROFESSOR AZIZ S. ATIYA

NOTE

This is a companion volume to
THE CRUSADE: HISTORIOGRAPHY AND BIBLIOGRAPHY
published simultaneously by Indiana University Press

Contents

Maps

Preface

THE PRESENT VOLUME contains the enlarged substance of a series of six lectures delivered at Indiana University under the auspices of the Patten Foundation. For the honor of my election as Patten Lecturer for the year 1957, I am truly grateful and appreciative.

My interest in the study of the relations between the East and the West is as old as my academic career; I started lecturing on the subject at the School of Oriental Studies in the University of London more than a quarter of a century ago in the academic session 1933–34. Of necessity, my material has undergone considerable emendation and development in the process of repeated lecturing on various aspects of it in the numerous educational centers where I was engaged in teaching or conducting historical research. After London, I held seminars on the same theme at the University of Bonn in Western Germany until the approach of the Second World War, when I moved to the Egyptian Universities of Cairo and Alexandria. For several years I developed various courses from the same material, with an eye on the Arabic sources in particular. In the meantime, I delivered occasional lectures on the Crusade at numerous institutions in America and in Europe, including the Universities of Chicago, California, Harvard, and Princeton, as well as Zurich in Switzerland. In 1955–56, when I was chosen Medieval Academy Visiting Professor of Islamic Studies at the University of Michigan, I gave a full course on the whole expanse of East-West relations. This was repeated by request for a graduate seminar in the Near and Middle East Institute at Columbia University during the following year.

Though the material of the subject kept accumulating and maturing over the years, I never had the courage to attempt a general treatise on this vast and variegated sphere of historical knowledge until the time of my invitation to give the Patten Lectures. Since a major condition was the delivery of the text of the lectures for publication by the Indiana University Press, I had no choice but to succumb to the temptation which I had been able to resist for many years.

In so vast an area, comprising contacts of East and West in most of the Middle Ages, with excursions into antiquity and modern times, I have found it unavoidable to dwell on the salient only. I have had to rise with my readers to the stratosphere of time and look down upon the historic configuration of my terrain from afar, in order to be able to grapple with the main features of our course without involvement in details and tedious minutiae. The great danger of this sytem is the tendency toward excessive generalization. The historian, while having his head in the clouds, must constantly keep and feel his feet planted on solid soil. Generalizations are acceptable only insofar as they are justified by concrete documents and data. Therefore, while I dealt with the bare generalities of my thesis, I have exerted every possible effort to keep the original sources within sight.

There is room in our historical library for a brief study on East-West relationship in its triple phase of Crusade, Commerce, and Culture. There exists virtually no satisfactory survey of the subject. Even if we single out the Crusade, which has received much greater attention than the areas of commerce and culture, it is difficult to point out any one-volume work which, while offering commendable presentations of all the orthodox materials, also incorporates the fruit of modern research and the new theories which have been epitomized in the following pages. The three volumes by Grousset and the equally large *History of the Crusades* by Runciman, as well as the monumental Pennsylvania *History of the Crusades* in five volumes—briefly discussed in my second volume, *The Crusade: Historiography and Bibliography*—are detailed accounts intended for the scholar and the specialist rather than the layman, who is bound to lose himself in the labyrinth of their contents. Perhaps the only work which fulfills the requirements of a general text within reasonable dimensions is Bréhier's *Crusades,* which has been relatively antiquated by new monographs, even if we overlook its inaccuracies. Since the issue of the fifth edition of that book in 1928, moreover, it has gone out of print, and no replacement for it has appeared.

It is hoped that the present study will help to fill part of this gap. But to do this, I have realized from the very beginning that the text should be enriched with bibliographical notices for the initiation of those who intend to embark on research projects in the field, and also for use by the advanced scholar whose need for a convenient up-to-date manual for ready reference to medieval literature has been seriously aggravated by the disappearance of A. C. Paetow's *Guide to the Study of the Middle Ages,* long out of print and out of date. To fulfill this dual purpose, I have equipped the present volume with a short general bibliography, and in a companion volume, *The Crusade: Historiography and Bibliography,* I have tried to round up the outstanding publications, source materials, and secondary literature.

In the latter volume, general reference works and monographs have been brought together in the form of a General Bibliography. A brief essay on historiography has been supplied. And I have included an analysis of the contents of selected Monumental Collections. I have chosen the *Recueil des Historiens des Croisades,* the *Palestine Pilgrims' Text Society Library,* the *Archives de l'Orient Latin,* the *Exuviae Sacrae Constantinopolitanae,* Michaud's *Bibliothèque des Croisades,* selected publications of the *Records of Civilization* of Columbia University, and the *Bibliotheca Geographorum Arabicorum*—all of which are often quoted but rarely explored, owing to their size and their involved substance.

I have departed from the usual method of just citing these sources, in order to provide a fuller statement of their contents, which will lay before readers the wealth of historical data in these collections. Nevertheless, I lay no claim to comprehensiveness either textually or bibliographically; and it is only hoped that this work may open up new channels of research in a field that still teems with immense possibilities.

In recent years, and since the delivery of my Patten Lectures, authorities in both the State Department and the Congress of the United States have realized the paramount value of language and area studies to America and to world peace and understanding. The Congress promulgated a National Defense Education Act empowering the Department of Health, Education and Welfare in Washington to subsidize and promote linguistic studies in American universities, with Arabic first in the list of critical languages needed in this country. The issuance of the present study is in keeping with the spirit of this program. It will be a most rewarding feature to the author if other readers interested in the cultures and politics of the Middle East should find in these pages some beneficial background material.

I have mentioned that the salient will be emphasized. Perhaps a word or two should be said about the scope of this work, which preeminently is to outline the general structure of three great historical movements in the relations between the countries and peoples of the Near and Middle East on the one hand and the states of European Christendom on the other. Crusade, Commerce, and Culture followed one another in successive stages as three chapters in the genesis of medieval society and the medieval mind. Though medieval in character, these movements contributed in varying measures to the shaping of modern civilization and modern thought. They are important phases in the story of mankind in general and in the history of the Eastern Question in particular. It is erroneous to define the Eastern Question as solely the problem of Turkey and the Great Powers in modern history. The conflict of East and West goes far back into antiquity; each age had its own special solution for this eternal problem.

The Crusade, hitherto almost constantly treated by scholars as a separate entity, should be viewed as only one of many phases or attempts at a solution of the Eastern Question. Throughout this volume I have attempted to emphasize my distinction between the Crusade, a movement with roots deep in the Greco-Persian-Arabic past, and with consequences extending far beyond the fall of Acre in 1291, and the Crusades as a series of military ventures initiated by Urban II and generally considered to be limited to the twelfth and thirteenth centuries.

The first four chapters of this work will be devoted chiefly to an inquiry into the Crusade, its antecedents and its repercussions. Although an attempt will be made at both comprehensiveness and novelty, it is necessary to warn the reader again that this is no orthodox history. An analytical presentation of the salient will be offered, together with a summary of new theories and orientations in the field. The Crusade in the latter Middle Ages, long and unduly overlooked or ignored, will be given its rightful place in the general cadre of the whole movement. The Counter-Crusade will be registered as a tremendous movement and a subject pregnant with immense possibilities in the world of Oriental research. The results of the Crusades will lead to a study of commerce in the Levant, which will be enriched considerably by Eastern and Arabic sources. And because the exchange of staples was spontaneously and necessarily followed by the infiltration of ideas from East to West, a measure of our attention will be given to cultural impacts. A brief epilogue will bring these developments to the threshold of modern times, and delineate the element of continuity, if not identity, in the basic factors at work in the interminable East-West conflict, which has been changing only in milieu and motivation.

I am deeply indebted to friends and colleagues—too many to be enumerated—whose encouragement and support rendered both volumes a reality. Mrs. Constance R. Pitchell of the Indiana University Press has been my editorial advisor and she has spared no effort to rectify my failures. With the patience of a true medievalist, she undertook the tedious task of editing my manuscript, correcting my proofs, and compiling my indices. Mr. Thomas Glastras of the Reference Department of the Indiana University Library has never failed to answer our requests and help in solving some of our bibliographical problems. Miss Miriam S. Farley, as Production Editor of the Press, has handled my text from the beginning with Mrs. Pitchell, and I have continuously availed myself of her wisdom. To all of them, I wish to express my personal appreciation. But responsibility for all shortcomings in both volumes must rest solely with the author.

In all humility, I put this material forward. May it serve some purpose for humanity and the humanities!

AZIZ S. ATIYA

Middle East Center
University of Utah
December 4, 1961

Crusade, Commerce and Culture

CHAPTER ONE

The Eastern Question: Earlier Solutions

DEFINITION OF CRUSADE

THE INTERPRETATION of the idea of the Crusade has varied from age to age. The medieval thinker regarded it as a holy war for a holy cause directed by the hand of Providence through the offices of the Holy Pontiff—the Vicar of God on earth. Here we sense the Providential view of history prevailing in the Middle Ages. Another medieval interpretation of the Crusade is that it was a pilgrimage or "passagium" conducted to the Holy Places beyond the sea for the remission of sins. The individual pilgrimage was known as a "passagium parvum"; whereas a communal or mass pilgrimage in which the participants were fully armed for offensive and defensive purposes was a "passagium generale," that is, a Crusade.

The opposite conception of the Crusade occurred in the time of the Renaissance, as well as in the course of the eighteenth century, when the rationalist philosophers of both eras described this movement as a mere outburst of medieval fanaticism and a demonstration of the bigotry of the medieval mind. These trends found a perfect outlet in Christian aggression against Islam and the Muslim Empire for the deliverance of the birthplace of Christ under the leadership of the Roman See.

The political historian, however, prefers to group the Crusades together as a migratory movement from the West to the East, another kind of "Völkerwanderung," or the wandering of needy nations and tribes in search of terrains more opulent than their own. Were not the Normans and the Franks, the chief initiators of the Crusade, highly famed for their migratory instincts from the dawn of the Middle Ages in the course of the fourth and fifth centuries of our era, the period of the decline and fall of the ancient empire of Rome?

The modern school of economic historians, on the other hand, views the Crusade from a totally different angle as a stage in the eastward expansion of Europe—a form of colonization and of medieval imperialism. During the eleventh century, the population of France and of some adjacent countries is known to have increased all of a sudden beyond the natural output of their meager resources, and it is not inconceivable that these hard-pressed people felt the expediency of exploring new areas for new opportunities. Conscious of the economic difficulties which faced the people, Pope Urban II, in his address of 1095, referred to Palestine as a land where rivers of milk and honey flowed freely. With the progress of the Crusading enterprise and the establishment of the Latin kingdom of Jerusalem, a continuous stream of settlers moved from the West to Outremer.

The general consensus of opinion among medievalists, however, is that the Crusades were military expeditions organized by the peoples of Western Christendom, notably the Normans and the French, under the leadership of the Roman Popes, for the recovery of the Holy Places from their Muslim masters. According to the older school of thought, the holy war as such lasted approximately two centuries, from 1095 to 1291 or

1292 A.D.—the lifetime of the Latin kingdom of Jerusalem on the Syrian littoral.

For a comprehensive definition of the Crusade, we have to make a somewhat detailed inquiry into the basic nature of the movement, as well as the circumstances of its realization in a world which it filled with thunder and lightning. In the first place, we must discard the usual treatment of that movement as an entirely separate entity in the annals of mankind. The Crusade should be regarded as one of numerous chapters in the relations between the East and the West. These relations go far back into antiquity beyond the confines of the medieval world. The bone of contention was the undefined frontiers of Europe, otherwise described as the spiritual frontiers of the West vis-à-vis Asia.

In fact, it was Greece and the miracle of the Greek mind and Hellenic culture that gave Europe a clear consciousness of its spiritual frontier, which it sought to defend and even extend over the territories east of the Propontic Sea, the modern Marmora. In the fifth century B.C. we begin to perceive unmistakable signs of that marked cleavage between Europe with its Hellenic civilization and Asia as identified with the way of life and thought prevailing in the Persian Empire. This gave birth to what may be described even at that early stage in ancient history as the Eastern Question, that is, the question of the mobile frontiers which separated the realms of Greece and Persia, or, more broadly conceived, Europe and Asia. The rising powers of the future tried to find successive solutions to that standing problem, age after age, from the Greeks to the Romans, the Byzantines, the Carolingians, the Latin Crusaders, and the Muslim Counter-Crusaders. Consequently, we may deduce in all simplicity that the Crusades in their technically limited sense were merely the Frankish Solution of the Eastern Question in medieval times.

In the second place, we must examine the state of medieval

Europe and medieval thought in order to be able to evaluate the nature and spontaneity of the Crusade. The Middle Ages were first and foremost an age of faith and of war. These two factors remained continually at work shaping medieval institutions and society and the medieval mind. But nowhere in medieval Europe did these two factors find a fuller expression than in the Crusade—war conducted for a holy cause and fought by the chivalry of Europe and the Church Militant in perfect harmony. The response to Urban II's pronouncements of November 1095 at Clermont-Ferrand in the Auvergne was unanimously "Deus lo volt!" God wills it! This was the only comment chivalry had on that memorable occasion.

Let us pause to examine Urban's speech, often mentioned but rarely quoted, which constituted the charter of the whole movement. A quick analysis of this document, the text of which was recorded more fully by Fulcher or Foucher de Chartres than by other contemporaries who heard it,* presents Urban's own definition of the Crusade. The logical sequence of the Pope's thoughts in putting forward his thesis is remarkable. A Frenchman himself, Urban addressed a French audience, not in Latin, but in their own native tongue in order to leave nobody in doubt about the solemnity of his summons.

1. In the preamble of his speech, Urban II begins by preaching internal reform within the moral state of Western Europe. He urges prudence, providence, modesty, learning, peace, watchfulness, piety, justice, equity, and chastity among mankind as a prelude to the Crusade.

2. Then he re-enacts the "Treuga Dei," the Truce of God, forbidding the violation of peace among Christians from Wednesday vespers to sunrise on Monday of every week, on pain of anathema, in order to enhance amity among all

* Excerpts below are based on original texts. Cf. A. C. Krey: *The First Crusade, The Accounts of Eyewitnesses and Participants,* reprinted, Gloucester, Mass., 1958, 24–43.

men in the West as a preliminary measure for concerted action in the East.

3. He gives an account of the state of the East. The conquests of the Arabs and Turks in the land of Romania (i.e., the Byzantine Empire) as far as the Hellespont (Bras de Saint Georges) call for action on the part of Western Christendom to deliver those areas, together with the Holy Places, from the yoke of an infidel oppressor, and to defend the Eastern Christians, whose lot has never been so lamentable.

4. He announces the Crusade, in the following impressive words: "On this account, I, or rather the Lord, beseech you as Christ's heralds to publish this everywhere and to persuade men of all ranks, knights as well as foot-soldiers, rich as well as poor, to carry aid promptly to those Christians and to destroy that vile race from the lands of your brethren. I say this to those who are present; I proclaim it to those who are absent. Moreover, Christ commands it."

5. The reward of all those taking the Cross is immediate remission of sins. "This, I grant to all who go, through the power of God with which I am invested."

6. He appeals to all princes to end their customary local feuds and transfer their belligerency to the East. "Let those who once fought brothers and kin now wage combat against the barbarians as they should."

7. In conclusion, the Pope beseeches his flock for an immediate beginning. He exhorts all Cross-bearers to refrain from procrastination, to lease their lands and raise the necessary funds for their expenses; "and as soon as winter ends and spring comes, let them eagerly set out on the way with God as their guide."

This call to arms explains the universality of the movement, which may be defined as the contest of the medieval "united nations" of Western Christendom against the forces of all Islam, the apple of discord being Jerusalem and the land of promise, of which the nations of both East and West disputed the right of possession.

The Crusade was initiated as a war of faith and principle on both sides, a duel of words turned into action. The two adversaries did not originally embark on that enterprise in a spirit of self-seeking interest and aggrandizement; and mystical enthusiasts for this cause in the West found their peers in the East in the fields of propaganda and warfare. The careers of Richard the Lion-Heart and the great Saladin have been immortalized by numerous records of their extraordinary feats of chivalry, valor, and honest pursuits. On the other hand, it would be an error to contend that their heroic conduct presented a solitary episode in the annals of the Crusade. The autobiography of Usāmah ibn Munqidh (1095–1188) and the Damascene Chronicle of ibn al-Qalānisī (d. 1160) provide us with innumerable examples showing that the genuine Crusade and the Counter-Crusade almost assumed the shape of daily sport in the borderland of the kingdom of Jerusalem. They were not wars of unmixed malice and treachery, as sordid and as devastating as the wars of Christians among themselves in Europe. Compare the horrors, atrocities, and ravages of the Hundred Years' War between England and France in the later Middle Ages with the local maneuvers between Muslim and Christian princes in the land beyond the sea, and you will ascertain the immense difference in the spirit in which the two conflicts were waged.

Moreover, the Crusade could sometimes paradoxically be presented as an affair of peaceful diplomacy. This approach is exemplified in the relations between Charlemagne and Harūn al-Rashīd on the eve of the ninth century, Frederick II's encounter with the Aiyubid sultan al-Kāmil in 1229, and the effective exchange of embassies between King Jaime II of Aragon and the Mamluk sultan al-Nāṣir Muḥammad ibn

Qalāwūn during the first three decades of the fourteenth century.

The Crusade was the Frankish attempt at solving the problem of the Eastern Question in the Middle Ages, whether the means was one of war or one of peace. A review of other attempts in earlier ages will illuminate the history of a movement that has its roots in antiquity and has been recurring across the ages. Pretexts for each outbreak of hostilities vary from case to case, but it will be found that the diagnosis of the real source of all phases of the problem bears unmistakable signs of continuity. At the root of most of these outbursts lies the miracle of the Greek mind, the legacy of the Hellenistic ideal, which kept pressing upon European frontiers and which aimed at encompassing the whole world.

THE GREEK AND ROMAN SOLUTIONS OF THE EASTERN QUESTION

The wars of the Greeks and the Persians in Asia over the spiritual frontiers of Hellenic culture constituted the first chapter in the struggle between East and West. The clash between the two cultures or world powers took place on the fields of Marathon (490 B.C.) and Salamis (480 B.C.), consummating in the Peace of Callias (449 B.C.), which confirmed the supremacy of the sons of Hellas over both the European and the Asiatic shores of the Aegean. With the extension of the Greek frontiers, there arose the idea of the Hellenization of the ancient world, which found its fullest expression in the meteoric career of Alexander the Great (356–323 B.C.).

Alexander was, in fact, not merely a world conqueror, but also something of a philosopher, a loyal disciple of Aristotle, who conceived of world hegemony as a means toward

Hellenized world citizenship. After unifying the Greek city states, the young Macedonian led the Panhellenic battalions around the Levant into Syria and Egypt, where he was hailed by the people as their liberator from the odious Persian yoke. In 332 B.C. he founded Alexandria ad Aegyptum, which was destined to become the chief center of Hellenistic culture under his Ptolemaic successors. Then he swept east over Asia and, in the following year, defeated Darius III in the battle of Arbela and won the vast kingdom of Iran. Finally his conquering arms penetrated Asia as far as Lahore and the Indus, and Samarqand and Kabul in Central Asia. Greek coins of the epoch have been dug out in recent excavations around Peshawar and in the valleys situated north of the capital of Afghanistan.

Curiously, Alexander, who Hellenized wide areas in Asia and who married his soldiers to the daughters of Iran in order to create a uniform Greco-Iranian nation, became himself in the end an Oriental potentate, an heir to Darius and Xerxes. But Hellenism remained a superficial imposition in Iran, and a relapse occurred with the Parthian revolt against the Seleucid successors of Alexander around the middle of the third century B.C.

Thus we turn a new leaf in the long story of the relations between the East and the West, representing one of the earliest phases in the metamorphosis of the Eastern Question. With the downfall of the Greek states in the Mediterranean, Rome became the soldier and defender of Hellenism. Julius Caesar had plans for the restoration of Alexander's empire beyond the Euphrates, and the project was resumed later by Emperor Trajan, who seized the Parthian capital, Ctesiphon, in 116 A.D. and extended the Pax Romana to the Persian Gulf. But his progress was foiled by the Jewish revolt of 117 throughout the Roman provinces of Africa and Asia, the first instance on record of what might justly be described as wars of religion.

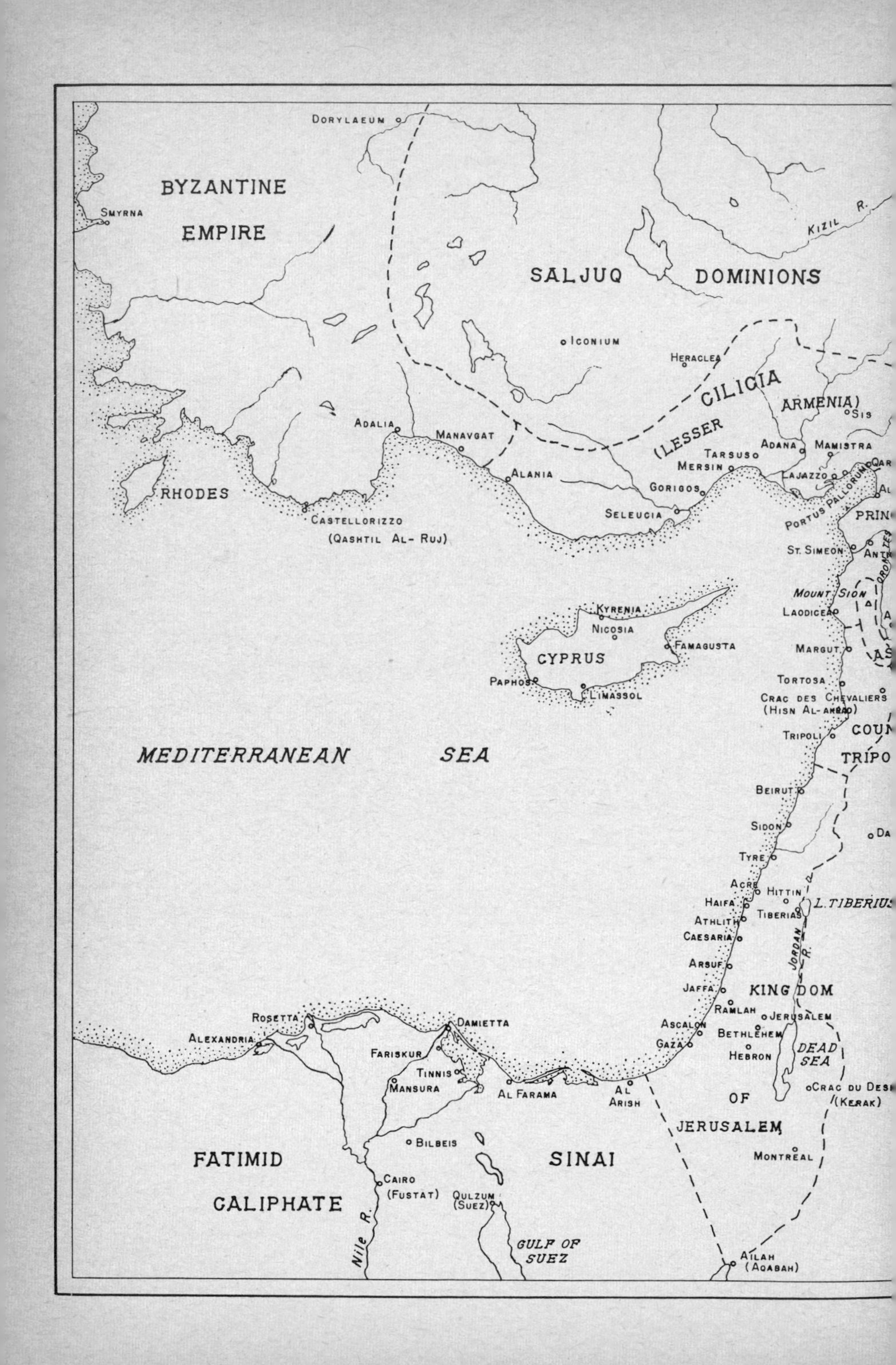

DORYLAEUM
BYZANTINE
EMPIRE
SMYRNA
SALJUQ
DOMINIONS
KIZIL R.
ICONIUM
HERACLEA
CILICIA
(LESSER
ARMENIA)
SIS
ADANA
MAMISTRA
TARSUS
MERSIN
LAJAZZO
PORTUS PALLORUM
GORIGOS
SELEUCIA
ADALIA
MANAVGAT
ALANIA
RHODES
CASTELLORIZZO
(QASHTIL AL-RUJ)
ST. SIMEON
MOUNT SION
LAODICEA
MARGUT
TORTOSA
CRAC DES CHEVALIERS
TRIPOLI
KYRENIA
NICOSIA
FAMAGUSTA
CYPRUS
PAPHOS
LIMASSOL
MEDITERRANEAN
SEA
BEIRUT
SIDON
TYRE
ACRE
HITTIN
HAIFA
TIBERIAS
L. TIBERIUS
ATHLITH
CAESARIA
JORDAN R.
ARSUF
JAFFA
KINGDOM
RAMLAH
JERUSALEM
ASCALON
BETHLEHEM
GAZA
HEBRON
DEAD
SEA
CRAC DU DESERT
(KERAK)
OF
JERUSALEM
MONTREAL
ROSETTA
ALEXANDRIA
DAMIETTA
FARISKUR
TINNIS
MANSURA
AL FARAMA
AL
ARISH
BILBEIS
FATIMID
CALIPHATE
SINAI
CAIRO
(FUSTAT)
QULZUM
(SUEZ)
Nile R.
GULF OF
SUEZ
AILAH
(AQABAH)

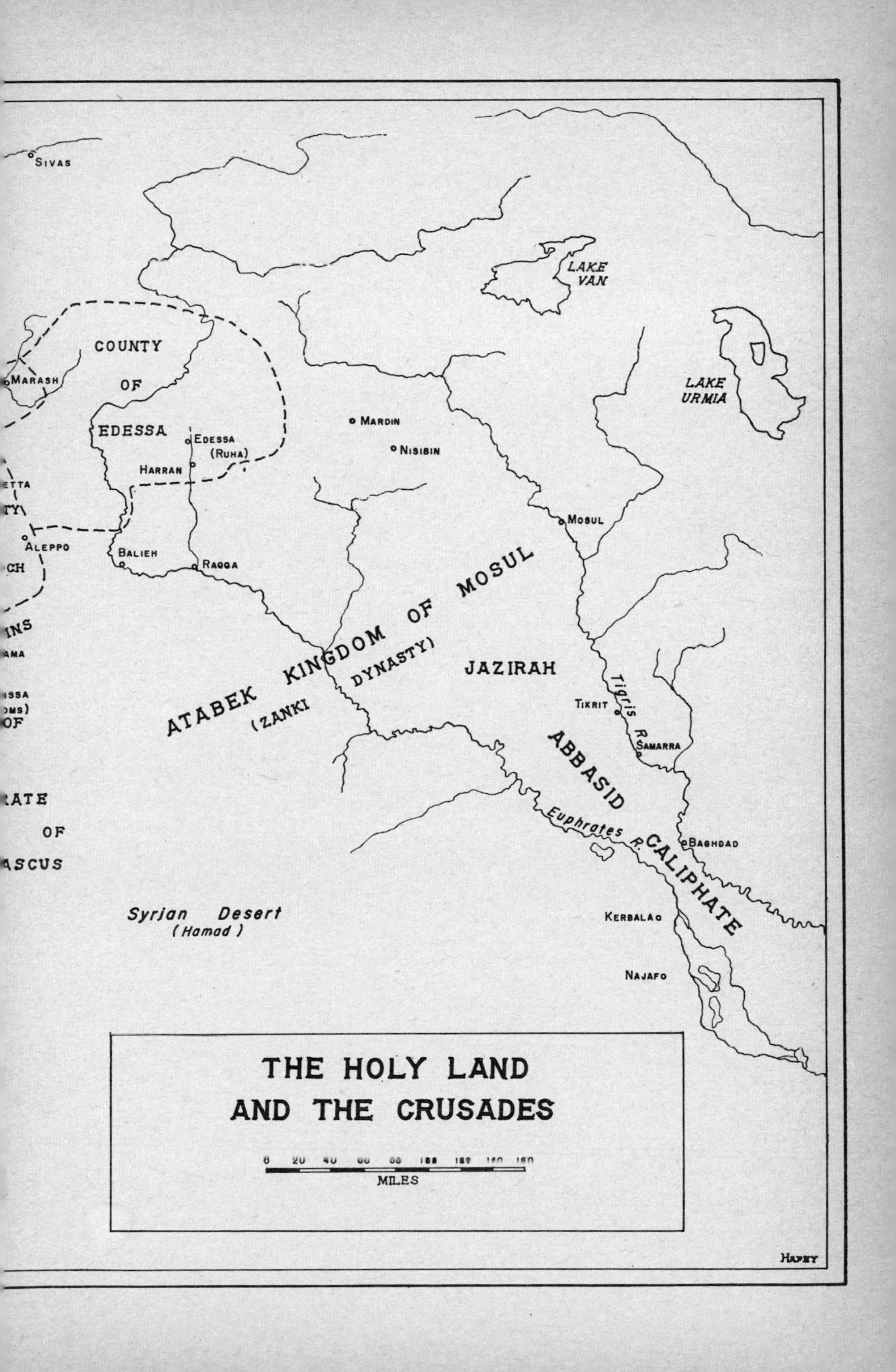
SIVAS
LAKE VAN
LAKE URMIA
COUNTY OF EDESSA
MARASH
MARDIN
NISIBIN
EDESSA (RUHA)
HARRAN
ALEPPO
BALIEH
RAQQA
MOSUL
ATABEK KINGDOM OF MOSUL
(ZANKI DYNASTY)
JAZIRAH
TIKRIT
Tigris R.
SAMARRA
ABBASID CALIPHATE
Euphrates R.
BAGHDAD
KERBALA
NAJAF
Syrian Desert
(Hamad)
THE HOLY LAND
AND THE CRUSADES
MILES
HAPEY

On the Asiatic side, however, the rising tide of Persian nationalism ultimately found its exponents in the monarchs of the Sassanid dynasty (224–640), who for four centuries kept fighting both Rome and Byzantium with a great measure of success. The humiliation of Rome was complete in the reign of Shahpour I (241–72), who seized Emperor Valerian in a raid against the city of Edessa in 260 A.D. That unparalleled disaster in Roman annals is commemorated by the Persians in a sculptured relief on a wall in the neighborhood of the ruins of the ancient city of Persepolis. Valerian is shown in a kneeling posture before Shahpour mounted on horseback; and the Persian potentate, with Oriental magnanimity, spares his opponent's life. No wonder he henceforward assumed the title of "King of Kings of Iran and of Non-Iran," to which occasionally were added "Sovereign of the Universe, Descendant of the Gods, Brother of the Sun and Moon, and Companion of the Stars."

The recent excavations in the ruins of Dura-Europus on the Euphrates east of Palmyra, a city which flourished from the third century B.C. to the third century A.D., provide us with testimony as to the furthest extent of Roman-Hellenistic culture in Mesopotamia. Yet even within this sphere of influence, we note that the emergence of the Palmyrene Empire of Zenobia under the guise of Romanism was in a sense a prelude to the next Asiatic upheavals—under the Sassanid Khosroes Parviz, and in the Arab invasion of both the Persian Empire and the Byzantine Empire after the rise of Islam in the seventh century A.D., with immeasurable repercussions on the whole course of history.

THE BYZANTINE SOLUTION

As we depart from antiquity and step into the medieval world, we find ourselves faced with a somewhat different set of circumstances. Hitherto, the Eastern Question had been one of race and culture. At this juncture, it became a religious problem. The early decades of the seventh century saw the star of the Sassanid dynasty in ascendancy. After a period of amicable approach and peaceful coexistence with the Greeks, Khosroes II Parviz, the Persian monarch, decided to avenge his Byzantine friend, Emperor Maurice, whose life was taken and his throne usurped by Phocas in November 602. War broke out in the following year, Phocas was ultimately routed at the battle of Arxamon between Nisibis and Edessa in Upper Mesopotamia, and Khosroes seized the fortified site of Dara in 605. The Persians ravaged the borderland of Syria and Palestine in 608; and in 609 they penetrated Asia Minor as far as historic Chalcedon on the Hellespont within sight of Constantinople.

The war dragged on for some twenty years, during which another usurper of the Byzantine throne emerged in the person of Heraclius (610–41), a man of courage and an experienced and resourceful general. In the meantime, the Persians finally invaded Syria in 613, inflicted a heavy defeat on the Byzantine garrison at Antioch, and occupied the important city of Damascus. In 614 they made a triumphant entry into Jerusalem, where they burned the Holy Sepulchre, seized the patriarch Zaccharias, and carried back with them to their capital, Ctesiphon, the Holy Cross and the relics and instruments of the Passion, which were presented to their Nestorian queen, Miriam. In 619, one Persian army conquered Egypt, and another pushed on toward the Bosphorus to lay siege to Constantinople from the sea, while the Avar hordes descended from Hungary and beleaguered the great capital from the land.

All seemed to be lost, and Heraclius began to contemplate flight to Carthage in the distant African province, when the patriarch Sergius persuaded the Emperor to declare Holy War and place the Church treasure at the disposal of the soldiers of the Cross. Heraclius found himself fighting what Archbishop William of Tyre described in his twelfth-century history as a Crusade, approximately five centuries before the advent of the traditional Latin Crusaders from Europe to fight another battle of the Cross in the Holy Land. The Emperor used the brilliant tactic of intercepting the enemy from the rear, with formidable results. In 622 he disembarked his forces on the shores of the gulf of Alexandretta at Issos, in the province of Cilicia or Lesser Armenia just south of the Taurus mountains, and forced upon the Persian besiegers of his capital a complete retreat from Asia Minor. Again, while Sergius, aided by a Byzantine patrician named Bonus, organized the heroic defense of Constantinople against the Avar hordes, Heraclius launched another campaign against the Persians in 623. This time, with surprising ingenuity, he bewildered his adversary by taking sail on the Black Sea to Trebizond, whence he sallied into Greater Armenia and Azerbaijan and harassed the heedless Khosroes in his royal nest at Ganzak.

Other campaigns were systematically repeated in the following years in the area of the upper Euphrates, until, in December 627, Heraclius finally descended into Assyria and destroyed the whole Sassanid army at Nineveh, in the neighborhood of the historic field of Arbela, where Alexander the Great had routed Darius nine centuries before. Next he stormed the royal palaces at Dastgard in January 628 and seized enormous booty, consisting of a great treasure of gold and silver, priceless carpets and silk textiles, and large stocks of sugar, spices, and aromatics. Khosroes, in flight, was dethroned and executed by order of his own son and successor in February. Heraclius then negotiated with the Persian general Shahrvaz for the evacuation of the rest of the posts still occupied by Persian garrisons. These were surrendered in 629 and Shahrvaz took the road to Ctesiphon to claim his old master's throne. At Hierapolis (the Arab city of Menbij) on the

Euphrates, Heraclius received back the Holy Cross and the relics of the Passion from Persian envoys; and, on March 30, 630, he entered Jerusalem triumphantly to deposit the precious acquisitions in their original places on Calvary. Thus ended the Crusade of Heraclius against the Persians. The two ancient empires had fought one another to the edge of annihilation. They had prepared the way for the lasting success of the imminent Arab menace.

In reality, Arab infiltration within the confines of Persia and Byzantine Syria had begun even earlier than the rise of Islam. The short-lived Palmyrene dynasty in the Syrian desert beyond Damascus is a demonstration of this. But the real Arab tribal establishments were stationed on the fringes of both countries. The Arab kingdoms of Banu Ghassan in the Syrian province of Hauran and Banu Lakhm in Hira on the right bank of the Euphrates were both Monophysite Christian and vassal states to the courts of Constantinople and Ctesiphon respectively. One Lakhmid king, al-Mundhir I, became tutor to a Persian prince, Vahram Gor, whom he advanced in 420 to the Sassanid throne. A Syrian bishop of the Arabs took his seat at Basrah, and a daughter of Mundhir founded Christian nunneries within the Arabian Peninsula near the Mesopotamian frontier. Between 604 and 611, on the eve of the Islamic revolution, the insignificant Arab tribe of Banu Bakr fought and defeated a Sassanid army at Dhu-qar between Wasit and Kūfah on the bank of the Euphrates. This was a portentous demonstration that the great empire was no longer invulnerable even to the nomadic Arabs.

The Arabs, hitherto divided in pre-Islamic times, were finally unified by the Prophet Muḥammad in one religion and under one banner, with the injunction of the principle of Holy War, "al-Jihād," against all non-Muslims until the whole world was subdued to Islam, a word meaning "surrender," that is, to the will of Allah. The Arab conquest was initiated in the reigns of the first two Orthodox Caliphs, Abu Bakr

(632–34) and 'Umar (634–44). In Syria, the first victory of the Muslim invader took place at the battle of Ajnadin on July 30, 634. Damascus capitulated in September 635. Heraclius suddenly became aware of the seriousness of the new menace and marshalled an army of 80,000, which the Arabs destroyed in the decisive battle of Yarmuk, a branch of the Jordan, on August 20, 636. Aleppo and Antioch surrendered in the north, but Jerusalem held out for two years under the leadership of the patriarch, Soffronius, who eventually opened the city gates in 638 after obtaining certain religious concessions and assurances for its Christian inhabitants. It was on this occasion that the relics of the Passion were removed from the Holy Sepulchre before the entry of the Arabs—the Cross went to Constantinople and the lance to Antioch. Finally, Caesaria succumbed in 640, eliminating Byzantine rule from the whole of greater Syria, Palestine included.

On the Persian side, the total collapse of the ancient Sassanid Empire came to pass at the hands of the virile Muslim Arabs after the two decisive battles of al-Qadisiya in 736 and Nehawand in 642. Fleeing for life with his royal treasure, the unhappy Sassanid monarch, Yazdagird III, was murdered in a hut outside the northern city of Marw by one of his subjects, a poor miller who coveted his old sovereign's gold. This brought to an end both the reigning dynasty and all hope of organized resistance. Unlike the Arabs, who were Semites, the Persians were of Aryan stock, and their Arabicization was a very slow, painful process, never really completed in either medieval or modern history. Nevertheless, Iran, which has preserved its ethnic and linguistic identity throughout that process to this very day, was destined to give to the Muslim Empire under the Abbasid Caliphate at Bagdad some of the most illustrious builders of Islamic thought and polity. Like the Greeks when conquered by Rome, the Persians captured their Arab conquerors culturally. Even in matters of religion, they swung toward the heretic Shi'ite * profession as against the prevailing Arab Sunnite ** creed, a factor not to be forgotten in the formation of their personality as a nation.

While the Arab armies were still gazing with bewilderment at the untold riches of Sassanid palaces in the east, a new offensive was launched in a westerly direction against Egypt, the richest wheat-growing province in the Byzantine Empire. The easy conquest of Egypt was made possible by the abstention of the native Coptic population from taking sides in the ensuing struggle. These Egyptian sons of the Nile had long been abused and persecuted by their Byzantine rulers because of their Monophysitic beliefs and their repudiation of the Chalcedonian profession † of faith after 451. The growing theocratic tendency at Constantinople was utterly inacceptable to the members of the Coptic Church, who accordingly were subjected to fierce persecution and much humiliation by the agents of imperial rule. The Copts thus fought a sustained battle of nascent nationalism, both political and ecclesiastical, though without any avail. Hence it became

* Islamic sect or sects which asserted that 'Ali, the third Orthodox Caliph at Mekka, and his progeny were divinely invested with the right of succession to the Caliphate after Muhammad's death. 'Ali was Muhammad's cousin and married his daughter, Fāṭima. Present-day Shi'ites are mainly located in Iran and Iraq, with formidable branches in Pakistan and East Africa.

** The Orthodox Muslim sect of the followers of the Prophet's tradition, as represented in his sayings (Ḥadīth) and deeds—the greater part of the Islamic world.

† The Council of Chalcedon was the fifth of the great Ecumenical Councils in which the nature of Jesus Christ, divine and human, was discussed. Rome and Constantinople adopted the exposition made in the Tome of Leo, the bishop of Rome, speaking for the two natures; but the ancient Eastern Churches led by Dioscorus, Coptic patriarch of Alexandria, stood for the indivisible unity of the two natures, which the council condemned. After 451 there arose two lines of patriarchal succession in Egypt and Syria—the Melkite or imperial, and the national, which repudiated Chalcedon.

impossible for them to participate in the defense of the enemy of their nation and their Church. The tolerant Arab, on the other hand, promised a much greater measure of religious independence and could be satisfied with less exacting taxation than the Byzantines; the Copts apparently had nothing to lose by the change of masters.

The Greek Cyrus, who combined the functions of prefect and Melkite or imperial patriarch, after several months' siege and futile negotiations, was forced to surrender the key fortress of Babylon (Old Cairo) to the Arabs under the generalship of 'Amr ibn al- 'Āṣ on Good Friday, April 6, 641. That triumph was soon to be followed by the seizure of Alexandria on November 8, 641. Apparently the city of Alexander the Great dazzled the nomadic children of the desert with its 4,000 villas, 4,000 baths, 4,000 royal palaces, and 40,000 wealthy poll-tax-paying Jewish citizens. With those two chief centers in Arab hands, the gradual conquest of Egypt became a foregone conclusion, and one of the richest provinces of Rome and Byzantium began to look eastward rather than westward.

As the Arab armies moved westward with incredible rapidity and seized both North Africa and the Visigothic kingdom of Spain, after the spectacular crossing of the Pillars of Hercules * and the fall of King Roderick on the field of battle near Medina-Sidonia on July 19, 711, their Eastern contingents harried the Byzantines in Anatolia and pursued them as far as the Hellespont. Daring Arab sea craft were seen in both the Aegean and the Propontis; in 673 and 717 they laid siege to Constantinople, during the reigns of Constantine IV and of Leo the Isaurian; but the capital was saved by the impregnability of its double walls and strong

* Representing the limits of maritime enterprise for the ancients, they became known after the Arab invasion as the Straits of Gibraltar, the Arabic Jabal Tariq, or mountain of Ṭāriq ibn Ziyād, the general who led the Moors to Spain in 711.

fortifications, combined with the use of the fearful Greek fire, a new weapon recently invented by a Greek architect from Syria by the name of Callinicus. The spell of the invincibility of the Arab broke down at the gates of Constantinople, and Leo the Isaurian or Syrian did for Eastern Christendom on the shores of the Hellespont in 717–718 what Charles Martel achieved in behalf of Western Christendom * in the battle of Poitiers in 732. The Arab tide began to recede to the south of the Taurus mountains in the East and to the south of the Pyrenees in the West.

After these decisive dates begins the slow counteraction: the reconquest of lost ground. The Spanish Reconquista remained limited to guerilla warfare for a considerable period before its results became noticeable against the Umaiyad Caliphate of Cordova. In the East, however, the idea of the recovery of Syria and the Holy Places kept haunting the Byzantine mind, though more for political expediency and self-aggrandizement than for sheer piety.

It would be idle to try to cover the whole story of Byzantine-Arab frontier incidents, occurring mainly on the soil of Armenia, which was wedged between those two empires. The first really serious enterprise to be undertaken against the Arabs took place in the reign of Emperor Nicephoras Phocas (963–69). He recaptured both Cilicia and the island of Cyprus in 965, and was emboldened to begin his inroads into North Syria for the restoration of Antioch, the old historic Greek capital of the East. The decease in 967 of the spirited Hamdanid amir of Aleppo, Sayf-al-Dawla, weakened the defense of Muslim frontier territory. After a long siege, the Byzantine legions wrested Antioch from its Muslim masters, and Aleppo became a vassal state to Byzantium. Its Arab amir was constrained to offer his allegiance to the Emperor and to sign a treaty whereby he promised to

* Before their progress was arrested beyond the Pyrenees, the Arabs seized Bordeaux and their irruptions covered all of Aquitaine.

fight in imperial lines, though only against non-Muslims. Moreover, he made a pledge to protect Byzantine trade and traders, to render imperial taxes on behalf of the Muslim population of his province, and to allow the free reconstruction of Christian churches in the city. The Orontes (Nahr al-Kalb) thus marked the southern boundary of the Byzantine Empire for the next few years. So high was the morale of the Byzantines now that one contemporary writer asserted that if the Emperor Nicephoras Phocas had not been assassinated in 969, he would have restored the imperial frontier eastward to India and westward to the Atlantic.

John Tzimisces (969–76), an emperor of Armenian extraction, continued his predecessor's campaigns in the Holy Land with even greater vigor, though with few results of a really permanent nature. He crossed the Orontes in 975 and approached Damascus from Lebanon. Without a single stroke, the Turkish lord of Damascus, Aftekin, who had been fearful of encroachments from the heretic Shi'ite Fatimid Caliphate in Egypt, decided on submission to the uncertain authority of the Greek invader and paid John a tribute for holding the city. Most of the other towns of Syria and Palestine followed the example of Damascus. Beirut resisted, but the Emperor succeeded in breaking through its defense and chastised its garrison, though he was unable to take Tripoli by storm. Arriving at Galilee, however, he made no attempt to recover Jerusalem, and thus failed to earn the title of the first liberator of the Holy Sepulchre. In one of his letters to Ashot III, king of Armenia, the Emperor tries to justify his position by asserting that he was distracted from entering the Holy City by pursuing "the pagan Africans" who hid themselves in the coastal castles. It is extremely difficult to explain the reasons for his withdrawal at that juncture. Perhaps he felt himself unequal to the task; at any rate, he retired to his base camp at Antioch in 975, after annexing the Orontes valley and imposing his shadowy suzerainty over the province of Damascus.

Basil II (976–1025) continued the policy of imperial incursions into Syria between 995 and 999. He succeeded in seizing a number of towns such as Shayzar, Homs, and Rafaniya. He recaptured Tortosa. But his arms again broke down at Tripoli. In the tug of war between Muslims and Christians over Aleppo, the city seems to have freed itself from any direct Byzantine rule. Finally, in the year 1000, the Fatimid Caliph, al-Hākim, sent an embassy to Constantinople to negotiate peace. It was agreed between the two parties to accept a ten-year truce on a status quo basis in the Holy Land. The Byzantine solution brought some gains to the Christians, since northern Syria remained in Byzantine hands for the time being, but it failed to deliver Jerusalem from the Muslim yoke. Nothing of great consequence happened after that date until the coming of the Saljuq Turks and the memorable appeal of Alexius Comnenus to the Pope of Rome in 1093.

THE CAROLINGIAN SOLUTION

While Byzantium was developing a new line of approach in solving the problem of the lost Holy Places, which led to the truce with Fatimid Egypt at the end of the first millennium of our era, there was a growing tendency toward another solution in a peaceful way between Carolingian Aachen and Abbasid Bagdad. The Arabs were no longer regarded as a mere race of conquerors temporarily imposed on the Byzantine provinces of the near East. The Byzantines had long jeopardized their position with the so-called dissident Eastern Churches, which they accused of heresy; and the Nestorians, Jacobites, and Copts enjoyed such religious autonomy under Arab rule as they had not experienced under the rule of the Eastern Roman Empire since the middle of the fifth century. The growth of peace, justice, and security in the countries of the Levant was accompanied by the steady development of a new superior Arab civilization to which the Eastern Christians contributed no mean share. The coexistence of Muslim and Christian, of Arab and non-Arab, became an accomplished fact which the original races accepted with grace; and the West could do nothing about it. In the meantime, the loss of Byzantine influence, not only in the East, but also in Italy, culminated in a movement of rapprochement between the Papacy and the developing Carolingian monarchy. This tacit alliance and the interest of the Popes in the Holy Places and in the position of the Eastern Christians was undoubtedly the starting point of a series of diplomatic exchanges between the Franks and the Abbasid Caliphs in the course of the eighth century. Though the original sources on this subject are meager, it is possible to construe the general course of these embassies and the issues at stake from a quick survey of the events.

The first embassy to go to Bagdad was despatched in the year 762 by Pepin III (741–68), king of the Franks. The ambassadors returned after three years' absence accompanied by other envoys of the Caliph, then al-Manṣūr (754–75), second in the Abbasid line of succession and famous founder of the city of Bagdad (Madīnat al-Salām, that is, City of Peace). Few details are available about the nature of their embassy other than friendly overtures, the exchange of presents, and some vague reference to negotiations. These diplomatic approaches were renewed under Charlemagne with a clearer purport. For a sound comprehension of the issue, we have to view these relations in the setting of world politics. The transfer of the Caliphate from Damascus to Bagdad, and its investiture with the Sassanid heritage, in addition to the continuous state of war with the Eastern Empire, must have revived acutely the traditional hatred of Persian and Greek. On the other hand, the establishment of the Umaiyad Caliphate of Cordova in Spain meant the survival of the chief enemy of the Abbasids in the neighborhood of the Frankish kingdom in the West. It was therefore natural for both sides to foster friendly relations, which, while giving the Franks a footing in the Holy City, involved them in the strife against the Spanish Umaiyads, with the help and the blessing of the Abbasids. In this way, too, the West aimed at filling the vacuum created by the disappearance of Byzantine influence from the Holy Land.

In the year 797 Charlemagne despatched three Frankish ambassadors to Bagdad, namely Lantfrid, Sigismund, and a Jew called Isaac, who was probably the interpreter of the embassy. The two Christians died on the way, and the Jew was destined to shoulder the whole burden of the mission. Two years after that date, a priest by the name of Zaccharias was also sent on another mission to the patriarch of Jerusalem. We can assume that the aims of both delegations were partly to foster the spirit of unity between the Abbasids and the Franks and coordinate their policies of encroachment on the territories of the Umaiyad Caliphate * of Cordova, and partly to procure privileges for Western pilgrims to Palestine and establish a fluid Carolingian protectorate over Jerusalem and the Christians of the East. Caliph Harūn al-Rashīd (786–809) was evidently favorable to all these propositions in principle. That he wished to undermine the Umaiyads as a dynasty surviving in Spain hardly needs explanation.

The idea of the protectorate over the Holy Sepulchre and over Eastern Christianity, rather difficult to accept in the light of modern political standards, is not really bizarre when viewed in the eighth-century setting. It has been customary from the early days of Islam for the Caliphs to leave the management of the affairs of the "People of the Book" or the "People of the Covenant," that is, the Christians and Jews

* The Umaiyad Caliphate resided in Damascus from 661 to 750. After having been routed by the Abbasids, the Umaiyad Caliphs fled to Spain, where they established themselves from 756 to 1031. Later, Spain became a prey to several adventurers known as Reyes de Taifas, that is Party Kings, until the advent of the Almoravid dynasty from North Africa.

under the protection of Islam, to the heads of their own churches, without any fear for Muslim world sovereignty. On the contrary, the Christian protectorate in the case of Charlemagne might well have put him in the position of a sworn liegeman to the Arab potentate. This is possibly why some historians tend to think that that idea could have originated at the court of Bagdad rather than at Aachen. It was no capitulation, certainly not in the modern sense of the term. What the envoys' deliberations may have been is likely to remain in the realm of the unknown. But the events of subsequent years point to the establishment of a nominal and undefined Carolingian protectorate of a spiritual or religious character over Jerusalem and the community of Eastern Christians.

Toward the end of 800, we hear of two Eastern monks coming to Rome on behalf of the patriarch of Jerusalem, one from the still renowned monastery of St. Sabas and another from the monastery of the Mount of Olives. They were accompanied by the priest Zaccharias, and brought with them the keys of the Holy Sepulchre, the standard of the city of Jerusalem, and some sacred relics which they presented to Charlemagne. This show must have impressed Pope Leo III, who hastened plans to place the crown of the Holy Roman Empire on Charles' head in the Basilica of St. Peter on Christmas eve of 800.

In the course of the following year, a direct embassy from the Caliph disembarked at Leghorn, port of the city of Pisa, and was granted audience by the Emperor at a place situated between Ivrea and Vercelli in the province of Turin, while he was on his way back to his German capital. The ambassadors, a Persian and a governor of Egypt called Ibrāhīm ibn al-Aghlab, no doubt reported to the Emperor about their master's willingness to acquiesce in his request, and gave him the news about his former envoys, who must have reached Bagdad probably before the departure of the Eastern ambassadors. The surviving member of the Christian embassy, Isaac the Jew, arrived later at Aachen in 802. The Caliph's presents included jewels, gold, robes, aromatics, sacred Christian relics, and the famous white elephant. In the same year (802), the Emperor sent another embassy headed by a certain Radbert, who, like his predecessors, seems to have died during the return journey. In 806 the Caliph responded by the despatch of new delegates from the court of Bagdad. A Muslim by the name of ʻAbdallah, accompanied by two monks chosen by Thomas, patriarch of Jerusalem, one called Felix and the other Egibald, proceeded across the Mediterranean and southern Europe toward Aachen with precious gifts of a polychrome linen tent and other material, as well as a miraculous sounding water clock, possibly a clepsydra, the first of its kind in European history.

Charlemagne's prestige must have increased considerably in the East during that period. He ensured safe conduct for pilgrims from Europe and defended the rights of the local Christians through diplomatic channels. Alms were sent by him and other pious Europeans to religious foundations in Jerusalem, which he kept in good repair, while new houses were built by imperial agents. Reference to such acts of charity is made in Charlemagne's Capitularies. Two new Latin monasteries were constructed in the Holy City, one on the Mount of Olives and another near the Holy Sepulchre. The Emperor's most impressive foundation consisted of a group of structures on a field known as the "Field of the Blood" (Ḥaql al-Damm), where he established a hostel for pilgrims, a basilica, a library, and a market; and he assigned to them the revenues accruing from twelve domains (mansiones) with rice fields and orchards in the valley of Josaphat. A certain Bernard the Monk gives an account of the intense activities in those foundations during his eastern pilgrimage in the year 870.

Donations came from the West with a stream of European pilgrims. On many occasions representatives of the patriarchs of Jerusalem travelled to Europe to raise funds for the repair of old churches, or for other special purposes; as in the case of the bishop of Amasia, who sailed to Europe in order to solicit funds for the ransom of a group of monks seized by the Turks on the Caspian shores in 900. Benevolent feudatories conceded the fruits of portions of their landed property for charitable causes in the East. At the beginning of the tenth century, Hugh, marquis of Tuscany, and his wife Juliet devoted the revenues of their counties of Orvieto, Sovana, and Aquapendente to the maintenance of the monks of St. Mary the Latin in Jerusalem, as well as to all pilgrims to whom they might extend hospitality.

The way of peace inaugurated by Charlemagne in the solution of the Eastern Question yielded security and justice to all Christians in the Near and Middle East. Theodosius, patriarch of Jerusalem, writing to Ignatius, patriarch of Constantinople, in 869, stated that the Saracens were just and never molested the Christians in any way. The story of tolerance in the days of primitive Islam and under the early Caliphate, still unwritten in the fullness of its splendor, was a remarkable feature which the traditional historians either contradicted or overlooked. Cases of sporadic persecutions occurred, but these must be linked up with the individual whims of such Caliphs as al-Ḥākim (996–1020), sometimes described as the "Egyptian Nero" for his cruelty to the Christians and his destruction of the Holy Sepulchre in 1009. But al-Ḥākim was insane. He also abused the Muslims and his end was obscure. It is said that he was murdered in the Helwan desert by his retainers, though a curious but unproved story states that he retired incognito to the oblivion of a Coptic monastery, where he buried his atrocities in austere penance.

Western Islam was equally tolerant in its general outlook. The survival of Spanish and Sicilian Christianity under the rule of the Arabs was a feature which surprised the Spaniards when they reentered Toledo and the Normans when again they seized Sicily. Christian churches were found intact and the clergy celebrated the Holy Liturgy without interference or interruption. The collaboration of Muslim, Christian, and Jewish scholars in the Iberian Peninsula was largely responsible for the efflorescence of the great medieval renaissance of the twelfth century.

Strictly speaking, Muslim terrorism as the order of the day in the Near East must be identified with the predominance of the Turks, who were new to Islam and had no comprehension of the language of the Qur'ān. The contention that the Christians were happier under the Saljuq Turks than in the Byzantine Empire is, of course, inacceptable. The real and systematic abuse of the holy places came to pass on the eve of the Crusades at the hands of those new masters who had wrested power from the Arab Caliphate and seized Jerusalem in 1078, while their irresistible hordes were spreading into Byzantine Anatolia.

THE AGE OF PILGRIMS

The ideas of pilgrimage and penance had a great appeal to the medieval mind, and some historians go to the extent of describing the Middle Ages as an era of pilgrims. Pilgrimage was regarded as an effective mode of redemption, and, moreover, it was held that the relics venerated by pilgrims often performed miracles of healing. A fine act of piety, pilgrimage was also an attractive occasion for those who loved adventure at a time when travelling was beset with great hardships and perils. It must be remembered, however, that pilgrimage and the cult of sacred relics became increasingly popular in medieval Europe from the tenth century onward.

Although pilgrims to sanctuaries and martyria are to be encountered from the dawn of medievalism, there has been divergence of opinion among the church fathers on the justi-

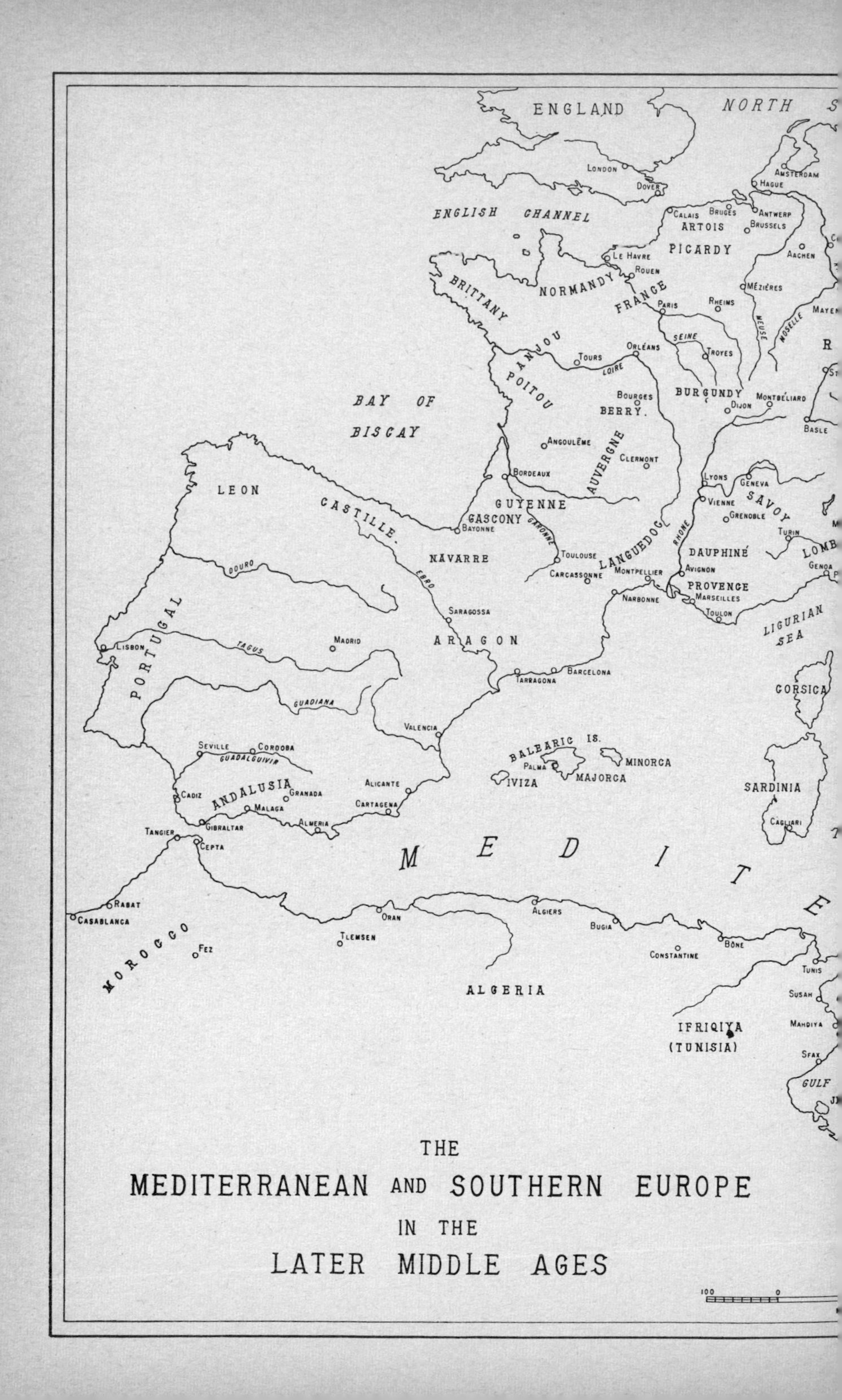

THE MEDITERRANEAN AND SOUTHERN EUROPE IN THE LATER MIDDLE AGES

BALTIC SEA
LÜBECK
HAMBURG
BREMEN
DANZIG
PRUSSIA
HANSEATIC LEAGUE
RUSSIA
ODER
VISTULA
WARSAW
SAXONY
ELBE
OLY
BRESLAU
POLAND
RANKFURT
MAIN
KIEV
NUREMBERG
PRAGUE
BOHEMIA
CRACOW
REGENSBURG
DANUBE
MUNICH
AUSTRIA
VIENNA
DNIESTER
THEISS
EMPIRE
BUDA
HUNGARY
PRUTH
MOLDAVIA
DRAVE
TRANSYLVANIA
TREVISO
VERONA
VENICE
AQUILEA
PADUA
CAPODISTRIA
CROATIA
SAVE
BOLOGNA
RAVENNA
LUCCA
PISA
FLORENCE
BELGRADE
ORSOVA
IRON GATE
WALLACHIA
BUCHAREST
DANUBE
BOSNIA
SIENA
ANCONA
WIDDIN
SERBIA
NICOPOLIS
ADRIATIC SEA
TIRNOVA
VARNA
VITERBO
MORAVA
RAGUSA
MESEMBRIA
BULGARIA
AXELLO
ROME
SOZOPOLIS
SCUTARI
KINGDOM OF NAPLES
OTTOMANS
PHILIPPOPOLI
ADRIANOPLE
BYZANTINE EMP.
CONSTANTINOPLE
MACEDONIA
THRACE
NAPLES
BARI
DURAZZO
TARENTO
BRINDISI
ALBANIA
SALONICA
BOTIAEA
BRUSA
IMBROS
GALLIPOLI
MIKALIJ
OTRANTO
BLACHIA
LEMNOS
TENEDOS
KARASI
SEA
CORFU
AEGEAN
SARUKHAN
MITYLENE
MANISA
NEGROPONTIS
SMYRNA
PALERMO
CEPHALONIA
CHIOS
ATHENS
MESSINA
SICILY
IONIAN SEA
CLARENZA
SASAN
ZANTE
MOREA
DODECANESE
SYRACUSE
ACHAIA
CYCLADES
MENTESHE
TELLARIA
MODON
CORON
SEA
MALTA
RHODES
CANDIA
CRETE
ES
A N E A N S E A
TRIPOLI
CYRENE
DERNA
TOLMETA
BARQA
LITANIA
BENGHAZI
GULF OF SIDRA
BARQA (CYRENAICA)
ROSETTA
ALEXANDRIA
SOLLUM
SIRTE
200
300
EGYPT

fication for this. We have two distinct schools of thought on that matter. One, inaugurated by St. Pachomius the Great (c. 292–346) of the Thebaid in Upper Egypt, and supported by St. Augustine (354–430) of Hippo in North Africa, discouraged pilgrimage as a remnant of ancient pagan habits. When St. Pachomius approached his end, he commanded Theodore, his pupil and successor, to carry his body under cover of night and bury it at an unknown place in order to save his remains from becoming an object of veneration and a center of pilgrimage. But other saints set a different example. St. Helena, mother of Constantine, led the way in the third and fourth decades of the fourth century. She went on pilgrimage to Jerusalem and excavated the Holy Cross and the instruments of the Passion, which she deposited in a church that she built for that purpose near the Sepulchre. She founded many other churches in various places, far and near, including the Chapel of the Burning Bush at the monastery of St. Catherine (formerly of the Transubstantiation) in Sinai. Others undertook the hazardous journey to Palestine from countries as remote as Gaul. The Bordeaux Pilgrim and St. Silvia of Aquitaine (known also as Cytheria and Aetheria) left written accounts of their visitations before the end of the fourth century. Foremost among the church fathers in popularizing pilgrimage was St. Jerome, who spent ten years (372–82) as a wanderer and a recluse around holy shrines throughout the Levant. Even when he returned to Italy, he stayed there only long enough to finish the Latin Vulgate translation, and then he went back in 385 to his Eastern peregrinations until his final settlement in a cave near the Church of the Nativity at Bethlehem, where he taught the youths of the area and established a new center for a community of female pilgrims from Italy.

Coterminously, a new phase arose around the middle of the fifth century when the Empress Eudocia started collecting relics, beginning with St. Luke's painting of Our Lady. This soon became a fashionable practice, and thousands of churches in Western Europe were founded and consecrated on relics brought by pilgrims from the East. The churches of Jerusalem were ransacked and relics in remote places were transplanted piecemeal through the centuries. The body of St. Catherine, an early fourth-century Coptic martyr in Alexandria, is said to have been enshrined intact in the monastery of Mt. Sinai during the ninth century. At present, Sinai has only the skull and the left hand of the Saint in a small white sarcophagus or casket with rich pious offerings of wrought gold and precious stones, on the side of the altar of the famous cathedral which Justinian built to commemorate the Empress Theodora. Those who visit the ruins of the Basilica of St. Simeon Stylites near Aleppo in northern Syria will find the column on top of which the holy man lived for nearly thirty years about the middle of the fifth century, once more than ninety feet high, now a stump, the rest carried away by relic hunters.

The pilgrim traffic was momentarily arrested during the Muslim invasion; but as soon as the belligerents laid down their arms, the flow of pilgrimage was resumed, even in the course of the eighth century. As early as the year 670, only thirty-three years after the triumphant entry of Caliph ʻUmar on a camel into Jerusalem, Arculf, bishop of Périgueux, went to the Holy Places and spent nine months in the Holy City. The written account which he left of his pilgrimage ("Relatio de locis sanctis ab Adamnano scripta") is typical of other known but unwritten ventures from England, Scotland, Gaul, Italy, and the rest of Europe. The pilgrimage of Willibald the Anglo-Saxon, begun in 722 and lasting seven years, is also recorded in another work of equal interest ("Vita sive potius Itinerarium S. Willibaldi episcopi Aichstadiani") .

The dividing line occurs in the establishment of the so-called religious Carolingian protectorate over the Christian East and the opening up of the route from Europe to the shores of the Levant as an immediate result. The pilgrim hostels established in the Holy City during that period were symptomatic of the increase in the number of Latin pilgrims. Three written accounts in the Carolingian era are worthy of note, namely, the pilgrimages of Fidelis (c. 750–60), of Bernard the Monk (867–70), and of Fortmund (*c.* 870–74). The first of these personalities is probably of Irish origin, and he is known to have visited and described the sacred sites of both Egypt and the Holy Land. The second was a monk of the Mont Saint Michel in Brittany, who undertook the voyage to the East with a certain Stephen from Spain and one Theudemund, probably a Frank. Bernard's story is entitled "Itinerary of Three Monks" or "Itinerary of Bernard the Wise" ("Itinerarium Bernardi Sapientis"), which contains interesting information on some aspects of ninth-century Egypt and the Holy Land. In Jerusalem, the three resided at the hostel built by Charlemagne for Latin pilgrims, and examined the contents of the library in the Church of St. Mary. Fortmund, who was a noble Breton, had been involved in a bloody crime for which he imposed a penance on himself in the form of perpetual pilgrimage until the Lord released him. Barefooted, with ashes on his head, wearing a coarse penitential robe, and chained round his waist and arms, he started toward the East. In his four years' wanderings, he visited Syria and stayed in Jerusalem for some time, went to Egypt, where he lived with the monks of the Thebaid, and was at Carthage, whence he crossed to Rome to implore Pope Benedict III's indulgence in vain. So he journeyed again to Jerusalem, Cana in Galilee, the Red Sea and Mt. Sinai, and the site of Noah's ark on the Armenian mountains; until in the end God had mercy over him and "delivered him from his chains of sin and iron" on his return to the tomb of St. Marcellinus in the monastery of Redon in Brittany.

Although the Byzantine wars of the tenth century must have depleted the number of travellers to the Near East, the flow of pilgrims from the West was never completely arrested.

Among the feudatories known to have undertaken the pilgrimage at the time were: Hilda, countess of Swabia, who died on the way in 969; Judith, duchess of Bavaria and Emperor Otto I's sister-in-law, in 970; and others at other dates, for example, the counts of Ardèche, of Vienne, of Verdun, of Arcy, of Anhalt, and of Gorizia. High dignitaries in the Church hierarchy did not lag behind. The bishop of Olivola performed the pilgrimage in 920. St. Conrad, bishop of Constance, visited Jerusalem three times, and St. John, bishop of Parma, no less than six times. Five more prelates * are known to have undertaken the same voyage beyond the sea at different dates, and we must assume that all these important people were accompanied by considerable bodies of retainers who were pilgrims of a humbler class.

Pilgrim traffic from Europe was conducted on the whole toward three main centers of great fame, namely, the shrine of St. James of Compostella in Spain, St. Peter's in Rome, and the sanctuaries of Jerusalem, the holiest of all holy cities. The abbots of Cluny in the tenth century encouraged the Spanish pilgrimage at first, and their monasteries on the southwestern route proved to be convenient havens for all pious travellers in that direction. Later, they extended their good offices to other leading centers and began to organize trips to the Holy Land. Numerous persons of standing in those days were able to perform pilgrimage under the sponsorship of Cluniac monks. These included, for instance, the abbot of Stavelot in 990 and the count of Verdun in 977.

Scandinavians also began to appear on the scene of pilgrimage, with one Kolseggr reaching Palestine in 992, succeeded by Harald Hardrada in 1034, and a number of isolated cases from Norway and Denmark in the course of the eleventh century. Even distant and derelict Iceland was represented by

* These were the abbots of Saint-Cybar, of Flavigny, of Aurillac, of Saint-Aubin d'Angers, and of Montier-en-Der.

its very apostle of Christianity, Thorvald Kodransson Vidtförli, who visited Jerusalem in 990.

Up to the eleventh century, the normal pilgrim routes converged on Rome with its numerous sanctuaries, and then across the Mediterranean from one of the south European maritime termini such as Venice, Naples, or Bari. The land route to Constantinople was opened only after the conversion of King Stephen of Hungary and his people to Christianity in the year 1000. It was chiefly used by pilgrims from Central and East Central Europe, and the First Crusade made it less unpopular. The conclusion of the peace treaty between Emperor Basil II and Caliph al-Hākim of Egypt in the same year (1000 A.D.) enhanced safety of travelling beyond the sea in the subsequent century.

Taken together, all these circumstances may help to explain the sudden jolt in pilgrim traffic at that time. In reality, the eleventh century may justly be reckoned as the age of mass pilgrimage. Hundreds of pious souls congregated on the eastern march to Jerusalem under the leadership of a bishop, an abbot or a great feudatory. Examples of these regimented assemblies of pilgrims are not wanting. Fulk of Nerxa, count of Anjou, conducted a communal pilgrimage in 1002. In 1026–27 a French abbot led a company of seven hundred pilgrims to the Holy Land; and Count William of Angoulême, together with a large number of abbots and nobles, took to the East in the same year. Duke Robert I of Normandy went with another group in 1035, though he himself felt ill on the return journey from Jerusalem and died at Nicaea near the western shores of Anatolia. Nevertheless, the pilgrimage from Normandy was repeated en masse during 1064. The great German pilgrimage of 1064–65 was organized by Bishop Gunther of Bamberg, who marched at the head of 7,000 men to Palestine, indubitably the most formidable company to be united in one "passagium" before the start of the Crusades. Some sources mention 12,000 instead of 7,000, which is apparently an exaggeration. Among them were other German bishops and archbishops as well as several feudal nobles and knights who crossed Central Europe to Constantinople and through Asia Minor, still in Byzantine hands, to Syria. Count Robert I of Flanders steered another pilgrimage in 1088–89. The eleventh-century registers of the abbey of Cluny contain more names of notable pilgrims from Germany, such as the archbishops of Trier and Mainz, others from England, and still more from France and Lorraine.

By that time the profound veneration for sacred relics and saintly shrines had become an integral part of the system of Latin Christianity, and pilgrims were not deterred in their penitential pursuits even by the changing scene in the Holy Land, where the Saljuq conquests reversed the enlightened policy of tolerance associated with the early Caliphate. As a rule, pilgrims proceeded unarmed except for their staffs, which they employed in driving away wild beasts. They walked most of the way, usually barefooted. The rich rode only donkeys. All were under the protection of the Church and customarily met with little or no trouble in Europe. Merchants frequently preferred to travel under the guise of palmers, that is, pilgrims carrying a Cross made of palm leaves from Jerusalem, for personal security. In the East, however, during the decades immediately preceding the Crusades, community pilgrimages became necessary for self-defense.

Not until 1074 do we begin to hear of a pontifical invitation for armed bands to fight their way to Jerusalem. This was made in a letter from Pope Gregory VII to Emperor Henry IV. After the success of the First Crusade, the establishment of the Latin kingdom of Jerusalem, and the creation of the military orders of religion, organizations for travel to Palestine multiplied. Apart from the Italian communes, notably Venice and Genoa, which possessed hostels in most cities of the Holy Land, the Hospitallers of St. John of Jerusalem and the Templars played a prominent role in supervising and facilitating pilgrim traffic. In fact, the Templars became the great banking agency whose branches in the European capitals, in Jerusalem, and in the majority of Eastern centers handled all manner of exchange transactions with enormous profits from the pilgrim service.*

EUROPE AND THE EAST ON THE EVE OF THE CRUSADE

A glance at the political map of the medieval world toward the end of the eleventh century will shed light on the genesis of events in the Crusading field and explain the factors at work in the position of the countries of both Europe and the Near East. First, it will be noticed that, of the two universal powers in the West, the Papacy rather than the Empire occupied the place of world leadership. As such, the Papacy became morally responsible for the defense of Christians wherever they might be.

In fact, the idea of Crusading in the East had been conceived at the Roman Curia even before the pontificate of its immediate promoter, Pope Urban II (1088–99). Pope Gregory VII (1073–85), the famous Hildebrand, had contemplated the project of holy war since his accession to the tiara. During his lifetime, the battle of Manzikert (Malazgard) in 1071 became a portentous omen of the fate of the Byzantine Empire, that last great bulwark of Christianity in the East against the Turks. Gregory realized that the Christian West must act if the Christian East were to be saved. It is not inconceivable that Urban II inherited this unfulfilled project from his great predecessor, the only difference being that Gregory had in

* Curiously, we hear only of pilgrims from Europe and none from Byzantium, although it is hard to believe that the Greeks refrained from going to the Holy Land at any time. This interesting topic calls for further inquiry from the Byzantinists.

mind the Eastern Empire whereas Urban aimed at the deliverance of Jerusalem after the relief of Byzantium. Moreover, the Popes were encouraged by the appeals for help from the Eastern Emperor Alexius Comnenus (1081–1118).

Early in the last decade of the eleventh century, the Emperor is said to have sent a personal letter to his old friend, Count Robert I of Flanders, asking Europeans for military support in his Anatolian struggles against the Turks. Unfortunately the original document is lost and the text survives in a rather ornate Latin version, sometimes regarded as apocryphal. In these critical years in the life of the Eastern Empire, however, there is no reason for doubting the historicity of the letter episode. After all, Robert of Flanders was an old pilgrim to the East; he even participated with the imperial ranks in fighting the Turks in Asia Minor during 1090; and it is not improbable that the Emperor should recall a friend to whom he might appeal for solace in the hour of his tribulation. In the meantime, the imperial envoys to Flanders must have stopped on their way across Italy at the city of Piacenza, where Pope Urban II had summoned a Church Council in March 1095, to deliberate upon the affairs of the East. That was an auspicious moment for the Byzantine embassy to appeal directly to the Holy Pontiff and the convened Roman hierarchy. In reality, Urban's mind appears to have been made up at Piacenza, and the next decisive step was reserved by him for the next Council in southern France. On November 27, 1095, the Pope solemnly declared the Crusade in his famous speech to the Church hierarchy and the French nobility in the Council of Clermont-Ferrand in the Auvergne. Since that moment, it may justly be said that the Crusade became the keynote of papal foreign policy until at least the close of the Middle Ages.

On the other hand, the Holy Roman Emperor was in a state of distress. Henry IV (1056–1106) of the Salian line in

Germany had been brought to his knees in the Investiture Contest at Canossa in 1077. Thus Charlemagne's successor was drowned in his own misfortunes, and Germany was torn asunder with local disaffection. Rival emperors kept springing up, sometimes with and sometimes without the blessing of the Holy See. Rudolph of Swabia, Herman of Luxembourg, and Conrad of Franconia fanned the fire of dispute over the imperial crown in an already enfeebled Germany. Although numerous crowds of Germans followed the itinerant preachers in the Peasants' Crusade, and although some responsible German knights joined the First Crusade, the Empire itself remained outside the movement in the early years of its life. Official German participation was deferred until the Second Crusade in 1146, when Emperor Conrad III led his imperial militia as far as Jerusalem.

In England, the Norman conquest of 1066, that capital event in English history, was still within living memory of the first Crusaders. The task of unification and centralization of the state was undertaken by William the Conqueror (1066–87), who was determined to free England from the vices of continental feudalism as he had known it in his old duchy of Normandy. The good work he began was still incomplete at the end of the eleventh century. His son and successor, William Rufus (1087–1100), the contemporary of the First Crusade, was unequal both to his father's heritage in England and to further involvement in foreign warfare in remote terrains.

Of the countries of Western Europe from which Crusading contingents were likely to be recruited, there remained Italy and Spain. The north of Italy was still under imperial jurisdiction and thus was dragged into the imperial disputes with the Papacy, a fact which rendered the area incapable of yielding any material contribution to the Holy War. Southern Italy, on the other hand, had just passed from Byzantine domination to Norman rule, and the new bellicose race of conquerors under

Robert Guiscard sought further fields of glory for more expansion. The First Crusade offered the Normans a golden opportunity for self-aggrandizement, and they hastened to throw all the weight of their power and vigor on the side of the movement.

In the Iberian Peninsula, the Christian principalities of Asturia, Castile, Navarre and Aragon, together with the nascent county of Portugal, had been fighting continuously a local Crusade * of their own against the Moors. The Popes not only absolved the Spanish people from the duty of Crusading in the East, but also invited the Normans and the French to lend them a helping hand in the pursuit of the Reconquista. In his southern advance on Toledo in 1085, King Alfonso VI of Castile was supported by French knights. At that time, the Moorish Caliphate was on the decline, and the local Arab princes sought independence, each in his own province. Thus a patchwork of Muslim kingdoms arose in the peninsula, known as the Kings of the Taifas (Reyes de Taifas), or Ṭawā'if, that is, tribes or separate communities, who fought one another and courted the alliance of their Christian neighbors and natural enemies against their own Muslim coreligionists.

The outlook for Muhammadan Spain would have been grim had it not been for the timely landing of the Berber Almoravids ** at Algeciras from North Africa under the able

* It is interesting to note that the first use of the word "Crusade" occurred in Spain at an earlier date. This is the Spanish "Cruzada."

** A Spanish corruption of the Arabic word "al-Murābiṭīn," that is, ascetics or religious recluses, sometimes translated as "Protagonists of the Faith." In French, the singular Arabic form "Murābiṭ" is corrupted into "marabout," signifying devotee. The duration of Almoravid rule was less than a century and came to an end with the rise of another more fanatical dynasty under the name of "Almohads," another Spanish corruption of the Arabic "Al-Muwaḥḥidīn," or Unitarians, who incorporated all North Africa and Southern Spain into a single unit during the period 1130–1269.

and spirited command of Yūsuf ibn Tashfīn, who succeeded in arresting the progress of the Christians. He defeated Alfonso VI at the battle of Zallaca in 1086, and Pope Urban II called on the French nobility to reinforce the Spanish Crusade. It was not until 1118 that the balance of power was again tipped in favor of the Christians with Aragon's recovery of the important and strategic city of Saragossa. The advent of the Almoravids occupied all the attention of the Spanish Christian hosts, who could hardly be expected to fight on two fronts by joining the new "passagium" to Palestine.

Apart from the Normans, the kingdom of France and its satellite feudal states proved in the end to be the rock on which Urban founded his Crusading aspirations for an Eastern campaign. With foresight, Urban, who was himself a Frenchman by birth and a Cluniac by profession, chose his own country of origin for launching the new movement. At Clermont in the heart of the Auvergne, he spoke to the clergy and nobles of France in French, and all conceded that his exhortations were divinely inspired. Thus the will of God (Deus lo volt!) became the battle cry of the Crusading hosts. The leaders of the First Crusade were essentially French and Norman. Whereas Gregory VII had contemplated going to the East himself at the head of the army, Urban was content with the appointment of Bishop Adhémar de Monteuil, the French bishop of Puy, as his apostolic legate for the coming expedition. This was a man of advanced years and great sagacity.

The French nobles, followed by the Flemings and the Normans, came forth in great numbers to take the Cross from the hands of Pope Urban himself. Foremost among them were Godfrey of Bouillon, duke of Lower Lorraine or Lotharingia, and his brother Baldwin. Other warlike leaders included Raymond of St. Gilles, count of Toulouse; Robert of Normandy, the Conqueror's son; Hugh, count of Vermandois and brother of the French king, Philip I; Stephen, count of

Blois; Robert, count of Flanders; Bohemond of Tarentum, son of Robert Guiscard, the great Norman warrior, and his nephew Tancred. They were all rich feudatories known for their valor, religious zeal, and determination. Their weaknesses were those of the age, chiefly obstinacy and a haughty character. Not one king took part in the First Crusade, often termed the Princes' or Barons' Crusade. In fact, the three great European monarchs—Emperor Henry IV, William Rufus of England, and Philip I of France—were all under sentence of excommunication at the time. The army, thus recruited, was not unified under one supreme authority, but was rather a series of contingents each serving under a liege lord. Even under those conditions, the first Crusaders proved to be sufficiently united in their ultimate aim to fight the battle of the Cross against the Muslim East, which happened to be suffering from symptoms of disintegration.

As a matter of fact, the state of anarchy which reigned in the Islamic Empire at the end of the century provides the chief explanation of the successes of the Latins and the discomfiture of the Muslims at the opening of the war. In the first place, the Near East was ruled by two hostile dynasties, the Fatimids * in Egypt with their heretical Shi'ite doctrines versus the Orthodox Sunnite Abbasid ** Caliphs in Bagdad.

* The Fatimid dynasty originated in Tunis under its first Caliph, 'Ubeid-Allah al-Mahdi, who assumed the title in 909 and reigned till 934. He founded his new capital, al-Mahdiya, from which the Fatimids spread their rule over the whole of North Africa. In 969 they conquered Egypt and transferred the seat of their government to the newly founded city of Cairo, which became the center of a vast empire extending from Morocco to Syria. They were descendants of Fāṭimah, daughter of the Prophet Muḥammad, who married the Prophet's cousin and third successor, Caliph 'Ali. They claimed for him the right of divine succession to the Prophet, and their Caliphs became the object of excessive veneration, contrary to the spirit of primitive Islamic orthodoxy. They became extinct in 1171, when Saladin completely suppressed them and returned Egypt from heterodox Shi'ism to Sunnite Islam.

** The Abbasid Caliphate succeeded the Umaiyad in 750 and transferred

Nothing could bridge the sectarian differences which separated them, not even the imminent danger of the Crusaders from Europe. But this was by no means the end of the trouble. The Abbasid Caliphs had become mere figureheads of the Islamic polity. Their commission ended with the ceremony of investing the strongest Turkish general with the title of sultan. The story of the Turks in Western Asia goes as far back as the reign of Caliph al-Mu'taṣim (833–42), the last great successor of Harūn al-Rāshīd, who introduced the employment of Turkish slaves as his bodyguard in order to free himself from the influence of the Arab aristocracy. Like the barbarian legionaries who were engaged by the later Roman emperors for a somewhat similar purpose, the Turks finally wrested all power from the Caliph's hands.

One of the Turkish clans or tribes, the Saljuqs, under the leadership of Ṭughril Beg, captured Bagdad itself in 1055 after invading Persia, and Ṭughril Beg wrested the title of sultan for himself from the impotent Caliph. His successor, Alp Arslan (1063–72), took a westerly direction in his expansionist policy and seized Jerusalem from the Fatimids in 1070. Then he turned to the northwest in the following year and inflicted the defeat of Manzikert (Malazjard) on the Byzantine co-regent, Romanus III Diogenes. Alp Arslan's successor, Malik Shah (1072–92), the last great sultan of the Saljuq line, completed the conquest of Asia Minor except for the marooned empire city of Trebizond on the southern shore of the Black Sea, which he reduced to a state of vassalage under his

the Arab capital from Damascus to Bagdad. Abbasid rule was suppressed in 1258, date of the fall of Bagdad before Hulagu and the Mongol hordes. The Caliphs then moved to Cairo under the protection of the Mamluk sultans. The Abbasids originally descended from 'Abbās, an uncle of the Prophet Muḥammad, and they retained a shadowy religious authority in Cairo until an Ottoman sultan, Selim I, took them to Constantinople after his Turkish conquest of Egypt in 1517. Ultimately, they became incorporated in the Turkish sultanate, which appropriated their title until the suppression of the Caliphate by Ataturk in 1924.

sultanate of al-Rūm, that is, of the Greeks. His death, however, marked the end of Saljuq supremacy.

The system of government practiced by the Turks contributed to the dissolution of their kingdom. The Turkish polity was fast growing into a kind of decentralized feudalism as a result of the habit of subdividing conquered territories among their commanders and their armies. Strong feudal lords awaited the first possible opportunity to appropriate their own fiefs altogether and declare their complete independence from the sultanate. The disappearance of Malik Shah's overpowering personality from the scene gave the turbulent generals their chance to assert full and undisputed authority over their provinces. This was followed by twelve years of internal chaos and mortal strife among various pretenders to succession to the sultanate.* It was at this propitious moment that the first Crusaders set foot in the East and succeeded in establishing the Latin kingdom of Jerusalem during 1099.

Thus was begun the Frankish solution of the Eastern Question in the Middle Ages, while the fortunes of the Muslims were at a very low ebb and they became an easy prey to the new invaders of the Holy Land.

* The picture of the internal factions in Syria itself at the time of the First Crusade is even more complicated. Sir Hamilton Gibb, in the introduction to his English version of ibn al-Qalānisī's *Damascus Chronicle of the Crusades,* London 1932, 14 ff, tabulates six distinct forces at work in the Syrian conflict: (1) the Fatimid Empire; (2) the local Arab tribes and princes; (3) the Saljuqid Turkmen princes; (4) the Turkish military officers or amirs; (5) the independent or non-Saljuqid Turkmen tribes; (6) the general body of the population. Each of these factions had its own course of action and its special interests. To the Crusaders, all were just infidel Saracens, a word borrowed from the Greek "σαρακεγοι," a corruption of the Arabic "Sharqiūn" meaning "Easterners."

CHAPTER TWO

Crusade: The Frankish Solution of the Eastern Question

OLD CONCEPTS AND NEW IDEAS

HISTORICAL WRITING * in the field of the Crusade has been slowly but steadily undergoing a series of fundamental changes in the course of the last quarter of a century, and recent works on the subject have displayed a new outlook on some of its principal phases. Most prominent among these is the problem of the chronology of the Age of the Crusade. There are two schools of thought about the beginning and the end of the Crusading Age. The foregoing chapter has revealed that the year 1095 was only a landmark, admittedly a most important one, in the genesis of a movement whose roots are deeper in history than Urban's speech. Indeed, Grousset's outstanding contribution, formulated in the introductory thesis to his

* See Atiya: *The Crusade: Historiography and Bibliography* (hereafter referred to as *Hist. and Bibl.*), essay on Crusade Historiography.

monumental work on the Crusades, is to push back the story of the war of the Cross from its traditional inception to pre-Islamic times—the mortal struggle between Byzantium and Persia. It must be noted, however, that Grousset followed in the footsteps of the older twelfth-century master historian of the Latin kingdom of Jerusalem, Archbishop William of Tyre, who began his annals with "L'Estoire de Éracles, empéreur." In other words, Grousset's originality lies in resuscitating a much earlier theory which had surprisingly escaped the vigilance of subsequent authors. Runciman starts his more recent work with "the abomination of desolation" which befell eastern Christianity on the rise of Islam and the spread of the Arab Empire over the Holy Land and elsewhere; and the same system of thinking recurs in the monumental and collective Pennsylvania *History of the Crusades*. The Crusades can be viewed properly only as one phase in the continuous relations between the East and the West.

The end of the Crusade, according to the older school and the cataclysmic view of history, came to pass outside Acre in 1291. The end of Latin dominion on the Asiatic mainland appeared to be a convenient date to close the story of the movement. Nevertheless, it will be seen that the Crusading momentum continued with considerable vigor at least throughout the fourteenth century.

Between these dates—1095 and 1291—there has been a growing tendency to discredit the use of fixed numbers in defining the successive campaigns. To label the Crusades numerically, it has rightfully been argued, would be a tacit admission that each expedition was rather a separate entity than an integral part of a continuous movement, which would be a misrepresentation of the truth. Apart from the First Crusade, which ended in the foundation of the kingdom of Jerusalem, the numerical conception of the movement begins to lose its accepted significance. Furthermore, the juxtaposition of the crucial campaigns of the fourteenth century renders the continuation of a numerical system even less meaningful. On the other hand, it seems inevitable for considerations of expediency, rather than historical aptitude, to make some allowance in connection with the Second, Third, and Fourth Crusades, long recognized as numerical entities; it is too late now to amend them. The remaining expeditions, however, must derive their names from their special character or their promoters.

Any comprehensive study of the results of the Crusade must necessarily lead to an inquiry into that much neglected phenomenon, the Counter-Crusade: the Islamic or Eastern reaction to action from the West. The importance of this aspect will be demonstrated. It led to the rebirth of the Islamic Empire, which appears to have been the most enduring outcome of the Crusade.

The growing interest in Arabic and Oriental material has been one of the chief features in the Crusading historiography of our time. Though much has been done in this field, more remains to be done. Before the bar of history, it is impossible to provide the correct appraisal of the position of the Crusade on an unbalanced record of Western and Eastern sources. In spite of due recognition of this, access to extant Arabic sources is still fractional, and the leading general historians of the Crusade are unfortunately neither Arabists nor Orientalists. With this in mind, it is not presumptuous to contend that the history of the Crusade has not yet reached the stage of adolescence.

In order to construe the general history of the movement between 1095 and 1291 as the Frankish Solution of the Eastern Question in the Middle Ages, it is essential to adopt the analytical method both to bring out the salient and to economize in the exposition of details, which are treated in other standard works. Grousset's system of classification is still the most acceptable, since it reflects with logical lucidity the true picture of events which he tried to paint in facile and enthusiastic style. According to him, there are three distinct phases in the development of the relations between the Western Christians and the Eastern Muslims on Asian soil in the era under review:

(1) First Phase. Muslim Anarchy and Frankish Monarchy.
(2) Second Phase. Frankish Monarchy and Muslim Monarchy: The Equilibrium.
(3) Third Phase. Muslim Monarchy and Frankish Anarchy.

Let us make a brief analytical survey of each of these phases.

THE CRUSADE TO 1291: THE FIRST PHASE

This is the age of the First Crusade, also known as the Barons' or Princes' Crusade, covering the period from the establishment of the Latin states in the Holy Land to the death of Baldwin II in the year 1131.

The First Crusade was preceded by the Peasants' Crusade, an inglorious prelude to the Holy War with which the problematic and somewhat dubious personality of Peter the Hermit is traditionally credited. His chief assistant, a poor knight known as Walter the Penniless, led a company of 12,000 disqualified irregulars, moved by faith and famine, while a German priest named Gottschalk headed an equal band from Franconia, Swabia, and Lotharingia. A veritable exodus took place, in which the whole population of villages enrolled in the battle of the Cross, with little armor beyond staff and sickle and wooden swords, and in expectation of miraculous triumph against the miscreants with the help of a host of angels. William, viscount of Mélun, Count Emich from the Rhineland, and Folkmar in Germany all led columns of recruits for the divine cause, and, after disgracefully molesting the Jews of Central Europe, proceeded along the Danube, where they suffered and inflicted suffering in Hungary and

Bulgaria. Finally they descended on Constantinople like a cloud of locusts, hardly what Alexius had requested in his appeal. The bewildered Byzantine Emperor had no choice but to acquiesce in their wish to be transported to Anatolia, where Turkish sabers cut them down at Nicaea in August 1096. A few who apostatized to save their lives were sent east in captivity, and only some, including Peter, escaped back to European shores and awaited the forthcoming feudal militias.

In the meantime, four regular armies were being mustered to follow the old pilgrim routes to Constantinople for the official Crusade. A substantial vanguard of Lotharingians and Rhinelanders under Godfrey of Bouillon and his brother Baldwin arrived via Hungary and the Balkans at the walls of the Byzantine capital on December 23, 1096. They followed the apocryphal route of Charles the Great, by which the first Holy Roman Emperor was believed to have gone to fight the infidels, undoubtedly a legend circulated to enhance the enthusiasm of the Crusaders in their sacred quest. Anna Comnena estimated 10,000 knights and 70,000 infantry apart from a multitude of camp followers. In the meantime, the bombastic Hugh Vermandois, brother of Philip I of France, together with a Franco-Norman band, crossed the Alps, Italy, and a tempestuous Adriatic, where he was shipwrecked near Durazzo and was escorted by Byzantine legions to Constantinople. He was followed by Robert Curt-Hose, duke of Normandy, Stephen, count of Blois and Chartres, and finally Robert of Flanders. The Normans from South Italy, numbering 10,000 knights and 20,000 career infantry warriors, under Bohemond, son of Robert Guiscard, and Tancred, his nephew, attained the eastern shore of the Adriatic below Durazzo and proceeded to join the others in November 1096. The Provençals under Raymond of Saint-Gilles, count of Toulouse, accompanied by Adhémar, the apostolic legate, traversed the Alps and North Italy to the shores of the Adriatic, where they suffered greatly until they also reached Durazzo and took the usual road (Via Egnatia) across the Balkan Peninsula to Constantinople via Thessalonica. The full array became complete in May 1097. The highest estimate is provided by Fulcher as 600,000, and the lowest by Raymond of Aguilers at 100,000, which is nearly the equivalent of the whole Byzantine army. Allowing for medieval exaggeration, even the lowest figure must have confronted the imperial household with a tremendous problem in the matter of logistics and of transportation to Anatolia.

After patching up a compromise on the application of the rule of international law regarding the position of the Western feudal magnates vis-à-vis the Eastern Roman Empire, arrangements were made for conveyance of the Crusaders to Asia Minor without further delay. They were persuaded to swear an oath of fealty to the Emperor and to owe him allegiance for their future conquests, an oath which they did not mean to keep, at least in connection with the Holy Places. The campaign was inaugurated with the capture of Nicaea, which they ceded to an imperial garrison, on June 19, 1097. Then the discomfiture of the main Turkish forces under Qilij Arslan at Dorylaeum, in the hot summer days of July 1097, opened up the Anatolian route to Syria, and some of the leaders began to envision prospects of principalities of their own. Friction between them became evident in the race of Tancred and Baldwin to capture the Armenian Taurus in September. Baldwin foiled his protagonist by marrying an Armenian princess and succeeding to the throne of Edessa after the murder of King Thoros in a local uprising.

Once within the confines of northern Syria, the Crusaders aimed at seizing Antioch, the fair and fortified "City of God" on the Orontes, where the followers of Jesus were called Christians for the first time in history. Bohemond coveted it for himself. After a protracted and agonizing siege of about eight months, the city * fell into their hands on June 3, 1098, only four days before the arrival of Kerbogha, the Turkish governor of Mosul, with a substantial army for its relief, and almost one year after Nicaea. The morale of the host, weakened by heat and hunger, was revived by the miracle of the discovery of the sacred lance with which a Roman legionary had pierced the Lord's side during the Passion, hidden in a chapel at Antioch. They were able to repel Kerbogha's mighty army in defeat, and Bohemond stayed at the head of the new acquisition; while the others pressed on to Jerusalem by devious ways for another year. Raymond, who had also wanted Antioch for himself and was ousted from it by Bohemond, had as his consolation prize the county of Tripoli.

In ecstasy the remaining Crusaders finally perceived the domes, turrets, and towers of the Holy City in the early days of June 1099. By the seventh of the month they managed to complete siege operations and started the construction of a tremendous wooden tower with a drawbridge in readiness for storming the walls. Battering rams, ladders, catapults, wheels, and all manner of engines were made and used in the successive daily attacks on the city fortifications. Jerusalem had recently been recovered from the Turks by the Fatimid Caliphate of Egypt, and a garrison of proved fighters was left on guard. In spite of the valiant defense of the city, it became evident that its downfall was only a matter of time, and the arrival of Christian reinforcements of men and material from Genoese galleys at Jaffa sealed the doom of the Muslims. On July 15 the Christians began to pour over the walls from the tower bridge, with Duke Godfrey always in the lead. The chroniclers of the event say that the storming of the city took place at the ninth hour, which was the hour of the Passion on

* The Turkish governor of the city was Yaghi Siyān, and the city's fall was precipitated by internal treachery in which the amir Fīrūz played a prominent role.

a Friday. Some descended swiftly and opened the city gates for the others to enter, and the rest of the story was simply a war of systematic extermination and fierce massacre. The anonymous author of the "Gesta Francorum," an eyewitness of the horrors of the assault, says: "Our men followed, killing and slaying even to the Temple of Solomon, where the slaughter was so great that our men waded in blood to their ankles." *

Archbishop William of Tyre calls the capture of the Holy City the "End of the Pilgrimage" and says that "it was not alone the spectacle of headless bodies and mutilated limbs strewn in all directions that roused horror in all who looked upon them. Still more dreadful was it to gaze upon the victors themselves, dripping with blood from head to foot, an ominous sight which brought terror to all who met them." ** The vivid picture painted by the twelfth-century archbishop continues thus:

> Each marauder claimed as his own in perpetuity the particular house which he had entered, together with all it contained. For before the capture of the city the pilgrims had agreed that, after it had been taken by force, whatever each man might win for himself should be his forever by right of possession, without molestation. Consequently the pilgrims reached the city most carefully and boldly killed the citizens. They penetrated into the most retired and out-of-the-way places and broke open the most private apartments of the foe. At the entrance of each house, as it was taken, the victor hung up his shield and his arms, as a sign to all who approached not to pause there by that place as already in possession of another.

This appears to be one of the earliest references to the use of coats of arms for identification, a custom which became more general among the Crusaders at a later date under the influence of Muslim heraldry. As the city became quieter and the

* A. C. Krey: *The First Crusade, The Accounts of Eyewitnesses and Participants,* Gloucester, Mass., 1958, 256.

** *A History of Deeds Done Beyond the Sea,* trans. and annotated by Emily H. Babcock and A. C. Krey (*Records of Civilization*), I, N.Y. 1943, 372. See Atiya: *Hist. and Bibl.,* Monumental Collections, section VI.

tumult subsided, the bloodthirsty and bloodstained pilgrims laid aside their arms and, with tearful sighs and heartfelt emotion, proceeded to pray in the Church of the Holy Sepulchre.

The Latin kingdom of Jerusalem was thus proclaimed, with its first custodian Godfrey of Bouillon, who accepted the modest title of "Defender of the Holy Sepulchre" (Advocatus Sancti Sepulchri). The chief duty of the "Advocatus" was to ensure the safety of the conquest, and this he did by defeating the first Egyptian army arriving from Cairo at Ascalon in the following month.

Apparently the winners of the day returned from that battlefield to Jerusalem laden with tremendous booty. Realizing the hopelessness of their plight, the Muslim amirs of the still unconquered coastal towns soon began to send Godfrey tributes in gold besants and presented him with horses loaded with provisions and fruits; and these peace overtures were accepted as stabilizing factors in the position of victors and vanquished who were destined to live together for many years to come.

At last, Godfrey died on July 18, 1100, and was succeeded by Baldwin of Boulogne as first king-elect of the new little theocratic state, who was crowned in the Holy Sepulchre on December 25, 1100. The genesis of this typically feudal monarchy,* viewed in the broadest outline, may be found to consist of two general stages in two successive periods: the first kingdom of the twelfth century, whose monarchs, though elective, sought to control the nobility; and the second kingdom of the thirteenth century, becoming hereditary but controlled by its feudatories. In both cases, the power of the Church was supreme and the advice of the Latin patriarch of Jerusalem usually was decisive. The kingdom consisted mainly of four semi-independent principalities: Jerusalem, Antioch,

* The feudal system adopted wholesale in the new kingdom was later codified in the famous Assizes of Jerusalem.

Edessa, and Tripoli. These in turn were broken up into smaller baronies and fiefs, while the administration of the coastal towns was largely confided to the greater merchant sea powers of Venice, Genoa, and Pisa.

The Latin Church also came into existence with two patriarchs at Jerusalem and Antioch, eight metropolitan provinces, and sixteen bishoprics, in addition to a considerable number of monastic establishments. It appeared at first as if Antioch, of ancient fame as the capital of the East from Seleucid days down to the Byzantine period, was going to regain the eminence which it had lost since the Arab invasion and become the new capital of another Christian kingdom; and indeed Bohemond worked hard for the realization of this ambitious project. But Jerusalem in the end won the day as the Rome of the East with the Holy Sepulchre, and Bohemond missed the chance of elevation to royal dignity, although the Church upheld his claims against those of Baldwin. It would even seem that the primate of Jerusalem, Dagobert, secretly envisaged some sort of Caesaro-papism in which the patriarchal throne, and not any temporal authority, should be the center of a great theocracy in the Holy Land. This accounts for the enduring struggle between Church and State in Jerusalem for at least the formative years of the first century of the existence of that monarchy.

Without dwelling on the internal political history of the new organization, or the daily military acts of reconnaissance and expansion of the various signories, detailed in many monographs and general works of reference, it would seem helpful for the comprehension of the salient in the Crusade to attempt an examination of the elements of strength and weakness in the new state. With the success of the Crusaders, the First Crusade was liquidated, and the burden of sustaining the conquest of the whole country was left for the new king to shoulder, along with those who tarried behind at his court. In fact, the invasion of the Holy Land was as yet virtually limited to a few important cities and a strip of land along the Mediterranean littoral, while the hinterland of Greater Syria remained wholly in Muslim hands. The important cities of Aleppo, Damascus, Homs, and Hamah were never completely incorporated by the Latins in the realm.

From within, the seeds of discord had been apparent in the semi-autonomous feudal divisions of the kingdom. The Christians were planted as alien colonists in preponderantly hostile Muslim territories. The pilgrim Crusaders had fulfilled their vow and left, homeward bound for Europe, while the defeated enemies remained near at hand in permanent bases, ready to seize every opportunity to start the slow and nagging reconquest of lost possessions. As early as 1100, Bohemond was captured by the Danishmend Turcomans of Siwas, to be freed only in 1103; and in the following year (1104) Baldwin du Bourg, the future king, and Joscelin of Courtenay were seized by the enemy while fighting in the province of Harran. They were released only in 1108 on payment of a large ransom. The position of the Christians in the East never ceased to be critical.

In addition to the perpetual danger from without and the continuous disaffection from within, Emperor Alexius claimed both Antioch and Edessa as Byzantine acquisitions by virtue of the original agreement with the Crusaders at Constantinople. Thus growing Byzantine hostility to the Crusaders resulted in Bohemond's abortive attack on Durazzo in 1108.

On the other hand, the reign of Baldwin I (1110–1118) was memorable for a number of points which strengthened the structure of the nascent kingdom. He was a man of vision and considerable ability. He fought the theocratic policy of the Church, which found a strong exponent in the Tuscan patriarch of Jerusalem, Dagobert, who was subsequently deposed. He sallied to the Gulf of Aqabah and seized the historic Red Sea port of Ailah from Egypt, thus achieving the cleavage of the Arab world into two sections, in Africa and Asia. Not having enough reinforcements of manpower from the West, he started a policy of rapprochement with the Eastern Christians, notably the Maronites and the Armenians, who were gradually drawn toward Roman obedience. The Latins, who were becoming ostensibly Orientalized, began to intermingle with the natives; and mixed marriages with the Eastern Christians, and sometimes with evangelized Muslim women, produced a new generation of "Pullani." Baldwin struck his own coins with Arabic inscriptions in order to facilitate trade intercourse with the Muslims. He encouraged the Venetian, Genoese, and Pisan merchants to avail themselves of the possibilities of the trade emporia on his shores, thus enriching the kingdom with new sources of revenue.

Both Baldwin I and his successors inaugurated the policy of building a chain of mighty castles on fortified sites from which the Franks were able to rule the country with effect—an accomplishment of great strategic importance. The Krak de Monréale,* built by Baldwin in 1115 to the southeast of the Dead Sea, is a fine example of the numerous citadels erected by the Crusaders in later times for both defensive and offensive purposes. Monréale was midway between Jerusalem and the tip of the Gulf of Aqabah and commanded the caravan routes from Cairo to Damascus and from Damascus to Mecca, thus enabling the lord of the castle to raise heavy tributes from passing Muslim traders and pilgrims. One of the largest and most famous castles was the Krak de Chevaliers on the mountain spur overlooking the caravan gorges in the north between Homs and Hamah on the one side and Tripoli and Tortosa on the other. Though it was occupied by and identified with the Knights Hospitallers, its foundations may have been laid down not long after the First Crusade on the invulnerable site of an older Arab, perhaps even Byzantine, citadel. The third of the great twelfth-century Kraks, known in Arabic simply as the Karak, was constructed east of the Dead Sea in the desert

* Known in Arabic as al-Shaubak, eighty miles south of Jerusalem and eighty miles north of the Red Sea.

of Moab. Here nestled Reginald of Châtillon, whose brigandage against the caravans of Damascus, Mecca, and Cairo precipitated the wrath of Saladin, who directed his attacks on it even more than against the other Kraks, and it was the first to fall into his hands in 1188. As a rule, these castles, the ruins of which are still standing, were tremendous structures with double enceintes, great halls, living quarters, chapels, magazines, stables, and water cisterns. They were partly hewn in the solid rock and a moat surrounded them between the two enclosures. A generous supply of water was customarily engineered from neighboring springs. Most castles were held by local knights and great feudatories, but very rarely by the kings.

The Latin kingdom received further strength from the creation of the military orders of religion. These consisted of groups of militant monks who combined the professions of monasticism and fighting the enemies of the Cross. The first of these organizations was that of the Knights Templar, inaugurated by a French knight, Hugh de Payens, and a few companions, who decided in 1119 to form a special contingent for the protection of pilgrims and the defense of the Holy Land. Baldwin II granted them a place of residence within the precincts of the Temple of Solomon, from which they acquired their name. St. Bernard of Clairvaux planned their rule for them on a Cistercian model of considerable asceticism, and Pope Honorius III gave them confirmation in 1128. They were robed in white with a red cross.

The second great order to play another role in upholding the Latin kingdom and the Crusading cause was that of the Hospitallers, or the Order of St. John of Jerusalem, whose remote origins could be traced to the year 1048, before the Crusades, when the merchants of Amalfi were allowed by the Muslim ruler of Jerusalem to build a hospital for Christian pilgrims. After the First Crusade, members of that hospital were actually engaged in caring for the sick and wounded warriors. About 1120 Raymond du Puy and his fellow workers in that hospital decided to set themselves up as Knights of the Hospital of St. John of Jerusalem, under the rule of celibacy, chastity, charity, helping the sick, and fighting in defense of the Holy Land. Their main headquarters during this period was the famous Krak des Chevaliers. They were robed in black with a white cross.

Other military orders on a similar model kept springing up, of which the Teutonic Order was perhaps the most famous. Members of those organizations were presumably men of free birth and an upright character. As time went on, they began to deviate from the tenets of their original rule, particularly the Templars, who became one of the richest banking concerns in Europe, until their suppression was engineered by the French monarchy, which had been heavily in their debt, and was executed by the Synod of Vienne in 1312.

The Templars and Hospitallers marred much of their valuable service to the Latin kingdom of Jerusalem by their continuous rivalry, not only in acquiring privileges and raising funds, but also in the dangerous sphere of war; and they are known to have occasionally allied themselves with Muslim princes against one another. Both became extremely rich and powerful. They owned commanderies and priories in Europe and practically all parts of the Latin Levant. They observed a strict rule and submitted to a close bureaucracy with a wide system of espionage. They owed allegiance only to the Pope of Rome directly, and consequently were able to defy local authorities, both ecclesiastical and temporal, even in matters of a military character.

It is interesting to note that the idea of Crusading never subsided in Europe between the First and Second Crusades. The influx of holy warriors, though far from being universal, was not arrested. During the present phase, record exists of two expeditions or minor Crusades reaching the Holy Land. The first has often been described as the Crusade of 1101, proclaimed by Pope Paschal II (1099–1118) on the arrival of the exciting news of the fall of Jerusalem, received just after Urban's decease. The first man to respond to the new call was an old objector to Urban's speech of 1095. This was William IX, duke of Aquitaine and count of Poitou, better known as the first of the French troubadours. Among his companions-at-arms were numerous feudal gentlemen such as Hugh de Lusignan, the half-brother of Raymond of Toulouse and a former Crusader, and Stephen of Blois, together with three French bishops and a multitude of recruits from France, Burgundy, Germany, and Lombardy. Constantinople was their common rendezvous, and they declared their aims to be the deliverance of Bohemond from captivity and the completion of the objectives of the First Crusade by seizing Bagdad, the seat of the Abbasid Caliphate. Following approximately the course of the first Crusaders, they were ultimately routed at Mersivan and Heraclea in Asia Minor. Many were massacred, some were carried into captivity, especially the women (Ida of Austria is believed to have borne the redoubtable Zangi in one of the princely harems) ; only a few reached the Holy Land by sea or by land.

Less abortive was the Norwegian Crusade of King Sigurd (1103–1130), who had been meandering in Norse fashion on the high seas with a host of Jerusalemfarers from Norway and a fleet of fifty-five ships for some four years, sojourning in England, fighting the Moors in Spain, fraternizing with the Normans of Sicily, and at last aiding Baldwin I in the capture of the port of Sidon in 1110. In the same year, the Genoese had also helped the king to seize Beirut. Baldwin's efforts to take Tyre, however, failed; and it remained for his successor, Baldwin II du Bourg (1118–31), to accomplish this conquest in 1124, with the support of the Venetians.

Baldwin II's reign was, on the whole, a continuation of his predecessor's in the policy of consolidating the kingdom. He brought with him to the crown of Jerusalem his old county of Edessa, in which he installed during the following year one of his close supporters, Joscelin of Courtenay. In 1119 he became regent of Antioch. He intensified the war against both Turks and Egyptians with mixed results. His foolhardy adventures led to his capture by the Turks in 1123, though he was freed in the following year. The advantages of his reign in general outweighed the disadvantages, although by his sustained pressure on the Syrian and Egyptian frontiers he drove his divided enemies into prospective alliance and stirred Muslim armies out of their pathetic lethargy. The seeds of Christian defeat were sown, but it took the next phase for them to germinate and bear fruit.

THE SECOND PHASE

The central period in the life of the kingdom of Jerusalem was one of unstable equilibrium between a consolidated Frankish monarchy and a consolidating Muslim monarchy. This is the age of Fulk of Anjou (1131–43) and his two sons, Baldwin III (1144–62) and Amalric or Amaury I (1162–74) in Jerusalem on the Christian side, and of the Zangi dynasty of Mosul, comprising the Atabeg 'Imād-al-Dīn (1128–46) and his redoubtable son and successor, Nūr-al-Dīn (1146–74), on the side of Islam. It is also the age of the Second Crusade of 1146–48, which was brought about by the fall of Edessa * (the Arabic al-Ruha). In fact, the height of Christian conquest had been attained by the end of Baldwin II's reign, and the capture of Edessa marked a slow turn of the tide which continued against the Franks in later years.

Perhaps the first note to be struck by Fulk at the beginning of his reign was his attempt to bridge the long-standing differences between the Latins and the Byzantines. His concilia-

* The first fall of Edessa occurred in 1144 under 'Imād-al-Dīn, and its final capture two years later in November 1146 was accomplished in Nūr-al-Dīn's reign and after his father's assassination.

tory policy was maintained by his immediate successors, and both Baldwin III and his brother Amalric I were betrothed to Comnenian princesses, while Manuel I Comnenus (1143–80) married Mary of Antioch, Raymond's daughter. Though it would be an error to assume that the mutual dislike and distrust of Latin and Greek were eradicated, there was a period of relative peace and understanding in the Levant. Fulk, too, scored another success with his Muslim neighbor, Anar, governor of Damascus, whose authority was imperilled by the expansionist schemes of 'Imād-al-Dīn Zangi of Mosul. In the years 1139–40, Anar sought and readily acquired an alliance with the Latin kingdom against his own coreligionist. The autobiography of Usāmah ibn Munqidh provides instances of growing amity and religious tolerance between the Christian settlers and the native Arabs of Syria at that time.

Nevertheless, the conquest of Edessa by the Zangis of Mosul alarmed the Christians, in whom the spirit of Crusading was aroused on the occasion by Bernard of Clairvaux, a French saint and an eloquent fanatic of tremendous prestige in the Europe of his day. Proclaimed by Pope Eugenius III (1145–53), and preached by St. Bernard at the courts of France and Germany, the Second Crusade materialized as a royal project of less popular and less international character than the First Crusade. King Louis VII (1137–80) of France and Emperor Conrad III (1138–52) of Germany marched at the head of some 70,000 recruits from each country. At Vézelay, where the men of France were enlisting, St. Bernard is said to have torn his own robe to make Crosses for the Crusaders when the original stock was exhausted—so great were the numbers of people swept by the zeal for holy war. Conrad thought the Crusade might be utilized to reunite his people, then divided between Guelf and Ghibelline factions.

While these two major armies pressed by the land route toward Constantinople, a smaller mixed contingent from Flanders and England sailed round the continent and landed in

Portugal for revictualling and to fight the Moors in the Iberian Peninsula. In 1147 they seized Lisbon and laid the foundations of the nascent kingdom of Portugal, which must be regarded as a byproduct of the Second Crusade. As to the larger armies, mistrust prevailed between the French and Germans, who kept at some distance from each other on the march; and both of them shared mutual suspicion of the Greeks. In Asia Minor the Turks crippled the invading detachments by destroying the crops and dessicating most of the water springs, thus depriving the Christians of all provisions for their daily livelihood. At the second battle of Dorylaeum in October 1147, they inflicted irreparable rout upon the exhausted Germans; and in January 1148 the French suffered a decisive defeat at Cadmus. Conrad retreated to Constantinople, sick and disheartened, then retraced his steps to Germany without having had a glimpse of the Holy Land. Louis managed with difficulty to reach Antioch, and he performed pilgrimage to the Holy Sepulchre at Easter, 1149, before taking sail homeward after a disastrous Crusade. On the way, he was harassed by the Byzantines, who rightly suspected his sympathies for their Norman enemies. Actually Louis landed in Calabria and crowned Roger as king of Sicily, and accordingly another kingdom came forth out of the Second Crusade. In France, Abelard's skeptic philosophy seemed to strike deeper roots in twelfth-century minds as a result of the failure of the Crusaders and his disciples scoffed at the policy of St. Louis.

The most serious outcome of the Crusade, however, was in the East, where the Muslim princes on the fringe of the Latin kingdom of Jerusalem were encouraged by the Christian defeat to harass the petty Crusader states without respite. Although the Muslims on the southern front lost Ascalon, surnamed "The Bride of Syria," to Baldwin III in 1153, the Syrians in the north constituted the most serious danger to the Latins. The Damascene-Christian alliance was broken by the foolish aggression of the Christians, who aimed at carving certain portions of the Muslim principality for themselves. In the end, Damascus submitted to Nūr-al-Dīn in April 1154, thus gaining in strength and stature along the vulnerable confines of its Latin neighbors.

Unequal to the Turks in the north, the Latin king explored another field for future expansion in the south. The Fatimid Caliphate in its latter days had been on the decline, and the situation in Egypt was apparently ripe for another conquest. The country was rich in resources, but impoverished in men of strong mettle for leadership. Both Amalric and Nūr-al-Dīn coveted this fresh prey, and there was a race between the two men to seize it. Amalric conducted five expeditions into Egypt between September 1163 and December 1169, the last one carried out with Byzantine military collaboration, which turned out to be little more than a nominal gesture.

Meanwhile Nūr-al-Dīn's general, Shirkūh, invaded the country three times. The internal conditions of Egypt afforded the Syrian his chance, and he was invited in by the Fatimid wazir Shāwar, whose position was endangered by the rise of a rival called Ḍirgham, the victor of the battle of Gazza (1163) against the Crusaders and an idol of the people. After Shāwar's restoration, he began to scheme against the Syrian, considering him a hateful Sunnite Muslim with a secret plan to end the so-called heretical Shi'ite rule of the Fatimids from Egypt. Shāwar turned to their common enemies, the Franks, for help. A treaty (1167) was concluded to the effect that Amalric should keep a garrison in Egypt until Shirkūh's army was destroyed or driven out of the country, and should meanwhile receive 400,000 gold pieces, half of which would be paid immediately.

Hugh of Caesarea was despatched to procure the ratification of the treaty from the Caliph in person, and William of Tyre reports the bewilderment of the envoy at the sight of the luxurious display in the Great Palace of the Fatimid in Cairo. Escorted through narrow passages guarded by armed Ethiopians, William of Tyre records in his history that the envoys

were conducted into a large and spacious court open to the sky which freely admitted the sun's rays. There, supported by columns of marble covered with designs in relief were promenades with fretted and gilded ceilings and pavements of various coloured stones. Throughout the entire circuit royal magnificence prevailed. So elegant was both material and workmanship that involuntarily the eyes of all who saw it were ravished by the rare beauty and never wearied of sight. There were marble fishpools filled with limpid waters; there were birds of many kinds, unknown to our part of the world. These were larger than those familiar to us, their forms were unusual, their colours strange, and their songs different.

As they approached the presence of the Caliph at the inner part of the palace,

the sultan showed the usual reverence to his lord, according to custom; twice he prostrated himself on the ground and humbly offered as if to a divinity due worship and a kind of abject adoration. Then for a third time bowing to the ground, he laid down the sword which he wore suspended from his neck. Thereupon the curtains embroidered with pearls and gold, which hung down and hid the throne, were drawn aside with marvellous rapidity, and the caliph was revealed with face unveiled. Seated on a throne of gold, surrounded by some of his privy counsellors and eunuchs, he presented appearance more than regal.*

After imprinting a kiss humbly on the Caliph's foot, the wazir explained the circumstances of the treaty and his master gave it ratification by putting his bare hand in the envoy's in response to Hugh's demand, much to the consternation of the Egyptians.

Actually Egypt by this extraordinary pact came directly under a Crusader protectorate for the first time in the history of the movement. Amalric besieged Alexandria, whose governor-

* *A History of Deeds Done Beyond the Sea* (*Records of Civilization*), II, N.Y. 1943, 319–21. See Atiya: *Hist. and Bibl.*, Monumental Collections, section VI.

ship was confided by Shirkūh to a young nephew by the name of Saladin, destined to become the real hero of Islam. The parties agreed to leave the city to the Egyptians instead of entering into a battle of doubtful issue. Amalric then marched back to Cairo, where he succeeded in persuading Shirkūh that both of them should leave the country—the Franks say through intimidation and the Arabic chroniclers say that Amalric bribed Shirkūh with 50,000 gold pieces to accede to this arrangement. Shāwar promised an annual tribute of 100,000 gold pieces and allowed the king to leave a Latin resident at Cairo with some detachments to guard the city gates, and then he went away.

Before the end of 1168, however, Amalric decided to break faith and descended on Egypt again, this time with the intention of a definitive conquest. At Bilbeis, east of the Delta, he massacred the population and then swiftly appeared outside the walls of the city of Fustat, just south of modern Cairo, the old Arab capital of Egypt for more than three centuries. The stunned authorities decided to burn the city, while couriers pressed to Nūr-al-Dīn to urge him to save Egypt and the Caliphate from the infidel. Twenty thousand barrels of naphtha and 10,000 torches were used in firing the hurriedly vacated city, and the conflagration lasted fifty-four days. The wastes and rubble of Fustat extending for miles have provided the modern archaeologist with a splendid site for years of excavation. Nūr-al-Dīn readily responded by sending his picked Turcomans under the command of the able Shirkūh, who was accompanied again by Saladin, his young nephew. They arrived in January 1169, while Amalric was still negotiating for more promised gold payments from the elusive Shāwar. Finding himself suddenly entrenched between the Egyptians within the city and the Turcomans in the rear from Syria, the Latin king was constrained to withdraw without a single blow.

In the meantime, Shirkūh was elevated to the wazirate by the grateful Caliph, as Shāwar lost his head, and his palace was thrown wide open for popular looting. On Shirkūh's violent disappearance shortly afterward (March 23), Saladin succeeded him in office. The anomalous sight of a Shi'ite Caliph with a Sunnite wazir resolved itself naturally with the decease of al-'Āḍid, last of the Fatimids, on September 13, 1171; and Saladin was immediately invested with all the powers of state in Egypt by the Sunnite Abbasid Caliph of Bagdad. Thus Fatimid rule became extinct and Egypt returned to the religious unity of Orthodox Islam. On May 15, 1174, Nūr-al-Dīn died too, and Saladin was able to seize his throne as sultan of the whole territory from Mosul to Aleppo in the north and Egypt in the south. Thus political unity on all the frontiers of the Latin kingdom of Jerusalem was accomplished.

The decisive hour was fast approaching. On the other side, the able Amalric died in the same year as Nūr-al-Dīn (July 11, 1174), leaving a young disabled leper, Baldwin IV (1174–85), on the tottering throne of Jerusalem to face on all his frontiers a new invincible giant with a unified sultanate. This was the unhappy ending of the middle phase.

THE THIRD PHASE

This decisive phase is the period of Muslim monarchy versus Frankish anarchy, in which the balance of power was reversed to the detriment of the kingdom of Jerusalem. It is the age of Saladin and his able successors, both Aiyubid * and Mamluk,** who accomplished the task of exterminating Latin

* The Aiyubid Dynasty (1169–1250) was founded by Saladin, whose full name in Arabic is al-Nāṣir Ṣalāḥ-al-Dīn Yūsuf ibn Aiyūb (1169–93). Of Kurdish extraction, he had begun his career in the service of Nūr-al-Dīn Zangi. The empire he built comprised Egypt, Syria, and the Muslim holy places of Hijaz, as well as Yemen and several districts in Upper Mesopotamia.

** The Mamluk sultans, of slave origin, continued the same policy as the Aiyubids. They consisted of two distinct dynasties: (1) the Baḥri (that is, River, since they lived on the Island of Rodah in the Nile) or Circassian rule within the Holy Land. Apparently Saladin might have chosen coexistence with the Latins on a status quo basis until he had slowly consolidated his position in north Syria. Twice he concluded and observed a truce with his enemy in 1180 and 1185; but Reginald de Châtillon, lord of Monréale, violated every truce from his desert nest at the Karak by intercepting and molesting innocent Egyptian trade and pilgrim caravans heading for Mecca or Damascus. In 1182 he transported by camels sufficient timber to the port of Ayla or Elath, which he occupied on the Gulf of 'Aqabah, and constructed a fleet of five galleys and a number of small craft, and set out to destroy the Muslim holy cities of Mecca and Medina. He reached Aden and pillaged the seaports of Hijjz and Yemen. It is said that he actually disembarked on the shores of Hijjz and advanced within a day's march of Medina. This was a mad project, romantic but futile, and foredoomed to failure. In 1187 Reginald seized the sultan's own sister in one of the passing caravans. Saladin requested the new king, Guy de Lusignan (1186–87), to chastise him, but Guy de Lusignan could not do so even if he wanted to. Saladin made a vow that he would separate Reginald's head from his body with his own scimitar.

While these vexations were mounting, the Christians were rapidly sinking into a state of anarchy. Every feudal lord acted independently in his signory. Then the death of King Baldwin the Leper caused immeasurable confusion over the problem of succession. When in the end Guy de Lusignan seized the crown, Count Raymond of Tripoli refused to give him recognition and concluded an alliance with Saladin in order to strengthen his position against the new liege lord. Their differences were bridged only after Saladin's conquests of 1187. Meanwhile, the divided nobles were forsaken by the West, for no substantial reinforcement seemed to be forthcoming, and

---

Mamluks (1250–1382); and the Burji (that is, Tower, since they lived in the Citadel of Cairo) Mamluks (1382–1517). The word "Mamluk" means possessed or owned, i.e., a slave in the sultan's bodyguard.

the death of the sympathetic Manuel Comnenus resulted in the massacre of the Latins at Constantinople in 1182. The usurpation of the Byzantine crown by Andronicus I Comnenus (1183–85) afflicted the impotent empire with a full measure of anarchy leading to dynastic upheavals. There was no hope at the moment either from Europe or from Byzantium.

In the meantime, Saladin had been gradually ridding the Islamic world of its rifts. From Egypt, he successfully spread his rule over the old homeland in northern Syria. Aleppo submitted to him in 1183 and Mosul joined his realm in 1185. The rest of the smaller principalities in Mesopotamia came to his side in 1186. Thus freed from trouble with his Muslim coreligionists, he proceeded to deal with the Christians at ease. At Nazareth, his army was engaged in open battle with the Templars (May 1, 1187). The Knights suffered a heavy defeat, and Saladin set siege to the important city of Tiberias. This was the beginning of the end, since it led to the decisive battle of Hittin, in which Saladin destroyed the Christian forces beyond repair.

The Latins had mustered their joint armies at the spring of Safouriya within a few miles' march from Tiberias for the relief of the beleaguered city. Despite his difference with the king, Raymond had to be present in the vanguard, for Tiberias was situated in his county and his wife was trapped in its citadel. The Christian host numbered about 10,000 knights and 18,000 footsoldiers, all ready for the fray but without farsighted leadership. Saladin, who knew the aridity of the waterless desert plain with its extinct volcanic hills, known as the Horns of Hittin, standing between the Christians and the distressed city, did his utmost to draw them into that merciless terrain before attacking them. When Raymond wisely advised the leaders to desist from taking that step despite his own paramount interest and the danger besetting his wife, the king and his impulsive consultants—such as Reginald de Châtillon—accused him of cowardice and ordered the march. It was in the early days of July with its sweltering summer heat and cloudless skies. The army encamped overnight in the middle of the desert at a point of no return, and the Muslims at once surrounded them and harassed them on all sides with their swift mounted archers who aimed at the horses after separating them from the infantry, and the dismounted iron-clad knights were left under the weight of their armor in a waterless inferno.

The battle of Hittin was fought on July 4, 1187, and the surviving men and horses on the Christian side were completely exhausted and scorched by thirst on blazing sands. To add to their utter discomfort, Saladin's men, seizing the direction of the breeze, set the neighboring prairies on fire to help suffocate the Christians with smoke. The Latins had taken the Holy Cross of the Passion with them as their standard in the decisive battle. This was sent from the Holy Sepulchre by the old patriarch of Jerusalem, who feigned illness at the time. Now the Cross was confiscated and sent to Bagdad; the most sacred of their relics was lost. A very few knights who realized the seriousness of the circumstances from the beginning, such as Raymond and Balian d'Ibelin, were able to fight their way back to liberty. The bulk of the army, with the king and the impulsive Reginald, were caught, and men began to throw away their armor while shouting for water. Saladin had scored a master stroke of good strategy and military wisdom, while the Christians attained the height of folly and paid dearly for it with their lives. The sultan ordered the Templars and the Hospitallers, 200 sturdy knights, to be executed at once. Reginald de Châtillon's head was reserved for Saladin's own scimitar in fulfillment of his vow. The king and the great nobles, on the contrary, were treated with magnanimity, given cool water to drink, and allowed to return after the payment of ransom. The rest were either killed or sold in the slave markets, which became oversaturated and prices reached a low level.

Now the way to Jerusalem was clear. But Saladin wanted

first to occupy all the territories around the capital so that the siege might be a short one. Tiberias capitulated on the following day. Acre was seized on July 9, and by September the ports of Beirut, Jaffa, Ascalon, Sidon, and Jubail (the ancient Byblos of the Phoenicians) had all been taken. The sultan did not tarry to set protracted sieges to strong castles. These, he estimated, were foredoomed with the spread of his Muslim hegemony over the surrounding territories, and their garrisons would indubitably yield in turn without a blow. Often, he wisely offered the inmates of those fortified centers their personal freedom if they chose to abandon their foothold in favor of the Muslims without open conflict.

Tyre, Tripoli, and Antioch were the only remaining seaports in Christian hands when Saladin decided to crown his career with the conquest of Jerusalem; and after a short siege of twelve days, the holy city surrendered on October 2. The operations of its seizure in 1187 stood in sharp contrast to the scene of its merciless storming by the First Crusaders in 1099. Saladin checked the fury of his men and controlled unbridled abuse. He made an allowance of forty days' time for wealthy inhabitants to raise their ransoms and go. He accepted sums of reasonable size toward liberating groups of the poor. He acceded to his brother's noble intercession on behalf of a thousand heads to regain their freedom unransomed. He responded to the supplications of his two chief enemies, the Latin patriarch and Balian, who conducted the city's defense, by granting the deliverance of another thousand. Then, with royal liberality and out of his own volition, he enfranchised some 15,000 from the ranks of older people, a charitable gesture and, in the language of the day, in alms for the solace of his soul. He protected the Holy Sepulchre from incendiaries and declared his will to permit the re-entry of unarmed Christian pilgrims. The Latin chroniclers of the events are unanimous on Saladin's chivalry, humanity, and magnanimity; and the Arabic annalists underline his devotion, righteousness, asceticism, and mystic mind. These sublime qualities must be combined with his indefatigable industry and military genius to complete the portrait of an immortal figure.

Consternation spread throughout Europe on hearing of the catastrophe that had befallen Jerusalem, and the three leading kings in the West at once took the Cross and launched the Third Crusade. Emperor Frederick Barbarossa raised a tremendous army and took the land route in 1190; after beating the Saljuqs outside Qonia, he reached Cilicia, where he was accidentally drowned under the weight of his armor while crossing the river Seleph on June 10, 1190. The remainder of his army was disbanded before reaching the Holy Land.

Meanwhile Philip Augustus of France and Richard I the Lion-Heart were persuaded by the Papacy to bury their differences and join hands in holy war. Philip sailed from Messena on March 30, 1191 and landed outside Acre on April 20. Richard followed on April 10, but his ships were blown to Cyprus, which he invaded, seized from a Byzantine usurper by the name of Isaac Comnenus, and sold to the Templars, who resold it to the Lusignans in due course. In June he landed at Acre, and in the face of a joint assault, the city capitulated on July 12. Then Philip returned to France after some bickering with Richard, though he left most of his troops in the Holy Land. Richard thus became the sole leader of the Crusade and he distinguished himself for his chivalry and extraordinary valor. In the end, he concluded peace with Saladin on September 3, 1192; the Latins were confirmed in the possession of the coast from Tyre to Jaffa and Christian pilgrims were to be accorded safe conduct to visit Jerusalem, which remained in Islamic hands.

Events in England and France forced Richard to sail back to Europe with a group of pilgrims on October 10, 1192, after the establishment of a modus vivendi marked by growing religious tolerance between the pilgrims from the West and the native Muslims in the Near East. (The story of Richard's captivity in Central Europe and his deliverance is outside the scope of this study.) In the following year (1193), the hero of the Horns of Hittin retired to Damascus, sick with fever, a weary man of fifty-five, to die on March 4, before seeing the elimination of the last Latin holdings in Palestine.

The idea of the Crusade continued to flare up in Europe during the next century from mixed motives. The son of Frederick Barbarossa, Emperor Henry VI (1190–97), wished to accomplish what his father's tragic death never permitted. He took the Cross in 1195 and brought together an army of 60,000 fighters and a fleet of forty-four galleys on the shores of Apulia in the southern part of the Empire below the Appennines. Then he conferred royalty upon Armenia and Cyprus, both of which became vassal kingdoms and allies in the forthcoming struggle. The Teutonic Order also came into existence at that time and joined Henry's forces. By 1197 preparations for the German Crusade were complete, and the fleet sailed, under the command of the bishop of Würzburg until the Emperor joined the host at a later date in the Holy Land. The Crusaders landed near Sidon and participated with the Franks in the recovery of Beirut. Afterward, while besieging the fort of Toron (Tibnin), news of the Emperor's untimely death in Europe demoralized the soldiers, who abandoned their posts and returned home. Perhaps the one enduring result of this abortive Crusade was the establishment of the Teutonic military order of religion, destined to play a historic role in the development of Prussia.

With the accession of Pope Innocent III (1198–1216), the Church Militant started clamoring for the resumption of holy war, and in the end the papal proclamations came to fruition. The Fourth Crusade, which Innocent inaugurated in earnest for the reconquest of Jerusalem, however, was diverted by personal greed from its normal course to an ignoble onslaught against Constantinople. The three delinquent parties in the disgraceful affair were the Venetians, the French, and the

Flemings. To Philip of Swabia and his half-Greek brother-in-law and protégé, a young pretender to the throne of Byzantium by the name of Alexius, was ascribed the first incentive to seize the Eastern Roman Empire. The blind old doge, Enrico Dandolo of Venice, was of course behind a project which would extend the trade privileges of his commune in the East beyond anything the Venetians had enjoyed in the past.

It was agreed that the Franco-Flemish contingents should converge on the lagoons of the republic of St. Mark from Flanders and Marseilles. In November 1202 they sailed on Venetian galleys and annexed the important Adriatic port of Zara to Venice before proceeding to Constantinople. Simon de Montfort and many disgusted Crusaders relinquished the campaign in protest and went straight to Acre in the Holy Land; while the bulk of some 20,000 men, evenly divided between the Venetians and the Franco-Flemings, sailed in the direction of the Bosphorus. The assault on the Eastern capital, which was far from easy, ended in the downfall of the enfeebled Greek Empire. After installing their own puppet Emperor, who was immediately assassinated by his subjects in a short period of utter confusion, the Crusaders decided on a Latin substitute in the person of Baldwin of Flanders, and the great city was officially given over to pillage for three days.

The sack of the most civilized city in Christendom, hitherto the bulwark of Europe in the East, was incredible. "Since the world was created," said Villehardouin, the contemporary French eyewitness and chronicler of the event, "never so much booty had been won in any city!" * Havoc and destruction became general. Robber barons, as well as Latin ecclesiastics in holy orders, shared equally in taking whatever they could carry. Works of art and priceless manuscripts were plundered or destroyed. The rarest scrolls and codices of an Aristotle or

* *La Conquête de Constantinople,* ed. by N. Wailly, Paris 1872, 147. Cf. Vasiliev: *History of the Byzantine Empire,* in 1 vol., Madison, Wisc., 1952, 461.

a Demosthenes were sold for a pittance. Palaces were denuded of their valuable treasures. Churches were looted of their sacred relics and reliquaries, gold and silver chalices and crosses, and every ornament. Sumptuous materials and furs of singular beauty were stacked in the galleys. The four magnificent bronze horses over the portals of San Marco's basilica in Venice were snatched from the Byzantine hippodrome, standing monuments of one of the greatest acts of brigandage in history. The altar of St. Sophia, loaded with precious articles, was swept away. Finally, the warriors of the Cross committed open rape, adultery, and fornication, and their violence did not spare even the matrons and virgins vowed to God. Nicetas Choniates, Greek eyewitness and annalist of those sordid events, bewailed the fate of the city in heart-rending lamentations:

Oh, city, city, eye of all cities, subject of narratives over all the world, spectacle above the world, supporter of churches, leader of faith, guide of orthodoxy, protector of education, abode of all good! Thou hast drunk to the dregs the cup of the anger of the Lord and hast been visited with fire fiercer than that which in days of yore descended upon the five cities.*

In this unspeakable fashion the Latin Empire of Constantinople replaced the Byzantine Empire until 1261. The partition treaty allotted the imperial throne and five-eighths of the city to Baldwin, and the new Latin patriarchate, together with the remaining three-eighths and St. Sophia, to Venice. Thomas Morosini was the first Venetian patriarch. Thrace and the coastlands of the Hellespont, as well as the greater Aegean islands, were given to the Franco-Flemish feudatories; while the

* The five Greek cities of Cyrenaica in North Africa (known as the Pentapolis), destroyed by the Arab invasion in the seventh century which eliminated Christianity from the area. The passage is quoted from Nicetas Choniates: *Historia,* ed. by I. Bekker (*Corpus Scriptorum Historiae Byzantinae*), Bonn 1835, 763. Cf. Vasiliev, *History of the Byzantine Empire,* in 1 vol., Madison, Wisc., 1952, 462.

trading points in Thrace and on the Adriatic, as well as the Dodecanese and Ionian Islands, the Peloponnesus and Crete, became Venetian. Such was the lion's share of one of the greatest robberies in the story of mankind, and Innocent had to swallow that fait accompli in spite of his rage over the deflection of the Crusade from fighting Muslims to a reckless assault on Christian territory. Though the Pope was somewhat appeased by the forcible Romanization of the Greeks, the temporary occupation of the country only prepared the way for the Turkish conquest two centuries later, and the gap separating the Eastern Christians from the West widened more than ever.

Innocent III wished to mend the scandal of the Fourth Crusade by awakening Christian consciences to the necessity of recapturing the Holy Places and fighting the Muslim Empire in the East. The response to papal exhortation at the time came from the children of Western Europe rather than from regular militias. This was in a sense a prelude to the Fifth Crusade, which, too, had a special character of its own, though neither Crusade seemed to suit the humor of the Holy Pontiff. The Children's Crusade of 1212 was one of the great tragedies of the age. It was preached by a twelve-year-old boy named Stephen, who appeared at the court of Philip Augustus with an alleged letter from Jesus to the king of France urging holy war under child leadership. In a credulous age where ignorance embraced superstition, the astute king's distrustful indifference could not arrest the spread of a movement which appealed to the masses. Some 30,000 children, it is said, including a number of noble birth, joined the Crusade and followed the new Peter the Hermit on the road to Marseilles, where the sea was expected to open miraculously before the pilgrims' progress.

The French contingent soon had its counterpart in Germany, where another host followed another boy by the name of Nicholas from Cologne. The Germans moved in two columns across the Alps to Genoa and to Brindisi by way of

Rome, where the Pope was able to dissuade only some from continuing the journey. Many died en route, others loitered in villages, and the rest stood by the seashore waiting for the miracle of the dividing of waters to the lands beyond. When this failed to happen, two men named Hugh the Iron and William the Pig from Marseilles offered free transportation to the Holy Land and conducted the children for sale in the slave markets of North Africa and of Egypt. The story is said to have been confirmed in 1230 by a young priest who had accompanied Stephen and, after a number of years of honest servitude in Egypt, was able to regain his freedom and once more attain his homeland. The Germans suffered less, since many of them were absorbed by Genoa and the Italian communes and seaports, while a few returned home, and some found means of reaching Palestine.

The origin of the Fifth Crusade must be traced to the coronation of Frederick II on July 25, 1215 at Aachen. The new Holy Roman Emperor, entirely of his own volition, took the Cross on that occasion. In his youthful days he was probably carried away by the idea of leading the whole Christian world in a universal cause. As it happened, he tarried in the fulfillment of his vow. Pope Innocent III, in the November Lateran of the same year, however, fixed the date of launching the Crusade at the beginning of 1217. Response to his call came, not from the Emperor, but from three minor sovereigns—King Andrew of Hungary, King Hugh de Lusignan of Cyprus, and King John de Brienne of Jerusalem. Their combined but rather meager forces launched a series of small fruitless campaigns from the Christian base of Acre into the Jordan Valley in the course of 1217. Afterward Andrew retired to Hungary and Hugh died. A few Germans were left with John until a fleet of Frisian reinforcements came to his support, and he declared that the key to Jerusalem was in Cairo and not in the Holy Land. Thus it was decided to embark on an Egyptian Crusade; they laid anchor at Damietta, to which they set siege from May 1218 to November 5, 1219, date of the capture of the city. News of this triumph brought forth further reinforcements, which arrived under the command of the Spanish cardinal legate, Pelagius of Albano, a spirited but haughty and obstinate prelate.

Sultan al-Kāmel Muḥammad (1218–38) inherited the task of defending Egypt from his father, al-'Ādel Sayf-al-Dīn Abu-Bakr, known to the earlier Crusaders as Saphadin, brother of Saladin, whose united realm was now divided. Al-Kāmel's brother, named al-Mu'aẓẓam (1218–27), reigned precariously in Damascus; both were below their ancestors in stature. Al-Kāmel of Egypt made the apparently incredible offer of ceding Jerusalem and the original Frankish possessions in the Holy Land prior to 1187 to the Crusaders in return for Damietta and peace. John de Brienne favored acceptance, but Pelagius insisted on the completion of the invasion of Egypt and the continuation of fighting until the advent of Frederick II's army. The Crusaders marched into the Delta in 1221. It was midsummer, hot and humid, and the Nile water was swelling fast in its annual inundation. The Egyptians broke the dams in all canals and the invaders found themselves in the middle of a vast lake with the enemy watching in the distance. Moreover, no imperial aid was forthcoming. The expedition failed miserably, and Pelagius was forced to accept al-Kāmel's new terms of safe retreat and the surrender of Damietta.

It was in the course of this campaign that the poor friar, Francis of Assisi, who accompanied the Crusaders, was able to persuade Pelagius to allow him to cross over the battle line to the sultan's camp outside Fariskur on Lake Manzalah under a truce flag to attempt the sultan's conversion to Christianity. The bewildered sultan listened with interest and amusement to the arguments of the shabby looking visitor, whom he considered insane, and then ordered his return unmolested to the Christian side.

The new peaceful orientation came not from the missionary

efforts of St. Francis but rather from a novel Crusade of a totally different character inaugurated by the enigmatic "Infidel Emperor," Frederick II (1211–50). One of the most controversial figures of his time, he was the consummation of the twelfth-century renaissance—versatile, tolerant, a great lover of learning, conversant with Greek and Hebrew and Arabic, a real "Stupor Mundi," as he was nicknamed. Yet he was also described as autocratic, unscrupulous, sensuous, and an atheist sometimes accused of having declared that the world was deceived by three great impostors—Moses, Christ, and Muḥammad—which is a dubious accusation. He incurred the wrath of the Pope, who excommunicated him. His court teemed with the enlightenment of Arab philosophers, and he was extremely friendly with the Muslims.

Whatever his vices may have been, Frederick's virtues rendered him a misfit in an age of bellicose bigotry and he set out on a special Crusade of his own invention in defiance of the Church—customarily labelled as the Sixth Crusade. At the outset, Frederick was probably in earnest about going to the Holy Land with an army during the year 1227, though it remains unknown whether he was really going to use the army in fighting or for diplomatic pressure. At any rate, the army was stricken with plague, and he himself fell ill and pleaded with the Pope for postponement. Gregory IX (1227–41), in keeping with the established hostile policy of the Papacy toward Frederick, refused to accede to any procrastination, whatever the cause. So Frederick, who was under sentence of excommunication and consequent deposition, decided as regent for his infant son Conrad to embark on a breathtaking peaceful voyage to the East on a small flotilla manned chiefly by Muslim sailors from Sicily and a limited company of his own retainers. He reached Acre by way of Cyprus and operated under the most disagreeable circumstances. Disowned by the Latin patriarch, he followed the sultan's movements from place to place, negotiating and bargaining for a treaty of liberation for Jerusalem. The sultan's envoys were impressed by his knowledge of Arabic language and culture, and at last the terms of a generous treaty were ratified by al-Kāmel on February 11, 1229. Frederick decorated with the order of knighthood one Fakhr-al-Dīn, the sultan's chief ambassador, in commemoration of this diplomatic triumph.

The three holy cities of Jerusalem, Bethlehem, and Nazareth were restored to the Christians, together with Toron (Tibnin) in Galilee, Lydda, Sidon, and a few other places forming a corridor from the Phoenician coast inland for the free passage of Christian pilgrims. The Mosque of the Rock and other Muslim sanctuaries remained in Muslim custody. The Emperor promised to desist from supporting armed Crusades against Egypt in perpetuity, and a truce was enforced for ten years Anno Domini, that is, the equivalent of ten Hejira years and a few extra months. Such was the master stroke of diplomacy by a man who understood the mind of his adversary. Frederick made a glorious entry into Jerusalem on March 18 and placed the crown of the Latin kingdom on his own head with his own hands in the Church of the Holy Sepulchre, since no ecclesiastic could officiate for an excommunicated renegade. Furthermore, in the name of the Latin patriarch of Jerusalem, the archbishop of Caesaria imposed an interdict on Jerusalem, which was accordingly forsaken by Crusaders and pilgrims; while the hero of the day was forced to race back home for the defense of his own kingdom in Italy, invaded by a papal army under the command of John de Brienne. This was the irony of fate.

Apparently the Papacy wanted Jerusalem only through conquest and blood. For the next two decades civil strife prevailed between the imperial bailiffs and the local Frankish feudatories, the Templars and the Hospitallers usually taking opposite sides in the fray, while the Italian communes cared for nothing more than their own trade interests in the seaboard emporia. The shadowy Latin kingdom was saved only by the fratricidal struggles on the Muslim side of the picture. The latter days of the Aiyubid rule somewhat resemble those preceding the First Crusade. The Latins allied themselves with the local Damascene chieftains against Egypt, and the Aiyubid sultan invited the Khwarizmian Turks to his aid. The Muslims seized Jerusalem in August 1244 and recaptured most of Palestine by 1245.

The second downfall of Jerusalem moved Louis IX (1226–70), the saintly king of France, to start a new Crusade against Egypt. Damietta surrendered in October 1249. Then the expedition proceeded in the direction of Cairo, and the same strategy was repeated, with disastrous results. Their progress was arrested at Mansura, where the Crusaders were beaten, and the king and most of his nobles were taken prisoner after the decisive fighting which occurred in the month of February 1250. The story of these stirring events has been poignantly recounted in detail by an eyewitness—Joinville, the court annalist, whose work is regarded as the first great French vernacular chronicle of the age. Negotiations concerning the terms of the king's liberation were opened while he was in prison. Damietta had to be evacuated at once, and a ransom was fixed at half a million livres tournois, the equivalent of a million besants. Early in May the survivors set sail with the king to Acre after the payment of all the funds they could raise, especially from the rich Templars. Louis remained approximately four years in the Holy Land trying to mend some of the damage which his Egyptian defeat brought upon the heads of the Latins in the East. He was able to consolidate the divided Franks in their meager possessions, and he concluded an alliance with the Assassins * in their Lebanese fast-

* A special Muslim sect of religious murderers, originating in Khurasan in the eleventh century under the influence of the Fatimid Caliphate and the Ismā'īli doctrine, which spread in Persia notably against Saljuq rule. The word is derived from the Arabic "Hashshāshīn," meaning opium or hashish addicts who fulfilled their religious leaders' orders of assassination

nesses. Then he sailed back home to France in April 1254. The king, however, remained in a restless frame of mind until he resumed Crusading in North Africa, where he died outside Tunis on August 25, 1270, with the words "Jerusalem! Jerusalem!" on his lips.

In the meantime, two other minor short-lived and ineffective Crusades took place, the first by the Bastards of Aragon in 1269, and the second by Prince Edward of England in 1271. As a whole, the thirteenth century witnessed a radical change in the meaning and spirit of Crusading. The conquest of Constantinople (1204), the Albigensian Crusade (1208), and the numerous European expeditions conducted first against schismatics, then against heretics, then against unruly Christians who antagonized the Popes,—all these elements contributed to alter the basic conception of the original Crusading ideal. All this happened while the Muslim East was gathering momentum and gaining ground. When the rule of the Aiyubids came to an end with the murder of Turānshāh in 1250, their heirs were the virile dynasty of Mamluk sultans who had been serving the old masters as a bodyguard of slaves. Aybak (1250–57), the first Mamluk, came to terms with Louis IX. One of his successors, Quṭuz (1259–60), witnessed the defeat of the invincible Mongols under Hulagu in the battle of Ayn Jalut in 1260. The hero of this decisive battle was Baybars (1260–77), who murdered his master and occupied his throne. Then one by one the Mamluks regained more and more territory from the Franks, until finally al-Ashraf Khalīl (1290–93) seized Acre in May 1291. By 1292 all the remaining Christian outposts, including Tyre, Sidon, and Beirut, surrendered, and the crown of Jerusalem was flung from Acre across the sea to the island of Cyprus.

---

of the enemies of the sect as a sacred duty. They became active in Syria during the Crusade, under the leadership of the "Old Man in the Mountain." The Agha Khan is the present imam of the surviving Ismā'īlis.

CHAPTER THREE

The Crusade in the Later Middle Ages

INTRODUCTION

CRUSADING HISTORIOGRAPHY, as already stated, has recently been subject to considerable revision and emendation, and older concepts have given way to new schools of thought. Until the last few decades, historians identified the span of the Crusade movement with the duration of the Latin kingdom of Jerusalem on the Asiatic mainland. Inaugurated by Urban II's memorable speech at Clermont-Ferrand in 1095, the holy war presumably ended with the tragic exit of the Franks from Palestine in 1291–92. This cataclysmic view of the Crusade has been repudiated in the light of cumulative research in the field; and in the present chapter an attempt will be made to outline the fate of the movement after the fall of Acre on the Syrian coast to the Egyptians toward the close of the thirteenth century. Notwithstanding ostensible changes in its basic motives, the continuance of the Crusading movement in the later Middle Ages will be proved beyond any shadow of doubt from a quick survey of the events. Strictly speaking, the fourteenth century was the age of the later Crusade in its fuller sense. Afterward in the course of the fifteenth century, the Crusade began to lose its real significance and ended in becoming a forlorn cause without hope of resuscitation.

The first half of the fourteenth century, extending roughly from 1292 to 1344, abounds in propagandist literature for the resumption of the Crusade. The second half of the century, lasting from 1344 to 1396, is a period of successive Crusading campaigns in the East. That century witnessed a number of monumental changes in the delineation of the traditional frontiers of Crusading terrain. Hitherto, holy war had been confined to the area of the Near East. In the later Middle Ages it reached distant horizons beyond the Holy Land in almost every direction. Though lacking in the qualities of vigor and valor, and in the sensational achievements of the early Crusaders, the fourteenth-century movement left its impression on the annals of mankind by the spectacular opening of the way to Cathay. The exploratory adventures of the Latin missionary at the court of the Mongol kingdom of Khān Bāliq * signalled a revolution in the geographical lore of the Middle Ages. The idea of collaboration with the Mongols, after their conversion to Christianity, in the struggle against the Mamluk sultans of Egypt and Syria has sometimes been described as the "Mongol" or "Tartar Crusade." This became a major feature in the propagandist literature of the time, and the idea was espoused by Popes and kings. The enlargement of the map of the Old World was, in a sense, a byproduct of the Later Crusade.

Though the final goal of the whole movement remained the acquisition of the Holy Land, the fourteenth-century Crusaders appear to have pursued their quests by devious ways, through attacking or sacking other ostensibly more important centers in the Muslim Empire, which, it was thought, should first be enfeebled and impoverished before making any serious landing on the shores of Palestine. As will be seen, the new

* Khanbalik or Cambaliech, otherwise Peking in subsequent history.

Crusades were conducted against Anatolia, Egypt, North Africa, and the Balkans rather than the Holy Places.

The seizure of Acre in 1291 by the Muslims, like the fall of Jerusalem earlier in 1187, and the collapse of Constantinople later in 1453, provided Europeans with a rude reminder of the sad state of the East. Other reminders were the wandering or "mendicant" kings from countries of the Near East. Peter I de Lusignan, called "athleta christi" by his chancellor, Philippe de Mézières, spent almost three years (1362–65) roaming from court to court throughout the continent of Europe soliciting aid for his bellicose projects. King Leo VI of Armenia, a disconsolate refugee without a crown, died childless in 1393 in Paris. Between 1399 and 1401 Manuel II Palaeologus left Byzantium on a tour of Western Europe to implore the Holy Pontiff and the strong monarchs of France and England for effective relief for his imperial city, long battered by a succession of Ottoman sieges and assaults. Even after the extinction of the Eastern Empire and the downfall of that great city, an imperial pretender by the name of Thomas Palaeologus took refuge at Rome in 1461. The Crusade, however, had become a defensive rather than offensive movement in the course of the fifteenth century.

FOURTEENTH-CENTURY PROPAGANDISTS AND MISSIONARIES

The fourteenth century was the real age of propaganda for the Crusade, notably in its early decades. This was the natural reaction of the European conscience to a situation which was steadily becoming desperate in the Levant. The failure of the Crusaders to save the Latin kingdom of Jerusalem and defend the city of Acre was one of the most poignant features of the time, and Europe had to search for the reasons of its discomfiture in the face of Islam. This accounts for the avalanche of propagandist literature which marked that era. In reality, the promoters of the idea of the Crusade seem to have come from all classes of medieval society and included Popes, kings, men of the sword and of the pen, ministers of state and of religion, and an endless stream of pilgrims returning from the holy city with fervent tales to tell about the East. Theorists pondered, not only over the reconquest of the birthplace of Christ, but also over the most effective manner whereby it could be retained in the hands of Christians after the reinstatement of the lost kingdom of Jerusalem.

A certain Thaddeo of Naples, an eyewitness of the Acre catastrophe in 1291, inaugurated the movement with a tract called "Hystoria," in which he described the fate of this last bastion of Latin Christianity on the shores of Palestine. His exhortations for union among all the princes of Catholic Christendom under the leadership of the Church Militant to save "our heritage" were in full conformity with the official policy of the Papacy. Nicholas IV (1288–92), his contemporary, actually planned a "passagium generale" in collaboration with Charles II of Anjou (d. 1309), whose interest in the project was enhanced by his claim to the crown of the Latin kingdom of Jerusalem. Even before the fall of Acre, a Franciscan by the name of Fidenzio of Padua advised Pope Nicholas on the details and plan of the projected campaign in a work entitled "Liber Recuperationis Terre Sancte." The maritime blockade of the Muslim Empire, the problem of military bases in Armenia and Syria, naval and land forces, routes to the East, and other important subjects were discussed by the author on the assumption that Acre was still in Christian hands, a fact which minimized the value of some aspects of his counsel. Nevertheless, the pontificate of Nicholas IV did witness the birth of a new phase in the literary and diplomatic propaganda for the Crusade.

The propagandist output of the time is bewildering in its dimensions, and a severe measure of selectivity must necessarily be observed in the treatment of some of its representative or outstanding landmarks. Perhaps the most novel approach to the subject was that ascribed to a Catalan by the name of Raymond Lull, born in 1232 and stoned to death by infuriated Muslims on the shores of North Africa in 1315 or 1316. Lull was one of the most extraordinary personalities of his age or any age. A poet, a philosopher, a writer of at least several hundred books, and the author of a new system of philosophy based on the unity of knowledge as demonstrated in his work entitled "Arbor Scientiae," he was also one of the earliest Orientalists, who mastered the Arabic tongue and even composed Arabic poetry. Though he began his life by promoting a new plan of Crusade in his "Liber de Fine," it soon dawned upon him that it might be more appropriate if he tried to win the Muslims over to Christ, and that by thus saving their souls from perdition, he would eventually bring the Holy Land and the whole world of Islam into the fold of the faithful without violence or the spilling of blood. To him, therefore, the study of Arabic and Islamic theology was a vehicle for the preaching of Christianity, and he became the apostle of missionary work among Muslims. Thrice he crossed over to North Africa with this perilous quest in view. In the first voyage he formulated his debates with a certain ibn 'Ammār, the grand mufti of Tunis, in a treatise called "Disputatio Raymundi Christini et Hamar Sarraceni." In the second, he was immediately seized by the Tunisian authorities and kept behind bars until his deportation by the lenient Muslim governor. In the third, he earned his much-desired crown of martyrdom when he was stoned by an intolerant mob outside the Algerian seaport of Bugia (the Arabic Bijayah), when he had reached the advanced age of eighty-two; his body was recovered by Genoese mariners and deposited in the cathedral of his native town of Las Palmas on the island of Majorca.

At the same time the traditional Crusading spirit was being nurtured at the court of France, where Philip IV (1285–1314), after humiliating Pope Boniface VIII (1294–1303) in Rome and establishing the Papacy within his realm at Avignon, envisioned the extension of French hegemony over most of the world. Among other things, he wished to install one of his sons at the head of a new Eastern Empire incorporating Byzantium, the Holy Land, and the Mamluk sultanate of Egypt. Apparently he regarded himself as the rightful heir to the universal leadership of the Holy Pontiffs, with the Crusade as the basic element of his foreign policy. Consequently his court harbored men who flourished on feeding royal aspirations with propagandist documents of the highest interest. Notable among them were two famous French jurisconsults, namely, Pierre Dubois and William of Nogaret. Eminent men of action, too, such as James de Molay, grand master of the Templars, Fulk de Villaret, grand master of the Hospitallers of St. John of Jerusalem, Henry II de Lusignan, Latin king of Cyprus, and Benito Zaccharia, the Genoese admiral of the French navy, came to solicit cooperation in executing the French monarch's plans.

The prevailing ideas at his court are best represented in Dubois's remarkable treatise "De Recuperatione Terre Sancte." A medieval publicist of the highest order, Dubois worked out a set of rules for universal governance with his imperious master as the central figure in authority. Political discord among the princes of the West must be eradicated, preferably by persuasion, but if necessary by force. A European tribunal consisting of three high clerics and three laymen should be set up for international arbitration, and economic sanctions could be imposed on recalcitrant states. The right of appeal to the Papacy was maintained; but the Popes must continue to live in France within the French monarch's sphere of influence, as they had done since the beginning of the Babylonian Captivity at Avignon. Church fiefs should be administered by the king, and the ecclesiastical hierarchy must return to the original rule of poverty. The Orders of the Templars and Hospitallers were to be merged into one organization, and their vast revenues confiscated for use in financing Eastern campaigns. The constitution of the Holy Roman Empire was to be transformed into an hereditary regime with a French prince at its head. The crown of Egypt and the Holy Land after the reconquest would be conferred upon Philip's second son. Details of the new reformed military government of the East were provided, and missionary work among the so-called dissident Eastern Christians, as well as the Muslims, was to be undertaken by scholars conversant with Oriental languages. The keynote to this incongruous patchwork of ideas was evidently the implementation of the Crusade to confirm French supremacy over the rest of the world.

Dubois was a propagandist with preconceived ideas and no personal experience in the field. Of a totally different character was another propagandist, Marino Sanudo the Elder (Il Vecchio) (1274–c. 1343). A rational thinker, Sanudo spent a lifetime in the Levant and was a descendant of the Venetian ducal dynasty of Naxos in the Archipelago. He was a man of great acumen and immense knowledge of an area in which he had travelled far and wide. During his comprehensive peregrinations he managed to collect a tremendous mass of concrete data about the countries of the Near East in the form of accurate descriptions, figures, and statistics. In fact, Sanudo could claim the title of the first statistician in European history.

His argument was preeminently based on economic considerations. If the sultan of Egypt were to be deprived of his chief source of revenue, which was trade, he would ultimately fall into a state of material and military bankruptcy. Consequently the Crusaders could defeat his armies and reconquer and retain the Holy Land without much difficulty. The trade emporia of the Mamluk Empire were the terminal points of the Eastern spice and pepper trade, ardently sought by the maritime powers of southern Europe. They paid a heavy toll to the enemy of the Cross for the acquisition of these articles. In addition to the enrichment of the sultan's coffers from these dues, Genoa and other Italian communes supplied him, in partial exchange, with war material and slaves from the markets of Caffa and elsewhere destined to swell the Mamluk battalions. Marino Sanudo recorded his reactions to this paradoxical position and his thoughts on the solution of the Western predicament in a monumental work entitled "Secreta Fidelium Crucis," of which the first edition was dedicated to Pope Clement V in 1309 and the second to King Charles IV of France.

After a detailed inquiry, he prescribed a ban on trade with Muslim territories on pain of excommunication and even of interdict. Further, a strict maritime blockade should be organized under papal leadership to watch over the execution of that ban until the resources of Egypt were completely drained and its army starved of men and war material. He estimated that three years would bring about the desired results. Though the plan received the Holy Pontiff's immediate support, it was ultimately defeated by two main circumstances: first the issue of papal dispensations to some Venetian ships to resume trade with the enemy; and second, perfidious Genoese smuggling of war material and slaves to the Egyptian markets in exchange for valuable staples and special trade privileges.

It would be futile to attempt a full parade of the fourteenth-century propagandists. Nevertheless, we should not overlook one principal idea, that of alliance with the Tartars for more effective Crusading against Islam. This new feature captivated the Western imagination and gave rise to the Latin mission to Tartary, with immense consequences for Crusading. Started during the pontificate of Innocent IV (1243–54) and the reign of St. Louis (1226–70), king of France, the most spectacular phase in the Catholic mission to Cathay may well be associated with the names of John of Monte Corvino and Oderic of Pordenone. John had, of his own volition and without any noise, made his way to the kingdom of Khān Bāliq and is said to have baptized 5,000 souls at Peking in 1304, built two churches and even translated the Psalms and the New Testament into the language of his congregation. A decade later he was joined by Oderic, who had rounded the continent of Asia by way of Iran, India, and the islands of Indonesia; Oderic returned to Avignon in 1330, completely exhausted, to die at Udine in the following year. Meanwhile, in recognition of his triumph, John was appointed archbishop of Sultaniya and the Far East by the Pope, who also despatched seven bishops suffragan to assist him in that vast new diocese. He died in 1328, and his last successor, John of Florence, was murdered at an unknown place in the heart of China during 1362. The knell of Roman Catholicism was tolled in medieval China; but the idea of joint action with the Mongols was later revived by Christopher Columbus, who wanted to reach India by the western route. The New World barred his way, and the discovery of America changed the whole face of history and of the Crusade.

AGE OF THE LATER CRUSADE

The outcome of sustained propaganda over a number of decades was the resumption of holy warfare in a series of campaigns of varying intensity during the latter half of the fourteenth century. The first chapter in these wars was the Aegean Crusade, in which the Holy League composed of Venice, Cyprus, and the Hospitallers, under the leadership of Pope Clement VI, succeeded in wresting Smyrna from Turkish hands in 1344. It remained in the Hospitallers' custody until Timur overthrew its Christian garrison in 1402, and the Turks ultimately took over the reigns of government in the whole of Anatolia, after the withdrawal of the Mongols from the Peninsula.

The new Latin foothold on the Asiatic mainland, though

insignificant, was hailed in Europe as the beginning of the end of the Islamic Empire. Thanksgiving processions and popular celebrations were held in numerous cities of the West, and the Avignonese Pope Clement VI invited Edward III of England and Philip VI of France to reap the benefit of this auspicious Christian victory in the East by joining arms for decisive action against their common enemy, instead of continuing their internecine strife in the Hundred Years' War. The position appeared to be pregnant with magnificent possibilities for a definitive Crusade, and Christendom lived in the expectation of a second Godfrey of Bouillon to lead its forces into the field.

At that time, an unknown and unhappy feudatory from the southeast of France by the name of Humbert II, dauphin de Viennois, espoused the cause of the Crusade and persuaded the Pope to grant him the title of "Captain-General of the Crusade against the Turks and the Unfaithful to the Holy Church of Rome" on condition that he should equip five galleys with twelve bannerets, 300 knights, and 1,000 arbalesters for fighting in the East, where he was to remain for at least three years. Humbert had lost his only son and heir and had become inconsolable. He had formerly quarrelled with the Church, and only the Pope's personal clemency had rescued him from the sentence of excommunication. The Crusade offered him opportunities for drowning his sorrow over the loss of his son and atoning for his past sins against Holy Church. So he renounced his hereditary rights over the Dauphiné, which consequently devolved on the French Crown,* and devoted himself to the service of the Holy Pontiff in the new cause.

Humbert's Crusade, a continuation of the Aegean campaign, was planned by the Pope first to relieve the Genoese at their mercantile colony of Caffa in the Crimea, which was be-

* The Dauphiné was given by the French king to his heir, who became identified with the title of dauphin after that time.

leaguered by the Tartars, and then to attack the Turks in Anatolia. The former dauphin, sailing from Marseilles in August 1345, crossed Lombardy after disembarking at Genoa to resume the voyage with his troops from Venice to Negropontis. Unable to risk the hazardous passage through the Marmora, he became involved in the petty squabbles and local differences of the Latin principalities of the Archipelago and only engaged in minor skirmishes with Turkish mariners in the Aegean and later at Smyrna. His subservience to papal command in practically all details enhanced his indecision, and the news of his wife's decease cast new shadows of hopelessness on his life. In the summer of 1347 he decided to become a Dominican friar and was absolved from his military obligations by the Pope, who bestowed upon him the honorific title of Latin patriarch of Alexandria and nominated him archbishop of Paris later in 1354. He died at the relatively early age of forty-three, while proceeding through southern France toward his new archdiocese after an unsuccessful career.

The first real "passagium generale" was reserved for the Lusignan kings of Cyprus, whose island was destined by its geographical and political position to become the meeting place of all Crusaders and of most Latin merchants. In this they were encouraged by the seizure of some outposts on the southern Anatolian coast, including Gorigos and Adalia in 1361. It was then that three champions of the idea of the Crusade were assembled on Cyprus: King Peter I de Lusignan (1359–69) ; Peter de Thomas (d. 1366) , the Latin patriarch of Constantinople and apostolic legate for the East since 1362; and Philippe de Mézières (d. 1405) , who became chancellor of the Cypriot kingdom and was one of the most celebrated propagandists of the age. Philippe spent his latter years writing extensively to promote his newly established military order of religion, which he called the "Militia Passionis Jhesu Christi." He dreamed of the creation of a unified military brotherhood throughout Europe under the banner of his novel Militia, which should incorporate all other military orders together with the feudal contingents of Europe as the only remaining hope for the reconquest of the Holy Land.

For the present, he accompanied the king of Cyprus during part of his European peregrinations lasting from 1362 to 1365 and extending from Poland to France and from England to Venice, in order to raise funds and recruits for his forthcoming project of Crusade. The various European detachments thus assembled were enjoined to converge in the waters of Rhodes, and Peter I sailed from Venice in June 1365 to lead a fleet totalling 165 vessels against an unknown target beyond the sea. The secret of his objective was closely kept by the king and his chief consultants—Peter de Thomas and Philippe de Mézières—for fear of Venetian or Genoese treachery in alerting the enemy. Their direction toward Alexandria was divulged only as the naval squadrons attained the high seas. They came within sight of the city on Thursday, October 9, 1365, and they landed on the shore of its western harbor on the following day. The storming and the sack of the city lasted seven fateful days with immeasurable consequences.

This occurred in the reign of Sultan Sha'bān (1363–76), who was only a boy of eleven, while the city governor, ibn 'Arrām, was in the Hijaz performing pilgrimage. The Mamluk court was torn asunder by disaffection, and the atabek Yalbogha, who acted as guardian of the sultanate, could with difficulty marshal enough manpower to press onward to Alexandria. Even then, he had to circle his way around the edge of the western desert, owing to the Nile flood in the Delta. As soon as the Egyptian army came within sight in the Mareotis area, the bulk of the Christian occupation forces evacuated the city on October 16, without making any earnest attempt at the defense of their conquest, contrary to the command of the king and against the advice of Peter de Thomas and Philippe de Mézières. Once they had completed the pillage of the city's treasures and set on fire its public buildings and principal warehouses, their only concern was to sail back to Cyprus in safety with their rich booty. Thus ended the tragedy of the most successful of all fourteenth-century Crusading adventures; the Egyptians could never forget its vandalism, for which the Cypriots had to pay a heavy price in the following century.

However, the immediate result of that untoward event was the promotion of another Crusade. News of the ephemeral triumph at Alexandria, as in the case of preceding campaigns in the Levant, soon circulated in the West, and Pope Urban V urged the faithful to pursue these occurrences to a successful conclusion. The most serious response to his call came from Amedeo VI, count of Savoy, who had previously taken the Cross with King Peter de Lusignan at Avignon from the Pope's own hand. His preconceived plan to go to Cyprus was changed by marriage between members of his dynasty and the Palaeologi. The course of his expedition was deflected to fighting for Byzantium against the Turkish invaders and some of their Balkan Christian allies and vassals. Sailing from Venice in June 1366 at the head of his own feudal militia, Amedeo VI was joined by an army of mercenaries from Italy, Germany, France, and England, meeting him at Coron in the Morea, whence a total of fifteen galleys advanced on Gallipoli, their first objective. That little peninsula, in Ottoman possession since the reign of Sultan Orkhān (1326–60), proved to be invaluable to the Turks both as a landing-place and as a base for expansionist operations in the Balkan Peninsula. Its garrison was surprised by the Crusaders, and its recapture in August was a serious blow to the Turks. Afterward the count went to Constantinople, where he discovered that his cousin, Emperor John V Palaeologus, had been taken prisoner by King Shishman of Bulgaria. So he was constrained to campaign for the deliverance of the Emperor, rather than reap the fruit of his recent brilliant acquisition from the Turks. After penetrating Bulgaria from the Black Sea as far as Varna, he successfully negotiated the liberation of the captive Emperor. By the end of 1366 his material resources were running out, and he was forced to retire to Constantinople, where John reimbursed him with 15,000 florins in exchange for ceding the conquered territory; this sum helped the count to pay off his mercenaries and ultimately dismiss them before the middle of 1367.

The next Crusade took place in 1390 against the kingdom of Tunis. A joint expedition was organized by the Genoese commune and the kingdom of France for different motives. Whereas the Genoese aimed to chastize the Barbary corsairs who had been harassing their merchant ships in the waters of the western Mediterranean, the French nobility, under the leadership of Duke Louis II of the house of Bourbon, cherished the idea of walking in the footsteps of St. Louis against the Muslims in Tunisia. Under the auspices of the Hafsid kings of Tunis, Muslim Moorish pirates had nestled in the strong town of al-Mahdiya, known in the French sources as the Cité d'Auffrique. It was agreed between the allied Crusading parties that Genoa should provide the expedition with a whole fleet fully equipped with an army of seamen, while the duke furnished the land forces consisting of feudal nobility, knights, men-at-arms, and squires. Pope Clement VII blessed the project and officially declared the Crusade, while gentlemen from France, England, Hainault, and Flanders swelled the ducal numbers to 15,000 strong. The Genoese totaled 6,000 of whom 2,000 were redoubtable arbalesters and men-at-arms, the rest being proved mariners, under Admiral Giovanni Centurione d'Oltramarino, whose first target was the island of Conigliera sixteen leagues off the African coast, within easy reach of the sea town of al-Mahdiya.

There the Christian ships reassembled after a rough passage, and the council of war decided the tactical procedure before setting siege to the city. Once on African soil, they became exposed to guerilla attacks from the joint armies of the kingdoms of Tunis, Bugia, and Tlemsen; the latter systematically avoided a pitched battle with superior contingents. The Europeans, on the other hand, used all manner of modern devices of warfare in their attempt to storm the city walls and gates, including one of the earliest examples of the use of gunpowder. Nevertheless, they remained unable to achieve their final goal; and the practical Genoese, seeing the difficulties with which they were beset, began secretly to negotiate a unilateral settlement with the enemy, who was approaching the point of exhaustion. A ten-year truce was approved together with a cessation of piratical practices, and the king of Tunis agreed to pay an annual tribute over fifteen years for peacefully retaining al-Mahdiya, as well as an immediate indemnity of 25,000 ducats to be divided between the commune and the duke. In the end, the council of war was summoned to ratify the proffered treaty, even against the will of the duke, who declared that he would be the last Crusader to board a galley. They finally returned home in October 1390, after the astute Genoese merchants had used the French as their cat's-paw for the solution of one of their major problems.

The greatest and indubitably the most disastrous of all fourteenth-century Crusading campaigns was still to come in 1396 in the face of the rising tide of Ottoman expansion in Eastern Europe. The new menace was sighted within the confines of Hungary, and was reported in 1395 at the French court by Nicholas of Kanizsay, archbishop of Gran and treasurer of Hungary, on behalf of King Sigismund, who solicited help from the West. It was around that date that Philippe de Mézières wrote his hitherto unpublished Epistle to Richard II (1377–1399) of England by order of Charles VI (1380–1422) of France, promoting peace between their two countries and urging unity of action in the East.

But eyes were fixed on the richest man in Europe, Philip

the Bold, duke of Burgundy (1363–1404), for an effective initiation of the movement. Philip, who was eager to have his son and heir, John de Nevers, the future John the Fearless, knighted in the field of battle while fighting the infidels, readily espoused the new cause and appointed John to command of the Franco-Burgundian contingents. Both the Avignonese Pope, Benedict XIII (1394–1415), and the Roman Pope, Boniface IX (1389–1404), issued bulls endorsing the Crusade, each within his own jurisdiction; and the most elaborate and lavish preparations were undertaken for a universal "passagium." Men of the highest distinction from France, such as John le Meingre, dit Boucicaut, marshal of the realm, Admiral John de Vienne, Enguerrand de Coucy, Philip and Henry de Bar, Guy and Guillaume de la Trémouille, and many others hastened to enroll under Nevers's banner, together with their feudal retainers and mercenary troops.

The response was even more general. German auxiliaries came under the Count Palatine, Ruprecht Pipan, count of Katznellenbogen, Count Hermann II of Cilly, and Burgrave John III of Nuremberg. John Holland, earl of Huntingdon, and John Beaufort, son of the duke of Lancaster, also joined at the head of a detachment of a thousand English knights. Further volunteers were recruited from Spain and Italy, while a Veneto-Genoese fleet was joined by the Hospitallers' galleys on its way to the Danube. King Sigismund of Hungary, who later became Holy Roman Emperor from 1410 to 1437, contributed the main bulk of the armed forces from his own realm, and other groups came from Austria, Bohemia, Poland, and notably from Wallachia. Not since the First Crusade had such a truly great army been assembled. The total has been estimated at 100,000, and their rendezvous was Buda, where the first general council of war was held in the midsummer of 1396 to draw up procedures and tactics.

Sigismund wisely favored defensive tactics, which he knew from past experience to be more effective in battle with the

Turks. But the Western leaders deprecated his advice, for, in Froissart's words, they came "to conquer the whole of Turkey and to march into the Empire to Persia, . . . the Kingdom of Syria and the Holy Land." * So lightly did they take their enterprise, and so confusing and misleading was their knowledge of Eastern geography!

The united hosts marched along the Danube as far as Orsova, where they crossed the river at the famous Iron Gate into Bulgaria, then under Turkish suzerainty. In seizing the towns of Widdin and Rahova, the Crusaders displayed no discrimination between hostile Turkish garrisons and friendly Orthodox Christian natives. On September 10 they received their first formidable check at the sturdy fortifications of the city of Nicopolis, situated on a hill overlooking the Danube to the north and a plain to the south. It was decided to set siege to Nicopolis from the land, while the galleys of the Venetians, Genoese, and Hospitallers encircled the city from the river. The siege lasted fifteen days, during which little or no constructive action was taken and the time was wasted in debauchery, orgies, and gambling.

In contrast to this was the position in the Turkish camp. On hearing the news of the Christian advent, Sultan Bayezid I (1389–1402) speedily called off a siege which he had been setting against Constantinople, summoned all his Asiatic and European troops, and marched to the relief of Nicopolis with about 100,000 men under his highly disciplined command. He reached the outlying hills on the south side of the plain in the neighborhood of Nicopolis on September 24, organized his army with great military cunning in a fortified position near the hilltop, and awaited the pitched battle which occurred on the following day.

Sigismund's appeal for placing the Hungarians, who were

* Froissart, Jean: *Chroniques,* ed. by Kervyn de Lettenhove, XV, Brussels 1870–77, 242. Cf. Atiya: *The Crusade in the Later Middle Ages,* London 1938, 441; and *The Crusade of Nicopolis,* London 1934, 55–56 and 180 n.

conversant with Turkish methods of warfare, and the Wallachians, whose loyalty was doubtful, in the van facing the enemy, while the French and foreign legions were saved in the rear for the decisive blow, was rejected outright by the impetuous French, who accused the Hungarian monarch of attempting to rob them of the glory of a great day. Bayezid's irregular light calvary (akinjis) formed the first Ottoman mobile line of battle, concealing behind them an extensive field of pointed stakes which separated them from the next line of foot-archers (janissaries and azebs), up the hill. The French and foreign knights on horseback had no difficulty in routing the first line of mounted Turks, who fled to the rear and reorganized their corps beyond the stakes and the archers. Confronted with the barrier of stakes, however, many Christians descended from their horses under showers of arrows, to uproot the stakes in order to make way for the rest of the mounted attackers. This, too, they soon accomplished, and they further inflicted heavy slaughter on the Turks after fierce hand-to-hand fighting. Then they pursued their fleeing victims upward to the hilltop, which they attained in a state of complete exhaustion, believing that to have been the end of a good day.

To their horror, it was only the beginning of the end, for they saw beyond the skyline Bayezid's picked cavalry (sipahis), together with his vassal Serbs under Stephen Lazarovitch, totalling some 40,000 in complete array ready to begin a fresh phase of the battle. The deadly massacre was reversed, and the pursuers became pursued; the survivors were carried into captivity. In the meantime, the riderless horses discarded by the French earlier in the battle, stung by Turkish arrows, stampeded in confusion to the rear across the plain and were regarded by both Hungarians and Wallachians as a sure sign of the discomfiture of their allies. The latter took to flight and Sigismund, grand master of Rhodes, and the burgrave of Nuremberg barely managed to save their skins by boarding a

Venetian ship which floated downstream, as the Ottomans began to make their appearance later in the day amid the remaining Christians.

As the sounds of battle were quelled, however, and the sultan had time to look around the field, he was alarmed at his own losses, which were estimated at 30,000, and he displayed his wrath in the cold-blooded massacre of 3,000 prisoners of war on the following day. Bayezid discovered among these captives Jacques de Helly, whom he had previously employed in his eastern campaigns and who understood Turkish. Through Jacques' intercession, the French nobility, including John de Nevers, Enguerrand de Coucy, Philip d'Artois, Guy de la Trémouille, and others, were saved from decapitation and held as precious hostages pending payment of a ransom of 200,000 gold florins. The news of this catastrophe overwhelmed Europe with deep sorrow and dismay; and the grim fate of the chivalry of the West at Nicopolis marked the end of one chapter and the beginning of another in the relations between the East and the West. The prospect for the Crusade became dimmer every day, and the Turk had to be accepted as a member of the European commonwealth of nations despite his race and religion.

After the great calamity which befell the Christian chivalry at Nicopolis, the nations of Western Europe became more and more unwilling to embark on hazardous adventures to overthrow the power of Islam and put an end to Turkish domination. The great propagandist upheaval of the early century began to subside, although we still encounter some writers clamoring for resumption of the Crusade. Most outstanding among these was Philippe de Mézières, who spent the later years of his life in a retreat at the Abbey of the Celestines in Paris, writing several voluminous works of high interest in defense of the old cause. After the defeat of 1396 in Bulgaria, he took up his pen to compose a penetrating epistle entitled

"Épistre lamentable et consolatoire," which he addressed to the duke of Burgundy.

De Mézières tried to analyze the causes of and prescribe the remedies for the downfall of the Christians in the East. He explained that the root of Christian impotence was imbedded in the lack of the four virtues of good governance—Order, Discipline, Obedience, and Justice. Instead of these, society was ruled by the three vicious daughters of Lucifer—Vanity, Covetousness, and Luxury. The "Summa Perfectio," declared Mézières, could be attained only by the adoption of his "Nova Religio Passionis," which provided for the redemption of the birthplace of Christ. This organization or military order of religion was the sole road leading to a successful Crusade, that is, if the old cause could be resuscitated. Meanwhile, it should be noted that de Mézières aptly described himself as an old pilgrim and an old dreamer, an echo of bygone days.

THE FIFTEENTH CENTURY

The complete discomfiture and humiliation of the hosts of Europe, and the massacre of the flower of Western chivalry in the Balkans, rudely awakened the Christian potentates to the stark realities of the Crusades and their futility as an implement for the solution of East-West relations. Furthermore, the fifteenth century resounded with other momentous problems of immediate consequence nearer home which distracted public attention from the old cause. The reopening of the Hundred Years' War between England and France, with its devastating ferocity, on the one hand, and the Conciliar Movement to end the Great Schism of the Church in the West on the other, were issues which consumed public attention throughout Western Europe.

Nevertheless it would be a serious error to contend that the

Crusade, both as idea and as action, was extinct. Although the movement had already started to lose its universal character, vestiges could be traced in a series of localized struggles to arrest Ottoman expansion in Eastern Europe and the Levant. In the first place, Burgundy, which bore the brunt of the heavy ransom paid to Sultan Bayezid I for the deliverance of the Nicopolis prisoners of war, became the center of deliberations for revenge. This yielded a new harvest of propagandist literature, which remained confined to the realm of theory. In the second place, the principalities of East Central Europe, led by the kingdom of Hungary, became the real bulwark of Christendom; and resistance in that area has frequently been termed the Hungarian Crusade. In the third place, the mid-century was characterized by the heroic but hopeless aspirations for the defense of the imperial city of Constantinople, which was almost continuously beleaguered by the Turks until the extermination of the Byzantine Empire. Afterward, practically all wars of defense fought against the Ottomans were conducted under the misnomer of Crusade.

Duke Philip the Good of Burgundy still entertained thoughts of leading the holy war, but preferred to proceed with the utmost caution and deliberation in order to avoid another disaster. For a perfect understanding of the position of his adversary, he commissioned two ambassadors in succession to go to the lands beyond the sea and attempt to gather original information about the Islamic polity in an intelligence report coupled with their recommendations. The first of these two was Ghillebert de Lannoy, who spent the years 1420–23 in the Near East, and the second was Bertrandon de la Broquière, whose embassy lasted from 1432 to 1439. While de Lannoy devoted most of his time and attention to Egypt and the Holy Land, de la Broquière, after performing pilgrimage to Jerusalem and the holy places as far as Sinai, retraced his steps to the north, where he conducted his inquiry on Armenia, Anatolia, Byzantium, and above all the Balkan territories subject to the Grand Turk. He visited the court of Sultan Murad II (1421–51) at Adrianople and remarked that the Turks were more friendly to the Latins than the Greeks were. He described the Turkish armies and armor as well as the whole Ottoman military system for the enlightenment of the duke.

Another propagandist of a different character, also from among the adherents of the Burgundian court, was Bishop Jean Germain, chancellor of the Order of the Golden Fleece, who compiled a political discourse to prove that the general position was still more favorable to the Christians than to the Muslims and that it was not yet too late for Crusading. Jean Germain wrote in 1452, on the eve of the downfall of Constantinople. He seemed to underline the shadowy religious union of the Christian East with Rome, concluded at the Council of Ferrara-Florence in 1439, which according to his estimate would bring to the Crusader ranks 200,000 combatants from Armenia, 50,000 from Georgia, some recruits from the Greek empires of Constantinople and Trebizond, the "Jacobites of Ethiopia," Russia, and "Prester John of India." The rosy picture he painted for Christian leaders was of secondary importance, since its author derived his arguments from wishful thinking rather than original knowledge. He had no direct acquaintance with the East and compiled his material from sundry sources.

The flickering ray of hope for the defense of Christendom was largely forthcoming from the hard-pressed peoples of East Central Europe in what has been described as the Hungarian Crusade, while reinforcements from the West grew less every day. The pivotal figure in this conflict was John Hunyadi (1444–56,), regent of Hungary and voyavode of Transylvania, whose heroic career passed into legend in contemporary Balkan annals. His spirited attacks on the Turks almost brought Murad II's reign (1421–51) to a disastrous end. The story began with the sultan's irruptions of the year 1438 into Transylvania across the Danube, as far as the strong city of Hermannstadt to the north and as far as the gates of Belgrade in Serbia to the west. It was at this precarious juncture that Hunyadi emerged on the scene in a coalition with Ladislas, king of Poland (1434–44) and also of Hungary since 1440, as well as George Brankovitch, despot of Serbia (1427–56).

At first each of the three leaders conducted hostilities against the Turkish battalions independently within his own realm. When Murad repeated the invasion of Transylvania in 1442, he was again beaten at Hermannstadt, leaving behind him 20,000 dead. In fury, he made a third and desperate attempt on the city and suffered the same consequences. Hunyadi captured 5,000 Turkish prisoners of war and 200 Ottoman standards. The myth of Turkish invincibility seemed shattered, and the voyavode, hitherto on the defensive, was further encouraged to take the offensive south of the Danube by the arrival of a number of detachments of Latin Crusaders under Cardinal Julian Cesarini in 1443. Again, joined by King Ladislas and John Brankovitch, John Hunyadi sallied into Serbia and scored a new triumph by routing the Turks at Nish, before he seized the Bulgarian capital, Sofia. Even the Albanians, who were Murad's sworn vassals, became so emboldened by these momentous victories that they seceded from Turkish suzerainty and declared open revolt under John Castriota, better known as Scanderbeg. On July 15, 1444 Murad was constrained to sign the Treaty of Szegedin with the coalition leaders. By its terms, George Brankovitch was reinstated in Serbia, a ransom of 60,000 gold ducats was paid by the sultan for the liberation of his captive sons-in-law, and a ten-year truce was approved; but it was later broken under pressure from Cardinal Cesarini. In the end, the despairing sultan decided to abdicate and disappeared from the scene of strife into the interior of Anatolia.

Hopes were revived in the West on hearing of the new triumphs. Duke Philip the Good of Burgundy (1419–67) received an embassy from the Byzantine Emperor, John VIII (1425–48), to court his support at Châlons-sur-Saône; and he consequently equipped four galleys under Geoffroy de Thoisy and Martin Alphonse, while Pope Eugenius IV (1431–47) contributed ships under the command of his own nephew, Francesco Condolmieri, to fight the Turks. The Crusading fire was rekindled, and Cardinal Cesarini's position was strengthened in persuading Hunyadi to break a truce held to be null and void in principle since it was concluded with an infidel. Moreover, the voyavode was promised the crown of Bulgaria on the final liberation of that country from the Turkish yoke.

The first great objective of the joint forces was the strong coastal town of Varna on the Black Sea. On the way, the Christian fleet from the West helped in the relief of the Hospitallers of St. John, who were under siege by the Egyptians in their island fortress of Rhodes during 1444. Afterward, the men-of-war proceeded directly to the Black Sea, to join the siege of the strong city of Varna, already surrounded on the land side and heavily battered by the coalition contingents under the command of the intrepid Hunyadi. Another shattering victory was within sight, when suddenly the old sultan emerged from his retreat at the head of 40,000 picked men whom the perfidious Genoese had transported from Asia to Europe for gain and the promise of trade privileges. During the mortal fighting which ensued outside Varna, both Ladislas and Cardinal Cesarini fell, leaving the weight of the defense operations solely on Hunyadi's shoulders. The Poles and Latins were demoralized by their leaders' sudden disappearance from the field, and the Hungarians faced extermination by an invincible enemy. Hunyadi had no choice but to take to flight on November 10, 1444 to save the remnants of his exhausted army.

Nevertheless, the Albanian rebellion continued to rage under the indomitable Scanderbeg; until, in 1448, Hunyadi reassembled another army of 24,000 men and crossed the Danube at the Iron Gate to invade Serbia. Murad was waiting for him with a superior army of 150,000. They met on the old field of Kossovo-Polye, where the heroism of Hunyadi and his desperate followers did not save them from disaster. Their numerical inferiority, the incoherence and absence of concerted tactics between the Albanians and the Hungarians, the doubtful loyalty of the Wallachians, and the exhaustion of ammunition in the hands of the German and Bohemian infantry, rendering their fearful gunfire utterly ineffective—all these were factors culminating in the tragedy of the Second Battle of Kossovo (October 17–19, 1448), which ended the Hungarian Crusade with irreparable rout.

Perhaps the only positive result of this painful chapter in Crusading history was the prolongation of the agonies of the tottering Byzantine Empire by a few more years. Even before the downfall of Constantinople in 1453, the sultan's suzerainty over the imperial city had in some way or other been tacitly recognized by most members of the imperial family. On John VIII's death in 1448, his three brothers appealed to Murad II for arbitration on their right of succession to the imperial throne, and the sultan's choice fell on Constantine Dragases, the last Emperor destined to defend the city with his life. The defense of this last bulwark of Eastern Christendom, in which a few detachments from the Christian West participated, was described by some contemporaries as a Crusade. Nevertheless, the story of the triumphant entry of Sultan Muhammad II (1451–81) into Constantinople, at midday on April 29, 1453, must be regarded as the consummation of the Turkish Counter-Crusade, and as such will be treated elsewhere in this book.

Although long foreseen and even expected, the final downfall of Constantinople to the Ottomans in 1453 was received throughout Christian Europe with utter bewilderment and great embitterment. The flight of many Greek personalities for refuge in the West became a living reminder of the fateful events in progress in Eastern Europe. The last of the Palaeologi, Thomas, brother of Constantine Dragases, ultimately settled down at the Roman Curia in 1461, taking with him the head of the Apostle Andrew, one of the priceless relics which he had saved from desecration. Pope Pius II (Aeneas Sylvius Piccolomini, 1458–64), who had previously associated himself with the moribund cause as a staunch propagandist for holy war, now espoused the cause of the imperial pretender and took the Cross himself. He invited all European monarchs to join him in a new universal Crusade for the recovery of Byzantium and the reconquest of the Holy Land. The only response to his call came from Philip the Good, who promised to follow the Holy Pontiff with 6,000 men. A little later, the Burgundian duke requested respite for a year and laid the blame on Louis XI's machinations against his duchy. As a matter of fact, Pius II himself was a very sick man at the time, and the whole project was ultimately buried with him on his decease in 1464. His successor to the tiara, Paul II (1464–71), was less ambitious and more practical. He decided to relegate the funds accumulated for the Crusade to Hungary and Venice as a contribution toward the cost of their intermittent wars with the Turks.

The call to Crusade was fading into a distant cry, though its echoes lingered in the minds of Western princes as late as the seventeenth century. Pope Innocent VIII (1484–92), attempting in vain to renew the plan of an expedition against the Turks, was heartened by the advent of Bayezid II's brother and rival Djem as a fugitive in Rome. Innocent VIII conceived the possibility of inciting rebellion in Turkey in favor of his protégé, but it is said that he was persuaded by the sultan's agents to give up the project, with Djem's body yielded in return for a prize of 300,000 gold ducats.

Alexander VI (1492–1503) succeeded Innocent and became the chief actor in this mysterious tragedy, in conjunction with King Charles VIII of France (1483–98). The Holy Pontiff surrendered his hostage to the king, and finally we hear of Djem's unnatural death in the course of 1495. The sultan was thus relieved of this menace, and immediately he resumed his irruptions into Hungary, Croatia, Moldavia, and even as far as remote Poland, until the peace treaty of 1503 provided Europe with a breathing space for some seventeen years. Both the Popes and the Western monarchs adopted a passive attitude and stood on the defensive, awaiting fearfully the next step to be taken by the Supreme Porte.* In the year 1515 Pope Leo X (1513–21) did indeed consider the renewal of hostilities against the Ottoman Empire in conjunction with King Francis I (1515–47) of France and Emperor Maximilian I (1493–1519) of the Holy Roman Empire, but their plan remained in the realm of discussion. Perhaps the only positive action of the period occurred when Emperor Charles V (1519–56) granted the Hospitallers a new abode on the island of Malta (1530) after their expulsion from Rhodes by Sultan Sulaiman the Magnificent (1520–66). Subsequently, a number of imperial detachments descended on Algiers in 1541, and again on the shores of al-Mahdiya in 1550, to chastise the Barbary corsairs. On the other hand, these minor successes scored by the Emperor induced his antagonist, Francis I, to swing French policy toward the conclusion of the alliance of 1536 with the Supreme Porte, marking the birth of the famous Capitulations. Only at the gates of Vienna (1529) and in the waters of Lepanto (1571) was Europe able to arrest the progress of Turkish invasions.

Henceforward, the Turkish wars became more or less localized in Central Europe; and in the following century we hear of the deliverance of Jerusalem only occasionally,

* "Al-Bāb al-'Āli" in Arabic and Turkish, equivalent to the "lofty gate," otherwise the "Supreme Porte" of the sultanate at the height of its power.

as a mere dream. Cardinal Richelieu (1585–1642) and the famous French diplomat Father Joseph (1577–1638) spoke about the Holy Land and how to save it. Ferdinand I of Tuscany went a little further when he landed on the island of Cyprus in the course of 1607–08 and tried to arouse the discontented Turkish subjects for joint action against their lord, Sultan Ahmed I (1603–17). The attempt yielded no practical results and Ferdinand himself died shortly afterward in 1609. It was in these years that a certain Father Giovanni Dominelli, an Italian priest living in Cairo, wrote what may be regarded as the last propagandist document outlining a project for saving Jerusalem and the holy places. He argued that the times were eminently suited for landing in Palestine since the sultan was engaged in fighting on several fronts in the continents of Asia and Europe, while his men silently harbored the spirit of insubordination and his Christian subjects were biding their time and chance for insurrection in order to throw off their heavy yoke of servitude. Father Dominelli's faint voice passed unheeded in a changing world, and Crusading days were mere memories.

CHAPTER FOUR

Aftermath: The Counter-Crusade

RESULTS OF THE CRUSADES

IN DISCUSSING the results of the Crusades, it is necessary to make a clear distinction between the wider issues of world history on the one hand, and the insulated and localized effects with a special bearing upon a given area, institution, or community on the other. The first category includes the Counter-Crusade, Commerce, and Culture, which will be considered here at some length. The Counter-Crusade was the immediate reaction of the Muslim world to the Crusading offensive in the Near East. The phenomenal development in Eastern commerce during the later medieval period came as a natural corollary to European acquaintance with the possibilities of Levantine markets situated at the terminal points of Asiatic caravan and maritime trade routes. In matters of culture, the areas of contact between Muslim and Christian must be extended beyond Palestine to Sicily and Spain in the central and western Mediterranean. In fact, the cultural impact of Arab civilization and Arab thought was intense in both Sicily and

Spain, where as it tapered off in the Near East. The extent of the role of the Crusade in each of these immense fields will be defined in the forthcoming pages.

At one time scholars had a marked tendency to overestimate the effects of the Crusade, and practically every change in European society at the close of the Middle Ages was ascribed in some way or other to the influence of that universal upheaval. Then suddenly this was reversed, and a more modern school of thought treated the Crusades as local and unrelated occurrences without any enduring impact whatever on the general course of history. Both extremes are objectionable, because neither of them represents the whole truth. The results of the Crusades are not uniform at all times and in all fields, and each case or sphere of influence will have to be considered on its merits as a separate entity for the correct appraisal of its relation to the movement as a whole.

To begin with, the effects of the Crusade were felt most acutely by the Church and its central administration at the Roman Curia. The Papacy had scored many decisive victories over the Holy Roman Empire in the Investiture contest, and the Emperors were humiliated and reduced to a secondary status in world politics. The Holy Pontiff had made enormous strides on the road to international domination, and the Crusade offered Urban II and his successors a potent new formula with universal appeal for papal foreign policy. The Church thus led in the war of the Cross, and each Crusade was accompanied by an apostolic legate to represent the Vicar of God in the field of action, and occasionally to assume supreme command of armed forces. Yet we must remember that within the Latin kingdom of Jerusalem, lay authorities opposed the tendency toward theocratization, and they succeeded to some extent in the restraint of papal ambitions in the new state. Ecclesiastical preeminence of the Popes, though tacitly recognized by all in the launching and preaching of Crusades, was not allowed a free hand in the conduct of the actual fighting, except in rare instances such as the later phase of the Fifth Crusade. Then the deflection of the Crusade from war against Muslims in the East for the deliverance of the holy places to the coercion of Christians in Western Europe, whether heretics as in the Albigensian Crusade or personal enemies of the Papacy, such as Frederick II, eventually became a factor in undermining papal authority and arousing skepticism about the spirit and significance of the whole movement. The tithes levied by clerics for that cause, and the substitution of money payments for Crusading and penitential vows by pious people, ultimately led to the development of a novel system of indulgences with far-reaching repercussions on the prestige of the Papacy.

One of the important offshoots of the Crusade was the creation of the military orders of religion. Most prominent among these monastic fighting forces were the Templars and Hospitallers. Though their participation in Crusading warfare was continuous, they soon began to foster independent leanings as semi-secular organizations with their own private policies, which often came into conflict and led to open friction between them. The Templars, moreover, became pioneers of international banking in medieval Europe, thereby alienating their brotherhood from its initial vow and spurring on their own downfall and ultimate suppression by the French monarchy in 1310—to be confirmed by the reluctant Papacy in 1312 after one of the most scandalous and horrible trials of any age. The Hospitallers, on the other hand, survived for several centuries. When they were thrown out of the Holy Land after the fall of Acre in 1291, they took refuge in the island kingdom of Cyprus, where they enjoyed the hospitality of the Lusignans for a few years. Then they seized Rhodes, which became their abode until Sultan Sulaiman the Magnificent drove them from it and annexed the island to Turkey in 1522. It was on this occasion that Emperor Charles (1519–66) gave them Malta, where they were established until their suppression by Napoleon Bonaparte in 1798 on his way to Egypt.

Other military orders emerged during that period outside the Holy Land. The Order of the Sword was founded by Innocent III in 1204, and the Teutonic Knighthood came into being during the Third Crusade. Both entered into alliance at a later date for the purpose of combating paganism in Prussia, a state which owed its creation to their concerted efforts.

Perhaps the most permanent reaction to the steady secularization of the military orders of religion was the rise of the new mendicant orders. First and foremost among them were the Franciscans or Lesser Brothers (Fratres Minores *), who owed their foundation to the great St. Francis of Assisi (1182–1226), after his return to Italy from the Egyptian Crusade of 1218–20. Next in importance was the Dominican order, whose members devoted themselves to opposing all kinds of anti-clericalism and to combating the new menace of the Albigensian heresy. Their founder was St. Dominic, an ardent Spaniard, who stressed the duty of preaching in the rule of the Dominicans (Fratres Praedicatores **), and their services earned for them papal sanction by Innocent III in 1215.

In reality, the rules of both these orders were modelled on the same pattern. Both strictly observed the principles of poverty and aimed at inspiring deference toward the Holy See, more especially in the urban regions, where they combined religious persuasion with public education. It is rather unfortunate that the Dominicans became involved in the violence of the religious Inquisition against heresy. The Franciscans, on the other hand, expanded their activities in a missionary campaign overseas. Their work in Asia has

* Known also as Minorites, Cordeliers, or Grey Friars from the color of their garb.

** Also called Black Friars.

often been termed the "Mongol Crusade"; because they undertook the unprecedented step of crossing the whole continent of Asia in an attempt to evangelize the Tartars, with the purpose of uniting the Far East with the Christian West in a comprehensive attack on the Muslim Empire in the Near East. All these historical developments must necessarily be tied in some measure to the age of the Crusades.

In the political field, the Crusades contributed to the development of the central power of the monarchy at the expense of the feudal nobility. The impoverishment of feudatories as a result of participation in a very costly war beyond the sea diminished aristocratic influence at home. Some nobles mortgaged their fiefs, some sold their rights over their hereditary possessions, and others died childless and forfeited their estates to the Crown. Meanwhile, royal taxation for the sustenance of the Holy Land was imposed by Louis VII of France in 1146 and 1165, by Henry II of England in 1166 and 1184, and by Philip Augustus in 1184 for three years. A Saladin tithe was exacted in both England and France in 1188, following the downfall of Jerusalem. In a sense, the modest beginnings of the system of modern taxation may be traced to the circumstances of Crusading imposts and impositions. Furthermore, while feudalism was just starting a long process of decline, the new middle class was slowly coming into existence. Townsfolk or burgesses purchased their franchises from the hard-pressed nobles going on Crusade, and allied themselves with royalty for defense against future feudal encroachments of local liege lords. It was this alliance between commoners or burghers and the Crown that signalled the original spark of modern "nationalism," at first in the form of "royalism," which was in the ascendant when the disintegration of feudalism became accelerated after the Crusades. It was in this way that the nucleus of modern states began slowly to emerge around the persons of kings. This proved to be an institutional, economic, and social revolution destined to change the face of Europe in the later Middle Ages.

The influence of the Crusade on the military system of medieval Europe was considerable through direct contact with both the Greeks and the Arabs. Being in the first instance an armed settlement on alien soil, the Latins were naturally susceptible to improvement of their art of war in the face of perpetual danger. The use of the concentric mode in castle-building, with double walls and a central fortified keep, is presumably of Eastern origin, although it is sometimes argued that it could have been a normal evolution dictated by the advisability of increasing the number of impediments in the way of hostile troops storming the castle. The fact, however, remains that the earliest example of a European castle built on the new model was the Château Gaillard, constructed by Richard I in Normandy after his return from the Third Crusade.

Other features may also be traced back to Eastern influence. Among them was the introduction of machicolation in military structures. A machicoulis was an opening between the corbels of a parapet, or in the floor of a gallery, or on the roof of a portal of a castle, for dropping boiling liquids or discharging missiles on assailants from without. This device had long been known in the East; examples of machicolation can be found in the battlements of fortified buildings, citadels, and city walls in Egypt and the Holy Land prior to their adoption by Western European military architects. Siege techniques, notably mining and sapping, as well as the employment of Greek fire and the mangonel, were innovations for which the Crusaders must be held responsible in Europe. The cross-bow was also a weapon of Eastern provenance. The idea of the surcoat was borrowed from Muslim warriors, who used it as a protective measure against the glare of the sun falling on metallic armor. The cotton quilts or padding under the Western steel mail were transplanted to Europe in imitation of

Arabian usage in the field. The scarf used to shield the head from the merciless Eastern sun is only the Arabic "kūfiya," with the same literal meaning. The tournament is very much akin to the "game of the stick" (la'eb al-Jarīd), a common game in the East. The use of carrier pigeons for the transmission of military communications had been an old practice in the East and was readily copied by the Crusaders. In heraldry, too, which became fashionable in the time of the Crusades, we can trace many Western emblems to Saracenic origins. The fleur-de-lis, the two-headed eagle, the lion, the cup, and the polo sticks are among numerous examples of heraldic signs known in the East before the Crusades.

It is noteworthy that French vernacular writing received a great impetus during the period of the Crusades. The "Estoire de la Guerre Sainte" by Ambroise, "La Conquête de Constantinople" by Villehardouin, the "Histoire de Saint-Louis" by Joinville, the "Histoire de Éracles" by William of Tyre, the "Gestes des Chiprois," the "Chanson d'Antioche," "La Prise d'Alexandrie" by Guillaume de Machaut, and the "Chanson de la Croisade des Albigeois"—all these and others form part of the Crusading literary cycle in the native Old French tongue. In spite of the hostility on both sides, one can read between the lines a growing tendency toward understanding and religious toleration in the literature of the times. Archbishop William of Tyre, for instance, writing of the Arabs at the time of the first Muslim conquest of the Holy Land, says: "They allowed the conquered people, however, to restore the ruined churches, to have their own bishop, and to follow the Christian religion without restraint." * He himself was conversant with Arabic and appreciated the Oriental world in which he had been living from early childhood.

Apparently the Crusaders brought back home with them

* *A History of Deeds Done Beyond the Sea,* trans. and annotated by Emily H. Babcock and A. C. Krey (*Records of Civilization*), I, N.Y. 1943, 62. See Atiya: *Hist. and Bibl.,* Monumental Collections, section VI.

numerous novel articles of archaeological interest. Gibbon points to the first importer of windmills from Asia Minor as one of the benefactors of the nations of Europe. Contacts with a highly superior civilization taught these rough warriors the use of public and private baths. It was by the same channel that Europe first became acquainted with and adopted the use of latrines. Crusading artisans and masons watched with wonderment the splendid stone carving and moulding in which the Syrians had excelled from antiquity; and they returned to their homes with new artistic ideals, to lay the foundations of the elaborate Gothic style in Europe. The Arab formulae for the manufacture of stained and enamelled glass and of the Damascus steel blade, hitherto kept as close secrets, were transmitted to European factories during the Crusades. Silk, sugar, and a multitude of other staples and delicacies also came with the Crusaders, but these belong to the discussion of medieval commerce.

The adventurous spirit of the Cross-bearers ultimately brought forth the age of exploration and discovery. Interest in the Mongols opened up the way to distant Cathay across the untrodden paths of Central Asia. The missionary activity of the Roman Church, which Louis IX fostered and the Popes sponsored, was a notable feature of the times. It must be noted, however, that with the death of Giacomo of Florence, last Latin patriarch of the see of Khān Bāliq, in 1362, the prospect of any union with the Mongols came to an abrupt end. Nevertheless, the dream of the Mongol Crusade lingered in the imagination of the Popes and princes of Western Europe, and an occasional attempt was made to revive the moribund cause.

Toward the close of the fifteenth century Ferdinand and Isabella embarked on their final Crusade against the Moors in Andalusia, and Granada surrendered to the Spanish Christians in January 1492. With the completion of the Reconquista, the two Catholic monarchs began to envision fresh fields of conquest for the faith beyond the confines of the Iberian Peninsula. It was for this purpose that they were persuaded to grant a charter to Christopher Columbus, an obscure but adventurous Genoese mariner, to attempt to reach India and the Great Khanate of Cathay by the western sea route. The object of that expedition is painted with remarkable precision in the journal ascribed to Columbus and preserved in the annals of the writer Las Casas. The explorer addresses his royal benefactors in these words:

> Your Highnesses, as good Christian and Catholic princes, devout and propagators of the Christian faith, as well as enemies of the sect of Mahomet and of all idolatries and heresies, conceived the plan of sending me, Christopher Columbus, to this country of the Indies, there to see the princes, the peoples, the territory, their disposition and all things else, and the way in which one might proceed to convert these regions to our holy faith.*

Ambitions to reach the Indies, however, were overshadowed by the spectacular discovery of America, which barred the western route to India and the Far East, and interest in Cathay was superseded by dazzling prospects of a whole New World. Indeed, it would not be imprudent to argue that the discovery of America was an indirect byproduct of the Crusading movement, a byproduct which was symptomatic of the new orientation in world history.

The expansion of human horizons beyond anything ever attained in the past, and the accumulation of wealth and consequent leisure in the trade communes of Southern Europe, yielded a rich harvest of works of art and literature denoting the new birth of a changing world. The Renaissance and the dawn of modern times are at least partly, though of course not wholly, the outcome of the Crusade and its long-range effects

* B. de Las Casas: *Historia de las Indias (Colleccion de Documentos Ined. para la Historia de España,* LXII), Madrid 1875–76. Cf. Atiya: *The Crusade in the Later Middle Ages,* London 1938, 258–59.

upon social, cultural, and economic life. The trends of normal progress from within, as well as European contacts with the advanced Arab civilization in Sicily and Spain, were parallel factors not to be forgotten in any appraisal of the imminent transformation in the European scene.

In the East—where the Crusades were inaugurated partly to save and strengthen the native Christians—it is paradoxical to note that the movement ended in a complete tragedy. Although Asia Minor was momentarily restored to the Greeks, the Turks relentlessly resumed their offensive against Byzantine territory whenever the Crusading tide receded. But the real calamity befalling the Eastern Roman Empire occurred in the Fourth Crusade, with all its irreparable implications, paving the way for the final collapse of Byzantium to the Turks in 1453, and intensifying the traditional hatred between the peoples and churches of the Christian East and the Christian West.

For the forgotten Christian minorities living within the Arab Empire, the Crusades were equally calamitous. These law-abiding Christians had learned to live with their Muslim neighbors in good fellowship, and to settle in the spirit of amity any differences arising between their communities. Now the Crusaders treated them as loathsome schismatics, worse than heathens, and deprived them of local rights which they had formerly enjoyed under Muslim rule. In the meantime, the new situation of Christian aggression from the West incurred the wrath of the Caliphate against all Christians, Eastern and Western without distinction. Some Eastern Christians, in desperation, either apostatized to Islam or became proselytized to Romanism in search of peaceful existence. The conversion of the Maronites of Lebanon and part of the Armenian people in Cilicia to the Catholic faith is largely a legacy of the Crusades, and the unity of the ancient Eastern Churches was thus impaired. Native Christians had to start again to mend their shaken status at home within the

Islamic polity after the liquidation of the holy war—a slow, painful, but indispensable operation.

THE COUNTER-CRUSADE: PROPAGANDA

Whatever the results of the Crusade might be, one thing appears to be perfectly clear from the examination of subsequent occurrences. Violence begat violence; and the wars of the Cross from the West revived the slumbering spirit of "al-Jihād" or early Muslim holy strife against all Christians. In other words, the Crusade precipitated the Anti-Crusade as its immediate and most destructive consequence. Notwithstanding the fact that this phase has been long and unduly overlooked, or at most casually studied in current works, it is impossible to minimize its place in the development of the map of the Near and Middle East. On close investigation the Counter-Crusade is revealed as a perfect counterfoil and an equal peer to the Crusade, with only one major difference—that the latter left its permanent impression on the course of history, whereas the former culminated in irrevocable bankruptcy.

The apparent lacuna in our knowledge and in existing literature on this highly interesting subject is largely due to the dearth of original material in print. Despite the tremenduous number of tracts and treatises left by medieval Muslim writers on this topic, the bulk of that literature remains in manuscript entombed or dissipated in far-flung repositories. From a preliminary survey of hundreds of those codices, the main constituent elements of this little-known subject become evident. Let us attempt a brief analysis thereof by way of introduction, leaving the task of fuller monographs on this unexplored territory to the inquiring minds of future students and Orientalists.

Above all considerations, it must be understood that the

sources and phases of the Counter-Crusade parallel those of the Crusade. Christian propaganda for the Crusade in the West was met by Muslim counter-propaganda for "al-Jihād" in the East. Attacks on Palestine and other Muslim countries automatically incurred Muslim hostility and resulted in a systematic invasion of the Christian states within their range as soon as the Muslims won relief from the Western menace. There ensued the new policy of Islamic conquest, with two chief sources: the Mamluk sultanate from Egypt, and the Ottoman Turks who broke loose upon Eastern and East Central Europe.

Muslim propaganda sprang, in the first instance, from the theological considerations of the principle of "al-Jihād" or holy war, which must be traced to the early days of the rise of Islam during the lifetime of the Prophet Muḥammad (570–632) and the four Orthodox Caliphs, his immediate successors. That principle of "al-Jihād" had been upheld from the very outset on the authority of a fair number of verses from the Medinese "Sūras," or chapters, of the Holy Qur'ān. It was soon recognized by the great Muslim jurists and commentators almost as a "sixth pillar" of the Islamic faith.*

* The other five "pillars" or fundamental doctrines are as follows. First there is the Profession of the Faith, the Arabic "Shehādah," that is, the declaration of the simple formula that "There is no God but Allah, and Muḥammad is the Prophet of Allah." When anyone declares this, he automatically becomes a Muslim; he surrenders himself to God—the word "Islam" literally stands for peaceful surrender to the divine will. Second is Prayer, consisting of a series of formal prostrations, genuflections, and pious statements and supplications to be repeated five times each day, at dawn, noon, afternoon, sunset, and nightfall. Third is Alms-tithe (Zakāt), a payment to the state in kind and in varying proportions according to the nature of the goods,—one-tenth, one-twentieth, or otherwise in accordance with juridical computation. The fourth pillar is the Fast of the month of Ramaḍān—complete abstention from food or drink or any extraneous material through the mouth or the nose, including perfume and smoking, as well as conjugal intercourse, from sunrise to sunset. Fifth is Pilgrimage to Mecca and Medina, binding upon all those who are able to undertake it.

Strictly speaking, the word "al-Jihād" stands for strife or struggle in the wider sense, both visible and invisible. The "imams," or religious leaders, distinguish four forms of "al-Jihād": that of the heart in fighting invisible sin, considered the hardest and most praiseworthy; that of the tongue against evil utterances; that of the hand in visible functions; and that of the sword against polytheists and the enemies of Islam (described as the "smallest Jihād"). In fact, "al-Jihād" became identified with holy war, defined as an obligation of all able-bodied Muslims (farḍ 'alā al-Kafāyah) to combat all non-Muslims until the whole world is subdued to Islam and submits or surrenders to Allah.

In theory, Islam depended for its expansion on "the mission" (risālah), that is, on winning others by the word of goodness. As the peaceful word of primitive Islam did not work fast enough, later jurisconsults recognized "al-Jihād" also as an acceptable means for spreading the faith. Even if we pass over the wars of Muḥammad's lifetime as essentially defensive in character, we soon find that the new ruling was made effective within a few years of the Prophet's death, in the case of dissenters (ahl al-riddah) who apostatized from Islam to the old pagan ways or followed other false prophets. Islamic rigor showed no mercy toward apostates. They were cut down by the sword, a usage which became acknowledged as a precedent for future generations; and the world was consequently divided into two camps of believers and unbelievers, of the "house of Islam" (dār al-Islām) and the "house of hostility" (dār al-harb). "Al-Jihād" thus became a binding communal duty without intercession or respite under the leadership of the Caliphate, until the whole world should be united in the "house of Islam." This elaborate doctrine is the starting point with which the whole multitude of Islamic propagandists inaugurated their treatises on the subject of holy war. All seemed to aim at the same goal of exhorting the faithful to fight in defense of the Holy Places and of every Muslim sanctuary. Their works may be divided into three main categories.

In the first place, we have the "Books of Pilgrimage" (Kutub al-Ziyārāt); the authors explain to the community of Muslims that the performance of a pilgrimage is not restricted to the holy cities of Mecca and Medina in Hijaz. To perform a complete pilgrimage, they contend, the faithful must extend their visitations to the main shrines and tombs of the Prophets of the two monotheistic religions of Judaism and Christianity. Muḥammad did not denounce the older prophets, nor did Islam abrogate their doctrines and Holy Scriptures. What Islam rejected in those faiths was the so-called element of corruption and subsequent interpolation in the original texts of the Torah and of the Gospels. Frequenting the ancient sanctuaries of the Prophets was binding to a Muslim as a supplementary duty. One author asserts that a single prayer said in Jerusalem (the Arabic al-Quds or Bayt al-Maqdiss, i.e., House of Sanctity) equals a thousand prayers said elsewhere. If the Muslim could not fulfill this office, he should send oil to the sacred shrines of the holy city. In reality, pilgrimage in the fullness of its meaning should further encompass the tombs of the companions of the Prophet Muḥammad wherever they might be outside the Arabian Peninsula, as well as the tombs of other holy shaikhs revered by later generations. From such works as were written by Abu Bakr al-Herawy (d. 611 A.H./1214 A.D.), Shihāb al-Dīn al-Maqdisi (d. 765 A.H./1363 A.D.) and Muwaffaq al-Dīn al-Khazraji (d. c. 780 A.H./1378 A.D.), the reader is left with the conclusion that the Muslim was bound by his religion not only to visit those places but also to preserve them within the pale of the Islamic Empire and defend them against the Crusader, who was considered to be an infidel Christian, a real heathen and polytheist whose mere presence polluted the shrines.

In the second place, a large collection of other works might be classified under the title of "Books of Virtues" (Kutub al-

Faḍā'il). Here the authors enumerate the virtues of Muslim countries, of Muslim towns, and of Muslim sanctuaries. Free territories under Muslim governance should be defended against any Christian aggression. Places which succumb to the Crusaders must be delivered from their yoke. Palestine is the heritage of the faithful Muslim alone. Impostors and Cross-worshippers should never be suffered in Jerusalem. An anonymous fourteenth-century tract entitled "Virtues of Syria" ("Faḍā'il al-Shām") advances a rather curious thesis that Syria (including Palestine, of course) comprises nine-tenths of the wealth of the world. It is further the land of resurrection. Thus, while being reassured of future admission to heaven, the resident of Syria will also enjoy material prosperity in the world here below. Writers of this category of books did not stop at the praise of pilgrim centers alone, but extended their eulogies to all manner of places in order to rouse public interest in every important city under Islamic rule. Even a man of Suyūṭi's stature found it worth while to compose an "Epistle on the Virtues of Alexandria," still in manuscript.

Jalāl al-Dīn al-Suyūṭī (1445–1505) ranks as one of the most outstanding Arabic authors of his age. He is prolific, monumental, and encyclopedic. His treatment of the subject of Alexandria represents well this type of writing. He begins by quoting traditional sayings (Ḥadīth) attributed to the Prophet Muḥammad on Alexandria. Then he describes its religious life and religious centers (ribāṭs), and argues that three days spent in one of them are equivalent to seventy years in the country extending between the Greeks (Rūm) and the Arabs, and that one month on its shore is valued as sixty pilgrimages elsewhere. Alexandria has two gates leading to Paradise, the one known as Muḥammad's Gate and the other as the Gate of Mercy. Four prayers for forty days in Ascalon, Caesarea, or Alexandria will ensure a prominent place in Paradise. Stories are recounted about people moving from afar, such as ibn Khudhaymah, who came in 1164 A.D.

all the way from remote Khurasan for retirement and worship in Alexandria.

The third category consists of "Books on Holy War" (Kutub al-Jihād), which are even more abundant than the other two classes. Holy war was the consummation of a Muslim vow. Discussion of the principle of holy war figures eminently in the unusually extensive literature of Islamic jurisprudence (Fiqh), from al-Bukhārī (810–70) to al-Suyūṭī, quoted above, both in the works of the Sunnites, with their four schools (Shafi'ite, Malikite, Ḥanifite, and Ḥanbalite), and in the works of the heterodox Shi'ites. There is no essential variance of opinion among commentators of the different creeds or sects of Islam on the matter of "al-Jihād."

More than a century before the outbreak of the Crusades, al-Qāḍī (Judge) al-Nu'mān ibn Muḥammad (d. 974 A.D.) wrote a work on jurisprudence entitled "Da'ā'imu l-Islām" (Pillars of Islam) from which the representative "Kitāb al-Jihād" (Book of Holy War) has been published in recent years. Since it remained as the chief Fatimid source in matters of jurisprudence, and since the Crusades flared up in Fatimid times, it is of special interest to attempt a quick analysis of the contents of that authoritative work. Al-Nu'mān begins by a series of quotations from the Holy Qur'ān commending strife for the faith, and then seconds these by excerpts from the "Ḥadīth" or sayings of the Prophet. He then classifies those divine injunctions under a series of different titles, including the urge for holy war, the place of the horse in battle, behavior of the members of a campaign, and the duties of the generals or amirs. He follows this with his own commentary on such subjects as the sermon to the army general, the practice of justice, the study of social classes and their relations with the governors, taxation, preparatory war measures, tactics, combating unbelievers, status of captives, safe conduct, truce, peace treaty and tribute, booty and its partition, fighting transgressors, and the ruling in regard to their booty. The minutest details of holy war received meticulous attention in the legal system of Islam (Sharī'ah).

But this is only one aspect of the works on "al-Jihād"—devoted to the theoretical treatment of the doctrine. The other aspect is even more copiously treated by writers. In fact, a whole literature arose to deal with the practical issues of the Eastern art of war, more particularly in the later Middle Ages. Treatises on equestrian art and chivalry, on armor and the proper manipulation of each weapon, the technique of fighting, tactics, and the order of battle were compiled by warriors and generals of proven experience and accurate knowledge of military science. The vast output of Muslim writers in this important field more than justifies a monumental study on the history of the Eastern art of war, as a counterfoil to the works of Köhler, Delbrück and, Oman * on Western Warfare.

Let us review briefly the Berlin manuscript ** of a fourteenth-century military writer called ibn Minkali (c. 1371)—an illustrative specimen of what we may expect to find in a hitherto untapped literature. This particular codex is dedicated to Sultan Qaitbay (1468–96) and is a real work of art, consisting of two general sections: one on equestrian art, and another on tactics and strategy. After the usual preamble derived from the Qur'ān and tradition, which are usually regarded as the fount of all knowledge in Islam, the author devotes a series of chapters to the technique of horsemanship, the numerous offensive and defensive positions in the field of battle, and the effective handling of all manner of war implements, such as sword, spear, bow and arrow, mace, shield, and mangonel. His exhaustive inquiry into all manner of detail is designed for the benefit of the individual soldier, as a practical

* See Atiya: *Hist. and Bibl.*, General Bibliography, section IV. 6.

** This is MS. Or. 588, which I have examined. Consult W. Ahlwardt: *Verzeichnis der arabischen Handschriften der königliche Bibliothek zu Berlin,* 10 vols., Berlin 1877 ff.

guide for basic training in the art of fighting. The writer afterward turns to the study of wider tactics and the order of battle, and he puts on record a number of well-defined plans of action to meet every emergency. He submits twenty-six drawings of different positions in the battle array and enriches his pages with a number of miniatures. The first part of his work was apparently prepared for the initiation of the rank and file, whereas the remaining set of chapters served as a brilliant manual for the edification of the generals who led the Muslim battalions to triumph. This and other similar works prove beyond any shadow of doubt that the Islamic East was in possession of an elaborate and scientific system of war, which accounts for the sweeping victories of Muslim armies in their encounters with Western chivalry, first in the Egyptian Empire and then in Turkey.

THE EGYPTIAN COUNTER-CRUSADE

The roots of the Counter-Crusade are almost as deep in time as the First Crusade itself, when the house of Zangi began its unflinching resistance to the Franks and even embarked on a policy of harassment toward the northeastern frontier of the Latin kingdom of Jerusalem. After the incorporation of northern Syria and Egypt in one united realm under the strong rule of Saladin, the Counter-Crusade entered a menacing phase in its history, culminating in the downfall of Jerusalem in 1187. Henceforward the gradual reconquest of Syria was resumed with varying degrees of vigor for a period of approximately one century, which was crowned in the end with the seizure of Acre in 1291 by the Mamluk sultan. Generally speaking, this is the first vital chapter in the story of the Egyptian Counter-Crusade. The momentum gained by the warlike Mamluks in the process of recapturing lost territory swung their armed forces beyond the Syrian border into the outlying Christian states of Asia and the Levant.

Owing to its proximity to the northern frontier of the Egyptian Empire, the Christian kingdom of Lesser Armenia or Cilicia became the primary target of Mamluk retaliation. The Arabic chronicles of the fourteenth century abound in references to the sporadic inroads of marauding Egyptian detachments within Armenia, which suffered repeatedly from pillage after the overthrow of Christian rule in Syria, even before the fall of Acre. In 1267 Sultan Beybars' men overran the country as far as Tarsus. This was repeated in 1275, and the Armenian towns of Massisa and Sis were put to the torch. In 1287 the Armenians were forced to buy a shaky peace with the payment of a million-dirhem tribute for a ten-year truce.

The thirteenth century was one of the most tempestuous periods in Armenian history. The country became an open field for fierce and continued fighting between the Mongol hordes and the Mamluk armies. Moreover, the sympathy which the Hethoumian dynasty of Cilicia harbored toward the Mongol khans embittered the Mamluk sultans, who intensified their plundering irruptions into Armenia. Then another new factor emerged to add to the growing vindictiveness of the sultans against Armenia. At that time a close blockade of the shores of Egypt led to the deflection of trade caravans to the Armenian emporia, more especially Ayas or Lajazzo. The Mamluks decided to chastise the poor Armenians by the total destruction of that maritime city, in the course of two successive raids during 1322 and 1337. After the second assault, King Leo V was forced to level the city fortifications to the ground himself. Large numbers of the Armenian population fled to Cyprus, and the Mamluks are said to have returned with some 12,000 Armenian prisoners of war to their base in the amirate of Aleppo. In 1347 they came back to seize what was left of the city permanently, and in 1359 Adana and Tarsus were also annexed to the Egyptian Empire. The kingdom of Armenia was then reduced to the two cities of Sis and Anazarb in the mountainous Taurus region; and both cities in turn succumbed to the irresistible military pressure brought to bear upon them by the amir of Aleppo. Finally, in 1375, Sis, the capital, was taken by storm and the whole country was doomed.

Hoping against hope, King Leo VI entrenched himself in the last of all his Armenian strongholds—the castle of Gaban—and after a heroic defense the castle fell into Egyptian hands. The king and his court were carried into captivity to the citadel of Cairo. After spending seven years in imprisonment at Cairo, Leo VI was ransomed by Venice and the Papacy, and he regained his personal freedom in 1382 on condition that he should never again set foot on Armenian soil. The dethroned monarch spent his remaining years as a mendicant and a fugitive wandering among the courts of Europe and in the papal Curia, until he died childless at Paris in 1393. Cilicia was retained as an Egyptian colony until 1516, when it was seized by Sultan Selim I for Turkey before his attack on Syria and Egypt. After the First World War it was temporarily occupied by French forces in the years 1919–21, when the Armenians received encouragement to seek independence; but bitter deceptions and unspeakable Turkish massacres followed.

The second Egyptian Counter-Crusade was directed against the Latin island kingdom of Cyprus under the Lusignans. The sultans of Egypt could never forget or forgive the disastrous Crusade of Peter I de Lusignan, in which their great Mediterranean city of Alexandria was sacked and plundered in 1365. From that very year the Mamluk sultans began to build up a strong fleet at the Bulaq docks on the Nile near Cairo for the punishment of the aggressor. Meanwhile the foolhardy Cypriot pirates continued to carry out a series of vexatious raids on the maritime towns of both Egypt and Syria. At home, the Lusignan hold on the island was steadily weakening as a result of the intervention of the Genoese commune. Then the assassination of King Peter I in January 1369 and the accession of an eleven-year-old boy, Peter II (1369–82), to the throne added to the mounting misfortunes of Cyprus, where the elements of decline ultimately brought about the imposition of a Genoese protectorate over the island.

The hour for Egypt to strike its deadly blow arrived during the reign of Sultan Bursbay (1422–38). The first of three naval expeditions was launched against Cyprus in 1424. This was in the nature of an experimental reconnaissance campaign which proved to be encouraging to the Mamluks. Their ships raided Limasol * on the southern shore and safely returned with a load of captives and booty. In August of the following year (1425), another naval squadron, consisting of forty ships under a Mamluk admiral by the name of Gerbash, surprised the Genoese garrisons at the strong seaports of Famagusta ** and Larnaca, and forced both of them to surrender. Limasol, too, was captured from the Greeks. In the end it was decided that the fleet would return to its base with more than a thousand prisoners of war and immense booty. The sources record the mercy of the sultan on the occasion; he commanded that parents and children should not be offered separately for sale in the slave markets.

Bursbay refused to lend an ear to attempted intercession on behalf of Cyprus from the Byzantine Emperor in Constantinople. In July 1426 he manned a more substantial fleet with proved mariners and a considerable force of volunteers and spirited Bedouins, all under the command of a famous Mamluk amir called Taghrī Bardī Maḥmūd, for the systematic and final annexation of the island. The army made a safe landing on the southern shores facing Egypt, at a place

* Know in the Arabic chronicles at Ḥiṣn al-Lamsūn.

** Al-Maghūṣ or Maghūṣah of the Arabic writers.

called Avdimou, and soon encountered the Cypriot feudal militia on the neighboring plains of Kherokitia on July 5, 1426. The Lusignan forces consisted of 1,600 knights and 4,000 foot soldiers, who were completely routed by the Egyptians. Leontios Makhairas, the Greek chronicler of Cyprus at the time, gives a vivid description of the demoralization of the Cypriot soldiers, their defeat and the capture of King Janus (1398–1432) by the Egyptians, the massacres that followed, and the raids on the island interior, until the Egyptians seized Nicosia, the capital, itself. In the end, the invaders sailed back with immense shiploads of booty and 3,600 prisoners, the king and his nobility in the front row of the captives. The prestige of the Latins in Cyprus was wrecked beyond repair, and the native Greeks, who had been kept by force under the heel of the Western Europeans, decided to revolt against their alien masters and at once elected one of their number, a certain Alexis, as their national basileus.

Like Leo VI of Armenia, his Lusignan cousin, Janus II of Cyprus was driven to the Citadel of Cairo in chains. His crown and banners were exposed at the head of a procession of about two thousand Cypriot knights in the streets of the Egyptian capital. Bareheaded and in iron shackles, Janus appeared at the sultan's court in the presence of delegates from the realms of the Muslim rulers of Turkey, the Turcoman amirates of Asia Minor, the king of Tunis, the sharif of Mecca, and a host of other envoys. The king of Cyprus kissed the ground at the foot of the sultan and succumbed senseless. The Venetian consul and a following of rich merchants from Europe later mediated on his behalf and guaranteed the immediate payment of 100,000 gold ducats as a first installment of the ransom, together with an equal sum after the king's return to Cyprus. Further, Janus made a solemn pledge to render to Cairo an annual tribute of a doubtful amount ranging from 5,000 to 8,000 ducats. Then he proclaimed submission to the sultan as his suzerain. At that point he recovered his personal freedom, was granted a house and allowed to ride in the city until his return to Cyprus, which occurred in May 1427. His first act was to hang the new Greek basileus; but an Egyptian occupation force had simultaneously landed on the island, and the king surrendered his financial authority at Famagusta to the Genoese. Cyprus became a tributary state to Egypt, and Janus paid a heavy penalty for Peter I's reckless sack of Alexandria in the previous century.

The third logical objective of the Mamluk Counter-Crusade was Rhodes, where the Knights of St. John of Jerusalem had established themselves and turned the island into a veritable fortress. The Egyptian triumph in Cyprus no doubt whetted the sultan's appetite to subjugate Rhodes, a natural corollary to his spreading hegemony over the waters of the Levant. The Hospitallers in Rhodes were a thorn in the side of the Islamic Empire, and there could be no peace in the area while such a strong organization continued to menace both Muslim shipping on the high seas and Muslim security on the mainland. But here the sultan was faced with a different set of circumstances, which rendered his attacks on this island ineffective and indecisive. The Knights were found to be of a different mettle from that of the Cypriots. Their military organization was unshakable, and the rigorous observance of discipline in the ranks of the Order was combined with a spirit of unity in counsel and action. Moreover, they had developed a closely knit system of international espionage, a kind of intelligence service of a unique character in medieval times, whereby their agents in hostile countries forewarned the grand master of any military movement against the island and thus kept the order in full readiness to repulse surprise attacks. Three times did the Egyptians attempt to reduce Rhodes to subjection, and three times their efforts were frustrated by the valiance and preparedness of the Knights. The first of these campaigns occurred in the summer of 1440, when a fleet of fifteen "grabs" * was manned at the Nile docks of Bulaq for an assault on Rhodes. Sailing by way of Cyprus and Alaya in Asia Minor for revictualling, the fleet was further reinforced by two more ships provided by the Turkish amir of Alaya, and the combined naval force proceeded toward Rhodes. To their dismay, the Muslims found the Hospitallers in full array awaiting their arrival. The Hospitallers were able to intercept the Mamluk landing in time and weather the attack; twelve Mamluks were lost and many others were seriously wounded. Realizing the hopelessness of their plight, the attackers withdrew to Egypt.

The defeat of the sultan's arms gave him a new grievance against the Knights of Rhodes, and he became determined to undertake another expedition to chastise them and destroy their power. He started preparation for the new enterprise in 1442, and approximately one year later a new fleet carrying 1,500 regular troops, in addition to a large number of volunteers under the able command of the Mamluk sea captain 'Īnāl al-'Alā'ī, sailed down the Nile to Damietta and then across the Mediterranean to Tripoli on the Syrian coast, to collect further reinforcements of men and material. The fleet was, however, battered and dispersed by a tempestuous passage, and its arrival was delayed. Some ships reached Beirut and others reached Tripoli, only to find that the Syrian contingent had become restive and decided to proceed to Cyprus—then a safe base for Muslim operations against Rhodes. The various forces at last became united in the Cypriot harbors of Larnaca and Limasol, and after plundering the defenseless inhabitants they set out to Paphos (al-Bāf of the Arabic chronicles) for revictualling, presumably at the expense of the king and people of Cyprus. Then they marched by way of the friendly Turkish towns of Alaya and Adalia on the southern Anatolian coast to the little island fortress of Castellorizzo (Qashṭīl al-

* From the Arabic "ghurāb," that is, "crow," known for its agility in preying upon exposed objects.

Rūj in Arabic sources), which belonged to the Knights of St. John. After some resistance the island fell, the garrison was massacred, and its fortifications were levelled to the ground in October 1443. At this juncture it was found that winter was approaching and, aware of the impregnability of Rhodes and the hazards of being cut off from Egypt for a whole season, the commanders of the army decided to retire directly to Damietta and Cairo for the time being. Like the first expedition, the second failed to achieve its main objective, Rhodes.

The third campaign was launched early in the summer of 1444 and turned out to be as luckless as its predecessors. In June of that year a body of one thousand Mamluks, together with detachments of volunteers from numerous provinces, amounting to 18,000 recruits, equipped with siege engines, left Alexandria and Damietta and sailed to Tripoli as usual for further Syrian reinforcements; the joint armed contingents then went on to Rhodes. While the city of Rhodes was beleaguered by sea and by land, a number of Muslim detachments raided the small neighboring villages on the island. Their efforts, however, proved to be without avail against the invulnerable fort of St. Nicholas. Their manpower was continually depleted in the course of the strenuous fighting. Three hundred Mamluks were killed in the field and 500 wounded, while a number of Latin renegades formerly converted to Islam deserted the Egyptians whom they had accompanied and went over to the Knights. The summer season was drawing to a close and the prospects appeared to be grim. Exhausted and disheartened, the surviving Mamluks raised the siege and sailed back to Egypt.

It is doubtful whether the Egyptian attacks on Rhodes had any permanent effect on the Order of St. John. The damage done to their stronghold was of a temporary character and the real strength of the Knights evidently remained unimpaired. Nevertheless, Egypt established a dangerous precedent for its

Ottoman successors, who twice besieged the island fortress and finally inflicted an inexorable disaster upon the Hospitallers. Sultan Muḥammad II (1451–81) launched the first great onslaught to subdue Rhodes in 1448, but it was not until 1522 that Sulaiman II the Magnificent (1520–66) succeeded in the final expulsion of the order from the island during the reign of Grand Master Philip Villiers de l'Isle-Adam, after one of the most heroic defenses in the whole Hospitaller history.

During the interval between the end of the Egyptian and the beginning of the Ottoman Counter-Crusades against Rhodes, many developments took place which radically changed the course of history in the Levant. The star of the Ottoman Turks was in the ascendant. Byzantine Constantinople had become the capital of their new Islamic Empire in 1453, and Ottoman power in Asia Minor was consolidated at the cost of the Turkish amirs, whose principalities were gradually incorporated in the Ottoman sultanate. In 1516 the battle of Marj Dabiq in the vicinity of Aleppo was fought between Selim I (1512–20) of Turkey and the Mamluk sultan Qanṣūh al-Ghaurī (1500–16) of Egypt. The latter fell in the field, and the discomfiture of the Egyptians precipitated the annexation of Syria to Turkey. Then, in 1517, the battle of al-Raydaniya (the modern Abbasiya quarter, northeast of Cairo) sealed the fate of Egypt itself; and after several minor encounters, al-Ghauri's successor, Ṭūmān-Bay (1516–17), was captured and hanged at the Zwailah Gate of the city of Cairo. The triumph of the Ottomans in both these decisive battles was due not merely to their numerical and tactical superiority or even to their unusual courage in hand-to-hand fighting, but also to their use of the new invincible artillery and gunpowder, unknown and demoralizing to the Egyptian soldier. Contemporary Arabic writers describe these mysterious and fearful weapons as "fire and iron" and contend that it was contrary to the spirit and law of Islam to use them against Muslims.

Whatever the causes of Ottoman successes may have been, the results were then clear. The Levant was transformed into one huge Turkish domain, with calamitous effects on the flourishing commerce between Egypt and the trade powers of Southern Europe, notably the Italian communes. All the trade routes were now in Turkish hands, and the marts of Cairo, Alexandria, Damascus, and other centers began to lose their medieval importance. Constantinople became the metropolis of the sultans and of Islam, and Latin embassies in search of markets and trade privileges made their way no more to Cairo, but to the new Ottoman capital on the shores of the Bosphorus. Meanwhile, the great movement of oceanic exploration, leading to the rounding of the Cape of Good Hope and the finding of the New World, was accelerated, and Near Eastern commerce rapidly declined and became a memory of past prosperity.

THE TURKISH COUNTER-CRUSADE

The disaster of the chivalry of the West at Nicopolis in September 1396 marked the end of the Crusades as an organized movement of all Christendom against Islam for the deliverance of the Holy Land. The Turks defended their foothold on the soil of Europe with so much success that the monarchs and peoples of the West became discouraged and left Eastern Europe to its fate. One of the early chapters in the history of the Eastern Question was thus closed in favor of the Ottomans, who forced their way into the membership of the commonwealth of European states in spite of their alien origin and their Muslim religion. Hungary became the bulwark of Catholic Christendom, and her only chance of survival lay in arresting the advance of the Turks into the heart of Europe. Toward the end of the fourteenth century, after the defeat of Nicopolis, the Hungarian armies were almost annihilated, and the meager numbers that survived the massacre of the Christians were dispersed without hope of immediate reunification for any orderly action. King Sigismund was incapable of offering any resistance whatever, at least for the time being, and the road to Buda was open to the invaders. Nevertheless, Bayezid I (1389–1402), probably owing to the exhaustion of his troops and his own illness, and perhaps in order to consolidate his conquests and his position in the Balkans, decided to remain south of the Danube.

The Ottoman Counter-Crusade had been launched in Europe for nearly half a century, and the rulers of Bulgaria and Serbia were already among the sultan's vassals, while the Byzantine Emperor paid him an annuity; but the Balkan Peninsula as a whole was still far from being an undisputed Ottoman dominion. Many wide areas were still unconquered, and for that matter, Asia Minor itself was divided among numerous Turkish feudal dynasties of which the Ottomans were but one, and not the strongest, unit.

It was to this primary task of consolidation that the far-sighted sultans of that transitional period chose to devote their attention for many future generations, and Bayezid was no exception to this general rule. North of the Danube, he limited his operations to the recovery of his suzerainty over the principality of Wallachia (the ancient Dacia Felix and modern Roumania) and to some raids on the Hungarian provinces of Styria and Syrmia. South of the Danube, on the contrary, he displayed more vigor in the exploitation of his great victory of 1396. The annexation of Bulgaria and Serbia was completed; and the Ottomans crossed the Morava and Drina tributaries of the Danube to the west, and penetrated Bosnia as far as Zwornik. In the south, too, a good opportunity presented itself to the sultan, when the Greek bishop of Phocis invited him to come on a hunting expedition into Thessaly and Epirus. The sultan, whose passion for the chase was great, welcomed the invitation. The hopes of both host and guest, however, were not confined to a mere pleasure trip. The bishop intended to use the sultan's formidable forces for the reestablishment of his shaken authority against alien Latin and native Greek rivals in his diocese; but the astute Bayezid and his armies hastened to lay their hands not only on Phocis but also on Doris, Locris, and several other districts in Livonia and the Morea. Turkish settlements were planted in many depopulated regions of Greece to replace the natives, who had fled or had been carried away into slavery.

While the sultan's generals, Everenos and Ya'qūb, were entrusted with the execution of the rest of his plans in the Morea, Bayezid himself resumed the siege of Constantinople. The siege, begun in September 1396 and interrupted by the Western invasion, was again undertaken without further delay. The capture of the great city had been the sultans' major objective, and its fall seemed imminent after the decisive Ottoman victory at Nicopolis. Western potentates, even if they could contribute to the defense of Byzantium, were reluctant to put more men in the Eastern field, where they had just suffered immense losses in their recent venture in Bulgaria. Emperor Manuel's western journey of 1399–1402 to beg for assistance against the Turks aroused little more than transient sympathy and empty promises from the Catholic rulers of Europe. The only material response to his appeal was the departure of the French marshal Boucicaut, at the head of a mixed band of adventurers numbering some twelve hundred men, who landed at Constantinople in 1399 while the mendicant Emperor was still moving around Europe. The Boucicaut episode could hardly be described as a Crusade, in spite of the fact that Pope Boniface IX (1389–1404) had twice proclaimed the holy war in April 1398 and March 1399. Monarchs and feudal princes capable of leading the Western hosts were much too engrossed in their own local affairs and troubled at home to lend ear to the words of the Holy Pontiff; and no one was in the mood to take his preaching earnestly, except perhaps the Venetians and the Genoese, whose trade interests in Constantinople were directly affected by the Turkish menace. The majority of Boucicaut's men were mercenaries and not pious volunteers for the defense of a religious cause. Their chief interest was the pay of their employer and booty from the victim. As soon as they discovered that the Ottoman offered no substantial material for pillage, and, moreover, that the Byzantine emperor was too impoverished to reward them, they sailed back west, after some minor engagements with the enemy in the neighborhood of the city. Boucicaut, marshal of France and governor of Genoa, then decided to depart and leave behind him John de Châteaumorand, with a handful of men, to supervise the defense operations until his return. It is said that he proposed that the Emperor should do homage to the king of France for his empire in exchange for French assistance, and that Venice, Genoa, and the Hospitallers sanctioned his suggestion. But Boucicaut himself never came back to the forlorn city, nor did the French king, Charles VI, accede to the plan of imposing his suzerainty over an empire which was tottering to fall.

It would, however, be an error to magnify the ease with which the Ottomans might have seized Constantinople at that stage in their career. Numerous adverse factors were still at work against them. They were not yet in possession of the heavy artillery capable of storming the strong city walls, nor had they built a fleet powerful enough to insure the complete blockade of the city on the side of the sea. If we remember that these, above all other considerations, were the two decisive elements in the final assault of 1453 by Sultan Muḥammad II the Conqueror, we may realize how difficult Bayezid's position must have been in 1399–1400. Moreover, the garrison received a little moral encouragement from Boucicaut's meager and transitory Latin reinforcement.

Although the siege under these circumstances promised to

be a long business, Bayezid seemed determined to carry it to a successful issue at all costs. So he pitched his camp outside the city and intercepted the supply of provisions to the interior, while his men began rebuilding huge siege machines for the next onslaught. Nevertheless, his operations against Byzantium were foiled by the Tartar invasion of Asia Minor under the invincible Timurlane. Bayezid had to cross the Bosphorus to defend his Asiatic possessions from the Mongol hordes. In the battle of Angora (1402) he suffered a terrible defeat and himself fell into enemy hands as a prisoner of war, to be carried across Asia to an obscure but unhappy end.

Thus the downfall of Constantinople was deferred for half a century, during which the Ottomans slowly but steadily recovered from the Tartar blow and commenced fighting the Christians with varying fortunes. Murad II (1421–51) started another siege of the city after his accession to the throne, but was compelled to raise it again for lack of effective artillery and a strong navy—the two factors which had handicapped Bayezid I in 1399. On the other hand, Murad's wars with the Hungarians under the leadership of John Hunyadi, the Transylvanian hero whose name passed into legend, culminated in a crushing defeat of the Christians at Varna in 1444. This campaign, like many others, was styled as a Crusade, and the Pope was represented in it by Cardinal Julian Cesarini; but actually it was little more than one episode in the Turco-Hungarian wars of the fifteenth century.

The crux of the Turkish Counter-Crusade was the final annihilation of the Byzantine Empire and the capture of the city of Constantinople on May 29, 1453. This event had long been awaited on all sides, and long-standing preparations by the Turks reached their consummation in the reign of Muḥammad II (1451–81). He concluded peace with John Hunyadi, regent of Hungary, renewed his truce with Venice, Genoa, and the Hospitallers in Rhodes, as well as with the

Albanian chief, Scanderbeg, and the despots of the Morea, Thomas and Demetrius Palaeologus, both brothers and rivals of Constantine XI Dragases (1448–53), the last Roman Emperor of the East.

In August 1442 the sultan finished the construction of the fortress of Roumili-Hissar on the European side of the Bosphorus, north of the city facing the older fortress of Anatoli-Hissar, built by Bayezid on the Asiatic side of the waterway, thus completing another preparatory stage in the forthcoming sea blockade of the city. On witnessing these ominous events, the Byzantine Emperor hastened in December 1452 to declare in St. Sophia the ancient formula of the Henotikon, or Act of Union, between the two Churches of East and West, thereby openly acknowledging the primacy of Rome, in spite of popular opposition to this measure under the leadership of George Scholarios, the future Patriarch Gennadios. Even high dignitaries such as Lucas Notaras vehemently protested against Latin union and asserted that "it would be better to have in Constantinople the rule of the Turkish turban than the Latin mitre." *

Judging from the details of the situation as a whole, Byzantium appeared to be a city forsaken to an imminent doom. There was no universal response to the imperial cry for succor. The Pope and the European monarchs showed no sign of initiating drastic action to save the city. Even a Christian patriot like Hunyadi failed to present himself in the field. Concrete aid from Venice and Genoa, the two parties most involved in the dark prospects, was scanty and unequal to the gravity of the position. Five Venetian galleys in the Golden Horn were requisitioned for the defense of the sea walls under the command of Gabriele Trevisano. The famous Genoese pirate, Giovanni Giustiniani, arrived from

* Michael Ducas: *Historia Byzantina,* ed. by I. Bekker (*Corpus Scriptorum Historiae Byzantinae*), Bonn 1834, 264. Cf. Vasiliev: *History of the Byzantine Empire,* in 1 vol., Madison, Wisc., 1952, 647.

Chios with 400 fellow buccaneers who enlisted in the service of the emperor. Another Genoese, a sea captain named Maurizio Cattaneo, forced his way to the Golden Horn through the Turkish maritime blockade with three Genoese ships and one Greek. They all fought valiantly and desperately, but they were a sorry match for a superior enemy with superior armor. Estimates of the Turkish army vary from 150,000 to 265,000, sometimes even more.

The defense within the city consisted originally of 4,973 soldiers, to whom must be added the 400 companions of Giustiniani and 1,600 foreign residents, mainly Venetian, under the intrepid command of the Venetian bailiff Girolamo Minotto. The city was depopulated and its inhabitants are said to have been reduced to 150,000 souls altogether. The Turkish fleet consisted of 140 ships, of which twelve were great galleys. But the Italo-Byzantine flotilla succeeded in guarding the entrance of the Golden Horn against the strenuous offensive of the Turkish naval blockade, and they further hindered enemy advance by means of a gigantic iron chain across the water exit.

On April 22, however, the defense of the harbor broke down before the mysterious and sudden emergence of Turkish ships inside the Golden Horn behind the Christian fleet. The Turks had quietly constructed a wooden platform along the valley from the strait to the inner harbor and had dragged the vessels on wheels by sheer manpower. Meanwhile the bombardment of the city walls by the heaviest guns hitherto known in history was continuously intensified without respite for fifty days, and all the remaining citizens worked night and day under heavy fire to repair breaches. Unfortunately, Giustiniani was mortally wounded and had to retire to his ship, to die two days later, and his departure disheartened the foreign legionaries.

Three general assaults were undertaken on three sides of the city walls simultaneously on May 28–29. Two failed, but in the third assault, near the ancient Gate of St. Romanus, where the Emperor was fighting in person, the Janissaries forced their way and relentlessly began pouring within the walls. Jumping into the fray with sword in hand, Constantine died like a hero, and Sultan Muḥammad II rode triumphantly over the dead and dying to St. Sophia, where he inaugurated the first Muslim prayers in Justinian's historic basilica, while the city was given to pillage for three days and three nights. Of the population, 50,000 were reduced to slavery. Treasures of art were flung into the flames and one besant fetched ten tomes of Plato and Aristotle. Nevertheless, amid conflicting views and evidence, it is hard to decide whether the Turkish conquest surpassed the horrors of the Fourth Crusade in that imperial city.*

The news of the fall of Constantinople, though foreseen for years, was received in Europe with consternation. A naval squadron brought together by the Papacy, Venice and Naples arrived at Chios after the seizure of the city. Talks of another Crusade were reopened, and hopes were fixed on Duke Philip of Burgundy, as well as the enthusiastic Aeneas Sylvius Piccolomini, later Pope Pius II (1458–64), whose diplomacy and eloquence were, however, without avail in bringing the project to a successful issue.

The Turkish conquest was slower in the reign of Bayezid II (1481–1512) because of troubles within the Turkish domain. His brother Djem claimed the throne and fled to the Knights of Rhodes, who handed him over to the Papacy; and Pope Alexander VI accepted 300,000 ducats as price of his acquiescence in the poisoning of the unfortunate pretender in 1495. Meanwhile Charles VIII of France took the Crusading vow in 1493, on the occasion of his conquest of Naples, but the project was forgotten after his expulsion from that area

* Vasiliev: *History of the Byzantine Empire,* in 1 vol., Madison, Wisc., 1952, 653, mentions the example of Th. Uspensky, who believed that the Turks in 1453 were milder than the Crusaders of 1204.

in 1495; and Bayezid resumed the gradual invasion of the Morea and the Aegean islands, taking them from the Latins in the course of the years 1499–1502.

Selim I (1512–20) went further by consolidating the lands of Islam under Turkish hegemony. After annexing Greater Armenia from Persian rule in 1514, he invaded Lesser Armenia, Syria, and Algeria in 1516, and crowned his career with the conquest of Egypt itself in 1517. His successor, Sulaiman I the Magnificent (1520–66), while appropriating Rhodes in 1522 and Bagdad in 1534, revived the Turkish Counter-Crusade in Europe. The Hungarian garrison in Belgrade surrendered in 1521, and King Louis II of Hungary was killed and his army completely routed by the Ottoman artillery in the decisive battle of Mohacs in August 1526. As a result, the city of Buda opened its gates to the victor in the following month. Louis's crown was disputed between Emperor Ferdinand I and John Zapolya, voyavode of Transylvania. Arbitrating between the two rivals, Sulaiman sided with the less important personality, Zapolya, who was a more amenable prey, and ultimately Sulaiman seized Buda himself. Afterward, in the year 1529, he found himself at the gates of Vienna, which he besieged for only a short time before retiring to the Hungarian capital. In fact, this turned out to be the furthest limit of Turkish expansion in Central Europe.

In the meantime the Ottomans were rapidly growing into a formidable naval power and Sultan Sulaiman started meddling directly in the maritime and political affairs of the West. He sent Turkish galleys to join the French fleet in support of Francis I of France against Emperor Charles V in the waters of Nice. He appointed the hardened Barbary corsair, Khair al-Dīn Barbarossa, as admiral (qapoudan-pasha) of the Ottoman navy and inflicted a heavy defeat on Andrea Doria, the Genoese admiral of an imperial naval squadron, when the Christians attempted a descent on Algiers in 1541. The Turks now dared openly to dispute control of the whole Mediterranean with Venice, the Hospitallers in Malta, and even the Hapsburgs. But their fortunes were not unmixed on the high seas. The wars to subjugate Malta in 1565 ended in Turkish failure, which was attributed to the extraordinary heroism of the grand master, John de la Valette, and the Knights of St. John. Cyprus, on the other hand, surrendered to the Turkish armada in 1570, and that year proved to be the high water mark for Turkish maritime expansion.

The battle of Lepanto took place in the following year and terminated in a conclusive defeat of the Ottomans in the Gulf of Corinth between Lepanto and Patras on October 7, 1571. The Turkish armada comprised 274 galleys carrying 25,000 men and 2,500 janissaries under the joint command of Admiral (qapoudan-pasha) 'Ali, Muḥammad Bey, and the pashas of Negropontis, Alexandria, and other ports. The allied Christian fleet consisted of 109 Venetian galleys, 50 from Philip II of Spain, 29 Genoese, 13 from Pope Pius X, and 3 from the Knights of Malta, totalling 204 altogether. The Christian vanguard was under the command of the Spanish Juan de Cardona, the main battle under Don Juan of Austria, the left wing under the Venetian Barbarigo, and the right wing under the Genoese Gian-Andrea Doria; and the Spanish marquis of Santa Cruz, Don Alvaro de Bazan, took a firm stand in the rear guard with reserve ships in readiness for any emergency. The Turkish discomfiture was signal. One hundred and seventy-seven of their galleys were seized and fifteen burned or foundered. The toll of the slain and drowned Turks ranged from 20,000 to 30,000 including the qapoudan-pasha 'Ali. Christian losses amounted only to twelve galleys and 7,500 men. Thus the Mediterranean waters were saved from total Turkish domination, which would have completely ruined Venice. In reality, the siege of Vienna in 1529 by land, and the battle of Lepanto in 1571 by sea, marked the end of the Turkish Counter-Crusade and the highpoint of Ottoman expansion in Europe.

RETROSPECT

It is evident from the foregoing survey that the idea of the Crusade passed through numerous metamorphoses. The student must guard against uniformity in the interpretation of the meaning of the Crusade from age to age. At its inception, the Crusade was virtually a collective act of faith, whereby Western humanity sought to liberate the earthly Jerusalem by the sword while mystically yearning to attain the celestial Jerusalem. Men literally accepted the words of the Lord according to St. Matthew * by carrying the Cross and walking in the steps of the Master. The true Christian was expected to espouse the cause of holy war, and the "passagium" to Outremer emerged as the shortest road to salvation. That road became the natural link between men's physical existence here below and the metaphysical life beyond. This basic concept in Crusading eschatology governed the medieval mind in the world which gave birth to the First Crusade, and the upsurge in the movement was likened to a new creed or regenerated faith (nova religio). When they accompanied the host of God and fell in the fray, soldiers earned the crown of martyrdom and gained entry to the higher spheres of sanctity and perpetual bliss.

Although it would be a serious error to lose sight of the religious factor underlying the progress of the Crusading enterprise in subsequent decades, we must realize that after the ecstasy of the violent seizure of Jerusalem and the Holy Sepulchre in 1099, events began gradually to take a different turn. As the tumult of the First Crusade subsided with the establishment of the Latin kingdom of Jerusalem, another stage was reached, and holy war came under the influence of numerous political, military, and economic circumstances of mundane life. The Crusade moved from the realm of un-

* Matthew, 16:24–25.

mixed piety toward worldly realities and a state of warfare where secular motives became increasingly perceptible, with phenomenal impact on the course of history. It may be noted that the Crusades, which were begun as a means to free the birthplace of Christ from an infidel yoke and to aid the Eastern Christians, ended tragically by inciting the Muslims to launch an unremitting Counter-Crusade against all Christendom. In reality, the ensuing Islamic onslaught on the Holy Land became widened in its scope so as to include the destruction of every Christian state within reach of Muslim arms.

Thus the Frankish Solution of the Eastern Question in the Middle Ages was immediately followed by the Islamic Solution in the form of the Counter-Crusade. There is one vital difference between the two solutions, in that the latter proved to be of longer standing and durability in world affairs than its transitory predecessor. The failure of Christendom to accomplish a permanent solution through Crusading, and the overwhelming success of Muslim arms, may be ascribed to many causes. Disunity played a prominent part in bringing disaster upon the leaders of the Cross and their contingents. This was symptomatic of the tenor of political and religious life in a changing Europe. Prominent among the wider issues of the times was the disruption of the older conception of world government by Empire and Papacy, and the rise of new states grouped around royal personalities, with a growing awareness of nationality.

Men's minds were distracted from the Crusade by multiple problems at home and in the Church. While England and France were involved in the ruinous Hundred Years' War, imperial prestige was sinking fast in Germany, Central Europe, and Lombardy. Italy was subdivided into a checkered pattern of independent republics and communes in continuous internecine warfare with one another, and their common aim was the defense of their own trade interests in Europe and overseas, with little regard for the cause of religion; the Venetians eloquently demonstrated this in the dictum that a native of the republic of St. Mark should be first a Venetian, then a Christian (Siamo veneziani, poi Christiani).

In the Iberian Peninsula, a different situation presented itself in which the native Christians were perpetually engaged in the reconquest of lost territories from the Moors. The Spanish "Crusades" were battles of national freedom—a subject apart—and must be left for separate treatment elsewhere.

Perhaps even more serious for medieval man than these grave developments were occurrences within the Church. The Babylonian Captivity, whereby for some seventy years (1305–78) the Popes were virtually incarcerated by the French kings at Avignon in Southern France, terminated in the demoralizing Great Schism of the Church in the West (1378–1409). It is hard to realize the subversive influence of the sorry sight of two or three rival Popes excommunicating one another in a public contest to snatch the tiara; the prestige of a time-honored institution fell low in the medieval mind. The Conciliar Movement developed out of all this as the only means to mend such ills; and it was only natural that it should monopolize the attention of both peoples and states in Western Europe. The tide of heresy was rising around John Wycliffe (c. 1324–84) in England and John Huss (c. 1369–1415) in Bohemia. Amid such alarums and excursions, the public mind was in no mood for Crusading.

The insincerity and arrogance which marked the behavior of many Crusaders added nothing to the justice of their cause, nor did it bring them any permanent triumph. The sacrilege committed by the Latins at Alexandria, and their unworthy flight on the approach of the sultan's real armed force, bore disquieting witness to the spirit of the late Crusaders. The earnest members of that expedition, such as King Peter I, his chancellor, Philippe de Mézières, and the apostolic legate, Peter Thomas, did not misinterpret these portents and admitted the guilt and ungodliness of the soldiers of the Cross.

Further, the Italian republics were engaged in constant secret intrigue against all Crusading enterprise in order to gain favor with the enemy of all Christians, particularly in the later Middle Ages. A war waged with the Muslims, who controlled all routes to the East, might impair their commercial prosperity and deplete their resources, and they were not disposed to sacrifice their material interest for the nebulous cause of God. The Fourth Crusade is a vivid illustration of the covetousness of the parties involved in that sordid international crime. Venetian avidity for trade privileges at any cost was equalled only by the absence of Genoese scruples in the slave trade with the Mamluks, in defiance of papal bans and bulls.

The haughty and impulsive character of the French chivalry, too, increased the difficulties of all orderly and serious undertakings against a redoubtable enemy. This led to ruin at Nicopolis, when the French rejected Sigismund's wise and farsighted proposals in the vain hope of gaining for themselves alone all the glory of the day.

In addition to all this, we have to remember that the Crusaders fought on alien soil, and that neither their armor nor their methods of warfare were suited to the new milieu. Their weighty coats of mail hampered free movement and exhausted their strength in a hot climate, while their bulky shire horses and their shock tactics proved to be of little avail in the face of the swift harassing attacks of the enemy's light cavalry. The Christians were under the illusion that they were going to fight a horde of disorderly miscreants. This false conception was a source of many and great mistakes and misfortunes. Both in Egypt and in Turkey, the sultans developed standing armies of the highest caliber in discipline —possibly the first of their kind in medieval history. Men whose sole vocation was war, trained in the best military tradition of the Mamluks and the Ottomans, with blind obedience and strict rule as the keynotes to their action, constituted the Muslim battalions which routed the heterogeneous medley of Western knights with their antiquated tactics. Like the Crusaders, Muslim combatants firmly believed that they were fighting a holy war for a holy cause against an aggressive infidel; and their loyalty to that cause on the whole surpassed that of the Christians. Medieval chroniclers tried on many occasions to find excuses for the discomfiture of their countrymen in the numerical superiority of the Muslims. This view, it is hoped, has been disproved in the foregoing pages. Victory was won, not by greater numbers, but by better tactics, stricter observance of discipline, finer leadership, and greater loyalty and devotion.

The final collapse of the Crusading impulse in the West had far-reaching effects on the course of events in the East. Egypt was left in full command of the situation in the Levant, and Turkey became a European as well as an Asiatic power. Egypt had embarked on a series of Counter-Crusades which precipitated the downfall of the Christian kingdoms near its boundaries. Armenia soon disappeared from the map as an independent state and became a Mamluk province, while the enfeebled Lusignan kings of Cyprus were constrained to pay annual tribute to the sultans in Cairo after the disastrous reign of Janus II de Lusignan. In the meantime the conquering arm of the Ottomans had been extended far and wide into southeastern Europe. After Adrianople, Byzantium became their capital, and the throne of Constantine devolved upon Muḥammad II the Conqueror and his successors after 1453. The process of incorporating the derelict Latin outposts in the Morea and the islands of the Archipelago was continued by the Turks with unflagging vigor; and once the conquests of the new empire became consolidated, the sultans began their northern march into East Central Europe as far as the gates of Vienna. The Crusaders of Nicopolis failed to arrest that sweeping thrust at one of its earliest stages, and the Eastern Question has remained one of the dynamic factors in European politics throughout modern history. At last, when Egypt and the Holy Land were subjugated by the Ottomans in the early years of the sixteenth century, their fate was henceforth bound up with that of a rising pan-Islamic realm whose ruler was simultaneously both sultan and Caliph.

The recovery of Jerusalem by recruits from Western Europe and all the continents, old and new, was achieved toward the close of the First World War. Muslims as well as Christians fought on both sides in a war waged not for the capture of the holy places as such, but primarily to defeat the Turks and their German allies. The budding spirit of nationalism in the heart of the long depressed peoples of the Arab commonwealth of nations in the Near East, combined with the interests of the Western powers fighting for their lives against the German peril, brought them together in a pursuit which led to the liberation of the Holy Land. The older cause of holy warfare had already sunk into oblivion centuries before the triumphant entry into Jerusalem of the Allied Forces on December 10, 1917.

CHAPTER FIVE

The Romance of Medieval Commerce in the Levant

GENESIS OF MEDIEVAL COMMERCE

THE ECONOMIC FORTUNES of the medieval world must be attributed in the main to the development of commerce and the international exchange of goods between East and West. It was in this process that the medieval merchant became enriched and the national wealth of certain areas soared to unprecedented heights. As a matter of fact, the birth of the economic revolution of the Middle Ages took place, not in the static agrarian feudal society of Western Europe, but rather in the dynamism of trade and industry inherent in most of the countries of the Eastern Mediterranean. The map of the medieval world, viewed in its broader economic outline, is divisible into three areas which passed through these successive phases in the genesis of commerce during the era from the fall of the Roman Empire to the dawn of modern history. The first of these areas is the Byzantine Empire, which commanded preeminence in the world market from the fifth to the end of the seventh century. The second is identified with the Arabs during the central Middle Ages, from the beginning of the eighth to the end of the eleventh century. The third, which roughly occupied the later Middle Ages, is associated with the emergence of the southern European trade communes and the development of sea power and industry in both Northern and Southern Europe. Each of these areas and phases, taken in sequence, presents a special set of characteristics governing the course of the events of its own day, which we should examine for comprehension of the genesis of medieval commerce with particular reference to the Levant.

In the first phase, the downfall of Rome, followed by the influx of the barbarian hordes in the West, had far-reaching repercussions on the progress of ancient commerce with the East across the Mediterranean. Though it would be a misrepresentation of the facts to contend that international trade, which had flourished under the Pax Romana, became extinct after the barbarian invasions, there is no doubt that the smooth flow of commerce across the sea was momentarily arrested at the outset of the Middle Ages. With the return of peace and the reestablishment of security and a measure of stability, dealings were resumed, but at a much less active rate. In other words, international commerce, though not completely obliterated from Western Europe, suffered a severe blow.

Meanwhile the survival of the Byzantine Empire offered another haven to compensate for the waning Western trade, and the new center of gravity shifted from Rome to Constantinople. Its felicitous geographical position within reach of the three continents of the ancient world at the meeting place of the land and sea routes of the Far, Middle, and Near East, as well as the countries of Northern and Western Europe, rendered the Byzantine metropolis a natural market where the merchants of almost all nations converged. The indisputable proof of Byzantine trade ascendancy in the high

Middle Ages is the fact that the Eastern Roman gold "nomisma" completely supplanted the old Western Roman gold "solidus" as standard money and means of exchange in Europe and the East.

Goods from all directions poured into the marts of Constantinople. Silk and porcelain from China, jewels and spices from India, rugs and tapestries from Persia, pearls from the Persian Gulf, ivory and ebony from Africa, textiles and grains from Egypt, glass and steel from Syria, furs and amber from Russia, leather work from Morocco, and slaves of all descriptions from every corner of the world were among the innumerable articles on sale in the great city. Moreover, numerous industries developed in the area, and able technicians and artists from the surrounding countries found a place in the rich capital. Perfumes, vestments of brocade and gold thread, ikons, mosaics, ivory carving, sculpture and stone moulding, jewelry, enamelled gold and silver, jewelled crucifixes and bookbinding, and all kinds of luxury articles were manufactured by accomplished artists in Constantinople and sought by the wealthy magnates of all countries. Moreover, trade and industry were regulated by the Byzantine state in such a way as to protect buyer, seller, and the imperial rights. The "Book of the Prefect" of the ninth century provided a closely knit code of laws regulating the trade markets and the rights and duties of manufacturer, merchant, and money-lender or banker. Its ordinances are reminiscent of the contents of the "Book of the Intendant," the Arabic "Kitāb-al-Ḥisbah" of later fame in the Islamic Empire, for control of the market and the policing of the populace. The Byzantine regulations were not always marked by a sense of balance and justice; nevertheless, the imperial trade policy with its excessive extortions did not greatly hamper commerce, and Constantinople remained the first city in Christendom and the peer of Bagdad and Cairo in the Islamic Empire during this period.

In Western Europe, the resolution of the position of the new states resulted in the establishment of a new social order which was basically agrarian; and commerce, though not banned, was discountenanced by the ecclesiastical authorities of the age of faith as being almost another form of usury. Local trade dealings were limited to primitive barter in articles of necessity, and money had little or no place in these transactions owing to its great scarcity. During the Merovingian and Carolingian periods international commerce became even more meager than internal trade. It was chiefly confined to peddling of Eastern light goods brought to the West by individual Syrians and Jews. The Syrians were the descendants of the ancient Phoenicians with their background of great maritime skill; and trade was their chief vocation from remote antiquity. The Jews, who were generally barred from agrarian settlement, and were dispersed among all nations of East and West, were fitted for commerce and money dealings, which they practiced from country to country. In the medieval Latin of this period, the term "mercator" became synonymous with "Judaeus."

It would, however, be wrong to exaggerate the role of the merchant in this early medieval society. Markets were few and far between, and people with real purchasing power were not in a majority in Western Europe. The Roman cities (municipia) had well-nigh disappeared and their places were taken by the smaller agricultural villages and manorial settlements. The ancient road system which furnished Roman charioteers and Roman legions with the means of swift movement from one end of the empire to another were ruined and reduced to mere footpaths fit at best for the pack horse or mule with its limited load of goods. Bridges were dilapidated. Travel was beset with tremendous hazards and the forests were infested by robbers. And with all these hardships, the returns were thinned by the fiscal limitations of that period, since the gold currency of the Romans had disappeared and silver coinage was minted by the Carolingians only in restricted quantities. The revival of town life, industry, and commerce in Europe belongs to a much later age.

The second phase in the story of medieval commerce is associated with the Arab conquest of the Asiatic shores of the Levant as well as the littoral of North Africa in the course of the seventh century. The eighth century witnessed the extension of Arab hegemony over the western shores of the Tyrrhenian sea, with catastrophic effects on Mediterranean trade. Ṭāriq ibn Ziyād, whose name is commemorated by the Rock of Gibraltar (Jabal Ṭāriq), seized Spain from Roderick the Visigoth in 711. In the eighth century Arab pirates intensified their raids on the islands of the Mediterranean, both eastern and western. As early as 648 and 652 we begin to hear of recurring pillage on Cyprus and Rhodes. In 717–18 Rhodes was occupied by the Syrian Muslims, and Cyprus succumbed to them later in the middle of the century. The Balearic Islands were seized by the Umaiyads of Spain in 798. Corsica and Sardinia, long harassed by Muslim corsairs, were finally occupied by the Aghlabids in 809. The conquest of strategic Sicily was a slow but steady process from approximately 827 to 902, when all the island, with the exception of the solitary fort of Taormina, was subjugated by the Aghlabids. From their Sicilian bases the Muslim forces sallied into Italy on periodic and devastating raids. In 868 and 872 they attacked Gaeta and Salerno respectively. They ravaged the countryside of Central Italy as far as the precincts of Rome itself, and Pope John VIII (872–82) could buy peace for his afflicted territory only by payment of 25,000 silver "mancusi" * to the enemy. Nevertheless, Pisa, further north, was again plundered during 935, and the fortified Muslim bases at Bari and Tarentum barred maritime traffic outside the Adriatic.

For all practical purposes, the whole of the Mediterranean

* Silver or gold coin of uncertain value, used in Italy, then in England, where it was reckoned as the equivalent of up to six shillings.

became an Arab lake, inaccessible to Christian shipping, but open to trade from all countries under Arab sway, with staggering results in the field of Arab economy and industry. The vast expanse of the Arab empire from Samarqand in Transoxonia and Lahore in the valley of the Indus on one side, and the Atlantic and Spain (Andalusia) on the other, increased trade potentialities beyond recognition. Commerce was held in high regard by the Muslims, unlike the Christians of Western Europe. In fact, the Muhammadan tradition recorded a saying of the Prophet whereby he blessed the triple resources of the faithful as agriculture, cattle raising, and commerce, all on an equal footing. Arab merchants had no doubt been to Constantinople and witnessed the splendor of its fabulous mercantile wealth. It was natural that they should seek for themselves a share in the brilliance of its commerce; and in the long run their rising cities such as Bagdad, Cairo, and Cordova began gradually to replace Constantinople. The major trade arteries from the East, both by land and by sea, terminated in or traversed lands under Arab rule. Ships laden with rich staples from India laid anchor on Arab shores in the Persian Gulf and the Red Sea, while caravans of thousands of camels crossed the Asiatic continent from China to the marts of the vast Arab Empire. Arab borders touched the Caspian and the Black Sea, which opened the northern and western routes to Russia and East Central Europe. Before the close of the seventh century, the Arabs minted their own coinage, and the gold "dinar" * and silver "dirhem" ** began to rival the Byzantine "nomisma" in international transactions. The Caliphs honored the merchant and established rigorous secu-

* The word "dinar," derived from the Roman "denarius," was the equivalent of 1/72 of a pound of silver until the reign of Nero, after which it varied. The Arab "dinar" is the gold coin of the same weight as the "dirhem," which is in silver, otherwise 48 grains or 3.11 grams, approximating in value $4.75.

** The "dirhem" is a corruption of the Greek "drachma" containing 48 grains or 3.11 grams of silver valued at about eight cents.

rity on the roads for peaceful and just circulation of commerce.

From the ninth century onward there was a steady deflection of trade and business to the emporia of the Arab world, resulting in an incredible enrichment of both the merchant and the state. By the tenth century, Arab annalists recorded fabulous figures representing the growth of wealth and prosperity in the lands of the Eastern and Western Caliphates. An estimate of the trade revenues of the cities of Aleppo, Damascus, and Jerusalem in Syria during the year 908 approximated 2,000,000 gold dinars, that is, the equivalent of some 9,500,000 gold dollars, uninfluenced by the inflationary tendencies of modern times; and we must remember the high purchasing power * of the money at that time. In Egypt the Tulunid ruler of that province raised a similar sum from the taxation of trade intercourse about the same date. Furthermore, as we move to the West, the imagination marvels at the degree of affluence in Andalusia, where the traveller ibn Ḥauqal (c. 975) asserts that the Umaiyad Caliphate of Cordova under 'Abd-al-Raḥman III raised revenues totalling 20,000,000 gold dinars (about 95,000,000 modern gold dollars) solely from the Sudanese gold trade carried by the caravans to Sijilmasa and Morocco between 912 and 951. The same author states that while in the oasis city of Andaghosht, situated at fourteen days' journey north of Ghana in the Dark Continent of Africa, he saw a check (the Arabic word Ṣakk) for 42,000 dinars transmitted to a merchant of Sijilmasa.

* It is difficult to determine purchasing power in medieval times with precision. Examples have been quoted from other fields. Will Durant: *Age of Faith* (*Age of Civilization*, IV), N.Y. 1950, 626 n., mentions Coulton's estimate of the value of English currency at forty times as much as its worth in the year 1930; and he raises this estimate to fifty times in the course of 1948. All this is rather arbitrary but significant. The correct evaluation of such equivalents depends on the purity of the metal used as well as medieval fluctuations, which are difficult to determine on account of the lack of economic source material for that age.

For some appraisal of the extent of the Muslim trade expansion, it may be sufficient to follow the economic conquests of the Arab "dinar" as currency in its wide peregrinations throughout the medieval world. Recent excavations in many regions have uncovered hoards of Arab coins in Russia, Finland, the Scandinavian countries, and the Balkans. Isolated specimens were even found in such distant regions as Britain and Iceland. The majority of the coins bore dates ranging from the close of the seventh to the beginning of the eleventh century. The famous gold coin minted by Offa, king of Mercia (757–96), with his name "Offa Rex" inscribed from right to left in the Arab manner on one side and bearing an Arabic inscription on the verso side, is a clear imitation of the Arab dinar and demonstrates the influence of Arab commerce and coinage in that age.

Arab ascendancy remained undisputed until the advent of the Normans in Italy and the Mediterranean during the second half of the eleventh century, as well as the outbreak of the First Crusade in 1096, which ushered in the third phase in the history of commerce. A band of pilgrims who also served as mercenaries under a Byzantine general, George Maniakes, in a campaign against Muslims, the Normans ultimately descended on Southern Italy as freebooters and decided to carve a kingdom of their own out of its confusion. Capturing Pope Leo IX in 1053, they served in the ranks of another Pope, Nicholas II, in 1059, and rescued Gregory VII from Rome when the city was sacked by a stray group of their own men in 1084.

The names of two Norman brothers stand out in this picture of anarchy and strife: Robert Guiscard (1057–85), duke of Apulia, and Roger I of Sicily (1061–1101). While the first concentrated on the extermination of both Byzantine and Muslim rule from Southern Italy, the second devoted himself to the task of supplanting the Arab amir of Sicily. The story of a new kingdom began in this way. Robert's capture of Bari in 1071 confirmed his rule over the whole principality of Apulia. Then in the following year, Palermo in Sicily was seized by Roger with the aid of his brother. The subjugation of the whole island was completed by 1091. This signalled the gradual re-Christianization of the Mediterranean waters, and Sicily continued to be the crossroads of intermingled Christian and Muslim commerce. In the meantime, the First Crusaders reopened the route to the East, and the Normans contributed their full share to the inauguration of the movement of Holy War. Bohemond, son of Robert Guiscard, and his brother Roger, together with Tancred and others, were among the earliest recruits for the new cause.

The impact of these momentous events on the course of medieval commerce was incalculable. It marked the rebirth of European trade with the East, and its gradual growth ultimately reached unparalleled heights in European history. The fleets of Venice, Genoa, and other trade communes and merchant cities in Italy and the southern Mediterranean countries expanded to meet the exigencies of the conveyance of increasing numbers of Crusaders from Europe. Meanwhile, the resumption of the Eastern trade came as a natural consequence to the Crusade, since merchants from Europe accompanied the various expeditions or followed in their steps and opened up fresh markets in every newly conquered seaport in the Levant. Direct contacts between East and West, though begun by the way of the sword, were soon destined to yield to the ways of peace in the fields of commerce and culture. Arab piracy was suppressed or at least considerably restrained on the high seas by the recapture of the islands of Sardinia in 1022, Corsica in 1091, and Sicily in 1058–90, which had served as bases and convenient nests for the ships of Muslim buccaneers from North Africa and Spain.

All this brought boundless prosperity to the merchant cities and led to the rise of the southern European communes as well as the establishment of the trade leagues of the north for the distribution of commodities throughout Europe. Venice, Genoa, and Pisa headed the list in Northern Italy. The League of Milan, which incorporated other Lombard cities such as Bergamo, Brescia, and Crema, designed originally to oppose Emperor Frederick Barbarossa, also played an economic role which was beneficial to trade. Naples, Salerno, Amalfi, and Bari flourished in South Italy, while Palermo on the island of Sicily gained an unusual position of importance. Marseilles, Montpellier, and Narbonne in France, and Barcelona in Catalonia, rose to fame at a later date.

In the interior, Hanseatic Leagues were formed for the promotion of commerce. The German or Baltic Hansa, begun by Lübeck and Hamburg in the thirteenth century, soon incorporated Bremen, Cologne, Dortmund, and distant Danzig, and reached the consummation of its political and economic power toward the end of the fourteenth and the beginning of the fifteenth century. It owned numerous trading centers and factories in the major cities of Europe, notably in Bruges, London, Bergen, and Novgorod. The Flemish Hansa of London under the leadership of Bruges specialized in the distribution of English goods, and its confederate cities were mainly Bruges, Antwerp, Calais, and Dordrecht. The Swabian and Rhenish Leagues are other examples—more economic and less political than the Baltic League.

But all these federations depended mainly for their Eastern goods on Venice and Genoa. While Venice chiefly devoted its mercantile fleet to trading with the Syrian and Egyptian emporia of the Levant, Genoa almost monopolized dealings with North Africa and the Black Sea, where the commune owned the important colonies of Caffa in the Crimea and Tana on the shore of the sea of Azov.

Cyprus also occupied a rank of the highest importance under the Latin kings of the Lusignan dynasty. Famagusta compared with the most prosperous sea towns in the Mediterranean basin. Leontios Makhairas, the fourteenth-century chronicler of Cyprus, provides instances of the immense fortunes accumulated by the merchants of that island from international trade. The graphic description of the wealth of two Nestorian brothers, Sir Francis and Sir Nicholas Lakha, in the reign of Peter I de Lusignan (1359–69), is impressive "And the riches which they had are beyond my power to describe, for the merchant ships of the Christians which came from the West did not venture to do their business anywhere else but in Cyprus; and all the trade from Syria was done in Cyprus." * Ships from Venice, Genoa, Florence, Pisa, Catalonia, and all the West, crowded the Cypriot harbors, where they were loaded with spices and all manner of merchandise for European markets. Sir Francis built the Nestorian church at Famagusta from its foundations entirely from his own pocket. One day, in a single stroke of business, he made 30,000 gold ducats and sent 10,000 to King Peter I as a gift. Another merchant from that island, Stephen de Lusignan, was able in one voyage from Syria to Cyprus with three ships to make so much profit that with one-third of his gains he could build the church of St. Peter and St. Paul, a superb edifice in Famagusta. The prosperity of Cyprus in the end rendered it a prey not only to the Muslims, who captured King Janus II in the battle of Kherokitia in 1426, but also to the Christians, who coveted the wealth of its markets. At first the Genoese seized Famagusta in 1383, and then the Venetians in turn annexed the whole island in 1489.

The Greek Empires of Constantinople and Trebizond, together with the Armenian towns of Asia Minor, also continued to be useful havens for the mercantile marine of the Christian West until their suppression as independent units. The paradox of the Fourth Crusade, which ended in the de-

* Leontios Makhairas: *Recital Concerning the Sweet Land of Cyprus entitled "Chronicle,"* Greek with English trans. by R. M. Dawkins, 2 vols., Oxford 1932, para. 92–95. Cf. Atiya: *The Crusade in the Later Middle Ages*, London 1938, 322, n. 2.

struction of the Byzantine Empire in 1204, helped in the acceleration of European trading with the new Latin principalities of the Aegean. Propagandists such as Marino Sanudo the Elder proposed the enforcement of a maritime blockade of the Egyptian and Syrian coasts in order to strangle Mamluk commerce with the West and deflect its course to the aforementioned Christian emporia of the East. But the project failed miserably, for even the Papacy, which had sponsored it on pain of excommunication, issued special dispensations absolving Venice from the ban on trade with Egypt.

The decline of Mediterranean commerce was precipitated, not by propagandist schemes or papal bulls, but through wider causes and circumstances of world history which will be reviewed shortly. The curious feature is that, in spite of the disappearance of the Latin kingdom of Jerusalem from the Holy Land in 1291–92 and successive Christian asaults on the Muslim countries, such as the sack of Alexandria in 1365 and the attack on al-Mahdiya in 1390, European trade with the East persisted and even flourished throughout the fourteenth and most of the fifteenth century. It was not until later that Mediterranean trade began to change its course away from Egypt and Syria.

ROUTES AND TRANSPORTATION

The height of Roman civilization has often been measured by the excellence of Roman roads, which were constructed of stone and connected all the important and strategic points of the Empire. Special care was taken to keep them in good repair. Bridges spanned rivers to insure continuous and speedy circulation, both military and civil. Judged by these ancient standards, the world of the Middle Ages, and Europe in particular, suffered a dreadful setback. With the establishment of the new barbarian kingdoms, the Roman roads fell into what amounted to almost complete decay. The medieval road became a totally unkempt horse track, either dusty or muddy, hampered by breaches and beset by dangers of wild beasts and highwaymen. The medieval merchant was called "piepowder" or "dusty-foot," * for his journeys were generally undertaken in the dusty summer season to escape from winter severities. Even the caravan routes across Asia and Africa compared favorably with European roads. In the East, the camel was the ship of the desert, though the horse was widely used for travel and postal service (the Arabic barīd); in the West, the pack mule, the horse, and the light two-wheeled cart were employed for transportation of merchandise. The use of heavy four-wheeled vehicles was confined to urban areas and large farm estates over short distances and paved streets. Further, the cost of the use of a wagon was equal to the profit drawn from three to five acres of arable land. The pack mule carried from 300 to 400 pounds of weight and covered a distance of fifteen to twenty-five miles per day. Expenses of such means of communication were more than doubled by local taxes, e.g. the gabelle or the "theloneum" exacted by land feudatories at every stage on the road from county to county. The main roads of medieval Europe could be traced between the large merchant cities and the districts of famous fairs such as Saint-Denis near Paris, Bruges and Ypres and Lille in Flanders, Lagny and Bar-sur-Aube in Champagne, Saint-Ayoul in Provence, and so forth.

The international circulation of the medieval merchant, almost impossible until the close of the tenth century, started modestly in the eleventh and became more general in the twelfth and thirteenth centuries, owing to the facilities offered by inns and stables along the main arteries, and, which was of greater importance, the construction of bridges across the waterways. In the later Middle Ages a new monastic brotherhood arose under the name of the Order of Bridge Brothers

* The French "pieds poudres" and Latin "pedes pulverosi."

(Fratres Pontis), whose vow implied the preservation of these vital links in a state of good repair for public service. Famous medieval bridges were those in London over the Thames, in Paris and Rouen on the Seine, at Avignon on the Rhone, and at Maastricht, Liège, Huy, Namur, and Dinant on the Meuse. Across the Alps, the passes of Mont-Cénis, the Brenner, Septimer, and St. Bernard were in use until St. Gothard was opened with its new suspension bridge connecting the plains of Lombardy with the northern mountain roads which lined the valleys of the sources of both the Danube and the Rhine in the thirteenth century. The wealthy merchant travelled with his own mercenary guards, while the lesser tradesmen travelled in companies for joint self-defense.

As a rule, river traffic was preferable in the case of heavy and bulky merchandise, though ships did not escape the vexatious burden of repeated tolls. The Rhine had 64 toll stations, the Loire 74, the Elbe 35, and the Danube 77. These were less than the hundreds of frontier tolls exacted on the land routes, but they were sufficiently great to result in a measure of price inflation. The transportation of wine by ship from Pisa to Florence, a distance of about fifty miles, cost 50 per cent of its original price; salt increased by 60 per cent.

The Eastern trade was brought by caravan across the traditional routes of Central Asia to the terminal cities within the borderland of Europe and in the Near East. Samarqand, Tabriz, and Bagdad were frequented stations. Novgorod, Kiev, and Caffa included famous markets. Aleppo, Damascus, and Acre were great centers of the Syrian trade, while Damietta, Rosetta, and especially Alexandria were freely visited by Western merchants.

The Indian trade was customarily carried by ship to the Persian Gulf and then up the Tigris to Bagdad or Mosul, whence caravans conveyed the cargoes to the marts of Aleppo, Damascus, or other merchant cities on the Syrian coast. Mostly, however, the Red Sea route was pursued as far as Aidhab and Qusayr or still further north of al-Qulzum, the ancient Clysma, at the head of the Gulf of Suez and roughly on the site of the present city of Suez, where the modern canal comes to an end. From Aidhab and Qusayr, caravans of camels and donkeys transported cargoes across the Arabian desert to the opposite city of Qus on the Nile in Upper Egypt, whence goods were shipped downstream by boat to Cairo and Alexandria. From al-Qulzum, merchandise was carried by land to Cairo and again by river to Alexandria, Rosetta, and Damietta. All internal transportation was reserved to the natives; and the foreign merchant was never allowed to penetrate the country beyond the terminal market cities, often located on the coast.

Ships usually sailed in convoys escorted by men-of-war for safety and defense at a time when piracy was practiced with the connivance of rival states and communes. Experience taught the medieval sailor in the Mediterranean that the favorable seasons for the eastward passage were April and June and the western journey should preferably be undertaken in August or September–October; rarely did sea craft embark on a winter passage. The progress in shipbuilding in medieval times was great. A galley was expanded to a capacity of 500 to 800 tons. Such ships ordinarily carried a total of 800 to 1,000 mariners and passengers besides cargo. In addition to sails, ships were driven by oars manned by chained slaves on the lower decks. The mariner's compass, though not unknown in Europe as early as the thirteenth century, was not generally used in navigation until the fifteenth century, after Arab sailors set an example with its use. Progress in seamanship and the seaworthiness of late medieval craft never eliminated the danger of foundering in storms as well as the terrors incurred from piracy. Though cheaper than transportation overland, shipping expenses remained rather high. It is said that grain shipped from Armenia to Italy by sea cost more than 160 per cent of the net value. It was deemed advisable to limit maritime transportation to merchandise of real worth and reasonable bulk.

FAIRS AND EMPORIA

International trade in the Middle Ages found a clearinghouse in the great merchant cities and more particularly in the medieval fairs, the French "foires." The most notable among them were the fairs of Champagne, a county with a geographical position admirably suited for trade exchange between many nations of Europe. Its location between France and Flanders on one side, and its accessibility to Lombardy through the passes of St. Bernard and Mont-Cénis on the other, made it a natural rendezvous for dealers from those countries. Furthermore, the central position which it occupied inside France brought it within easy reach of both northern and southern French provinces, while its westernmost confines were in close contiguity with Paris. Champagne was thus ideally fitted for the role which it was destined to play in the diffusion of commerce at the crossroads of Western Europe. Its able counts were fully aware of the possibilities of the area and encouraged all mercantile activities in the lands under their jurisdiction by opening up their fairs in rotation almost the whole year round. The fairs of Lagny, Bar, Provins, and Troyes were held each for about six or seven weeks at Christmas and Lent and in May and June respectively.

Fairs were generally intended for wholesale trading. Considerable store-rooms and halls were allotted to the merchants, and the count's agents kept a detailed inventory of all incoming merchandise to ensure the right toll levies without vexatious and unjust extortion. The fair opened and closed during set hours by means of bell signals. Security was stringently enforced by the count's representatives or custodians (custodes nundinarum). A special court of justice (jus mercatorum) was held to decide differences and to punish violations. A prescribed number of days was reserved for the exhibit and sale of all merchandise. All the preliminary transactions were concluded by paper checks, which were exchanged at the end of the season in the counting house of the fair, a real money market. Worsted from the Italian and Flemish looms, linen and fine wines from France, leather goods from Germany, iron from Sicily and Spain, spices and silks and rugs from the Orient, gold and silver from Africa, alum from Asia Minor—all these and numerous other valuable commodities were exchanged by a world clientele.

Outside Champagne near Paris, the Fair of Lendit at St. Denis was solemnly inaugurated by a procession of students from the Quartier Latin of the University of Paris for the purchase of their annual stock of stationery. In another area of France, the fair of Beaucaire in the neighborhood of Marseilles and Aix-en-Provence served other purposes. But Champagne remained in the lead until the fourteenth century. Already in existence during the twelfth century, the fairs of Champagne reached the consummation of their vigor in the thirteenth, and began to decline in the course of the fourteenth when the Venetians and Genoese passed through the Straits of Gibraltar and sailed directly to Flanders and England. It was then that the Flemish fairs of Bruges, Ypres, Lille, Thourout, and Messines experienced rapid growth and began to replace the fairs of Champagne as international marts. England, too, had its more modest fairs at Winchester, Stanford, St. Giles, St. Ives, Stourbridge, and Bartholomew. The towns of the Hanseatic League had much more activity than the English centers, while Novgorod in Russia and Kiev in the Ukraine became lively focal termini for the fur trade from the north as well as other items arriving overland by caravan from the Far East.

The fair was also one of the most attractive features of medieval life, and people of all classes of society came to it for amusement as well as business. Minstrels and jongleurs made their appearance on the occasion. Indoor and outdoor games were played there. Miracle and mystery plays were performed. Bears and animals were brought for attraction. The gay nature of the whole show must have been colorful and impressive.

Western fairs had their counterparts in the East, where practically all the villages or groups of villages in every district had their own fairs (sūqs) on given week-days from time immemorial. This practice is still employed, and usually the fair is associated with a commemorative day, either of a Christian saint or of a Muslim holy man. It is equally interesting to know that a combination of the annual pilgrimage and the intertribal fair was celebrated at one and the same time in pre-Islamic days. The fair or sūq of 'Ukāẓ in Mecca around the holy Black Rock of al-Ka'aba was the most famous gathering place of all Arab tribes before the time of the Prophet Muḥammad. Here the bartering of goods was done, while poets and public speakers delivered their annual literary harvest. After the rise of Islam and until the present day, perhaps the only change in the nature of the pilgrimage to Mecca could be detected in the development of its international character. Pilgrims from India and beyond met with people from Morocco and the intervening Islamic countries for participation in common prayer and for the exchange of their native products.

The rise of the medieval town as a center of economic enterprise, though seen from a very early date, became a sizable reality only in the course of the later Middle Ages. This phenomenon must be tied up with the steady progress of both industry and commerce. The industrialization of Flanders, for example, may be measured by the fact that at least half of its population became engaged in the textile manufacture in the course of the fourteenth century. Urban industry animated both local and international trade, and this led to the formation of a new class of bourgeois or burgesses. The increasing prosperity of the communes and cities of southern Europe is attributable in part to this industrial revolution and also partly to the enormous enhancement of the Eastern commerce. It is beyond the limits of this survey to go into the details of the organization of the scores of important European towns which accumulated fabulous fortunes by means of trade. Yet it would be illuminating to depict some aspects of exemplary towns known for their prosperity in the East and West, such as Venice and Alexandria.

The annalist Marino Sanudo "Torsello" the Younger recorded under the year 1420 in his "Lives of the Doges of Venice" a very interesting speech delivered to the Venetian Senate by the doge, Thomas Mocenigo da Campofregoso (1413–20), in which da Campofregoso submitted his annual report on the trade of the republic of St. Mark in the preceding year. The goods exported from the warehouses of Venice were valued at 10 million ducats.* The net profit on the exchange of articles was 4 million gold ducats. The military and merchant ships owned by the Venetians amounted to 3,000 units of varying dimensions. They were manned by a regualr army of mariners numbering 17,000. Three hundred ships carried 8,000 seamen, and forty-five heavy galleys were manipulated by 11,000. This averages about 244 sailors to the ship, which is a sizable crew even for a modern vessel. The dockyards in the lagoons employed a regular body of 16,000 workers. The mint of Venice coined, evidently in addition to the money already in circulation, one million new gold ducats, 200,000 silver pieces, and 800,000 solidi. Half a million pieces were sent to Egypt.

The Genoese also amassed great riches and rivalled the Venetians. A fourteenth-century Genoese chronicler, Stella, gives instances of Genoa's overseas affluence. The seizure of

* Roughly about $25,000,000. See below, section on Money, Credit and Banking.

two Genoese state galleys in the Black Sea in 1330 and 1344 revealed surprising aspects of the extent of Genoese overseas trade. One galley was found to contain goods valued at 460,000 pounds sterling, and the other 470,000 pounds. Under normal conditions, some merchants could more than double their fortunes in a single year. Representatives of Egypt were stationed in Venice and a number of other trade centers in order to issue letters of introduction at a given fee, as the equivalent of the modern passport and consular service.

The bazaars of Constantinople, Trebizond, Alexandria, and Damascus were frequented by Western merchants for Eastern goods. The fair of St. Demetrius at Thessalonica reflected all the trade activities of the Near East. Silken stuff from Boetia and Corinth, skins and salt from the Carpathians, Syrian damasks and Egyptian linen were among the wares sold there. But it was in Alexandria that the mercantile world was fully represented. Ibn Baṭṭūṭa, the Maghribin traveller who visited the city in 1326, recorded that he had never seen the like of it in the Mediterranean, and Guillaume Machaut, who wrote in 1367, called it the "Queen of the Mediterranean." Its two harbors were constantly crowded with merchant ships loading and unloading. The eastern harbor, the old Portus Magnus, known in medieval times also as the "Chain Harbor" because of the gigantic chain drawn up at its entrance during the night, was devoted to Christian vessels; the western harbor, the ancient Eunostos of the Ptolemies, was kept for Muslim ships coming directly from Muslim Spain and the Maghrib. The double walls and massive fortifications of the city, and its sea and land gates, enclosed some of the most magnificent buildings in any medieval town. Hostelries, or fundacos or fontecchis (from the Arabic "funduq"), were constructed by the Venetians, Genoese, Pisans, Florentines, Neapolitans, Marseillais, Catalans, Templars, Knights of St. John of Jerusalem, Northern and Southern Frenchmen, and the citizens of Montpellier, as well as by Africans and the merchants of the

Near and Far East; each of these structures was under the care of a responsible consul or fundicarius. Practically all the nations of the East and of the West were represented in Alexandria and came with loads of goods for sale at this terminal emporium. The booty carried away from Alexandria by the Crusaders of Peter I de Lusignan in 1365 revealed the immensity of wealth stored in that city.

COMMODITIES

What commodities were exchanged in the marts of Alexandria and other trading towns? They may be classified under three categories, namely, slaves, natural products, and manufactured goods. Of the three, the slave trade was probably the most lucrative for the West and the most eagerly sought in the East. A quick glance at the origins, structure, and organization of the Mamluk state (1250–1517) will explain the unusual importance of this trade in human beings. Originally a slave bodyguard of the Aiyubid Dynasty (1171–1250), the Mamluks ended up by taking over the sultanate and they ruled Egypt and Syria as a foreign legion. Their numbers were continually reinforced by new purchases from the slave markets. Every Mamluk amir had his own retinue as far as his means permitted. Qalāwūn's bodyguard numbered 6,700 Mamluks, but his first son, Khalīl (1290–93), increased his heritage to 10,000, and his second son, al-Nāṣir Muḥammad (1293–94, 1298–1308, and 1309–40), to 24,000. On some occasions, the sultan's Mamluks fell to as low as 4,000, as in the reign of Barqūq (1390–98). These were generally divided into special battalions representing numerous nations such as the Turks and Turcomans, the Mongols, Circassians, Kurds, Armenians, Greeks, Slavs and Slovenes, Albanians, and Serbs.

The Mamluks were afflicted by a high degree of mortality, not only because of falling on the field of battle, but also because of the frequent wholesale slaughter and massacre of all men of doubtful loyalty. Though professing Islam as the official state religion, the Mamluks were on the whole quite unscrupulous and most of them paid only lip service to religious functions. For survival as a special clan living in a military camp, they had to devote enormous sums annually to the purchase of new recruits, averaging two or three thousand slaves per annum. Some of them rose to high office. Sultan Kitbugha (1294–96) was a Mongol prisoner of war. Lājīn (1296–98) is said to have been a knight of the Teutonic Order who fought the pagans in Livonia round the Baltic and afterward became a Crusader in Syria, where he apostatized to Islam and joined the Mamluks.

Most of the European merchant cities participated actively in the slave trade, but Genoa was in the lead. The Genoese colonies of Caffa and Tana in Southern Russia were perhaps the greatest fairs for the sale of Mongol children, male and female, sometimes offered on the market by their own parents, who aspired to give them a brilliant career in Egypt. Moreover, they often replenished their stock with captives from among both the pagan and Christian inhabitants of Eastern Europe as well as from the Anatolian markets. A Mongol slave fetched 130 to 140 gold ducats,* a Circassian 110 to 120, a Greek around 90, an Albanian, Serb, or Slovene 70 to 80. Famous fourteenth-century Genoese merchants, such as Niccolo di S. Giorgio, Gentile Imperiali, Segurano Salvago, and others indulged in this remunerative business and defied the papal decrees forbidding it. While Pope Martin V (1368–1431) issued a bull in 1425 excommunicating all those engaging in this evil practice, the secular powers openly recognized and encouraged the illicit commerce; and in 1466 Emperor Frederick III (1463–1525) granted Genoa full authorization

* For a rough estimate in pounds sterling, divide by two; and in dollars multiply by two or two and a half. Such estimates are very approximate and rather arbitrary owing to the changing purchasing power of money from age to age.

to trade in slaves of both sexes. The value of a slave depended on his age and health. It is interesting to know that the same intermediaries who carried slaves from Europe and Asia into Egypt also imported Muslim slaves from North Africa and Asia into Christian Europe. Felix Faber, the noted fifteenth-century traveller, mentioned the existence of about 3,000 Muslim slaves in Venice; they were used as oarsmen in Venetian sailing ships.

The natural products which were eagerly requested in the European markets were first of all spices and pepper, imported from India and bought by Venice and other mercantile organizations at high prices in the Egyptian emporia. Spices were known as early as the sixth century, as is demonstrated by the cosmography of Cosmas Indicopleustes, who visited India at that time. All travellers in the Middle Ages who touched the subcontinent talked of spices. In medieval Alexandria a whole street or rather quarter was devoted to trade in pepper, and Guillaume Machaut cites the "Avenue du Poivre" in 1365, which appears in the Arabic literature as Shāriʿ al-Filfil (Pepper Street). The historian of trade in the Levant during the Middle Ages, Wilhelm Heyd,* has compiled an alphabetical list of the commodities and articles of exchange in the Eastern commerce. Without entering into the details of the material which he accumulated from the contemporary sources as well as from secondary studies, it will be

* *Geschichte des Levantehandels in Mittelalter,* 2 vols., Stuttgart 1879; French trans. by Furcy Reinaud: *Histoire du Commerce du Levant au Moyen Age,* 2 vols., Leipzig 1885–86, reprinted in 1959. The standard revised and enlarged edition of his work is the French and not the original German. It is interesting to note that Heyd used exhaustively the European sources of his time, but his knowledge of the Oriental and Arabic sources was limited to fragmentary translations into a European language of a relatively small fraction of the extant material. The field of inquiry into Arabic writings to supplement Heyd's work remains open to scholars. The French edition was reprinted in 1959, thus showing how essential it still is for the historian of commerce.

sufficient to enumerate some of the contents of the list without comment, merely to give the reader an idea of the magnitude of this commerce. The list included: aloes, alum, amber, balsam, benzoin, aloe wood, sandalwood, Bresil wood, camphor, cinnamon, cardamon, Cassia fistula, clove heads, coccusilicis, coral, costus-root,* cotton, frankincense, galanga (Arabic k͟hlunjān), rubia tinctorum, ginger, gums, indigo, ivory, laudanum, macis or musky nuts, manna, mastic, mumia or tar mineral, musk, myrobalani or prunes, cynips gallae tinctoriae, pearls, precious stones, black pepper, long pepper, rhubarb, saffron, roots of convolvulus scammonia, silk thread, tutia, and root of curcuma zedoaria roscoe. Some of these products were indispensable for certain industries; alum, for example, was widely used in fixing colors and dyestuffs in the textile business, and was imported from the Balearic Islands, North Africa, and some islands of the Archipelago and Asia Minor. Others were used in medical concoctions. Pearls and precious stones from the Persian Gulf and India were items of great attraction to the rich feudal nobility. Gold dust and silver, though not mentioned in Heyd's list, should occupy a special place, together with the base metal ores such as iron, copper, and lead. The last was used in the roofing of churches and cathedrals as well as in the framing of stained glass windows. The gold mines in Nubia and the Sudan furnished the markets with most of the stock in circulation in Egypt and the European communes.

Manufactured trade articles included gold and silver thread from Cyprus, porcelain from China, sugar from India and the Far East, variegated textiles from the ṭirāz looms of Egypt, from Damascus, Bagdad, Persia, and the Far East, rugs from Persia, as well as glassware from the kilns of Syria, Egypt, and North Africa. The interest shown by scholars and museums, particularly in the United States of America, in ancient and

*Native to Kashmir, known for its fragrance, and used in the manufacture of perfumes and incense, as well as in medical prescriptions.

medieval textiles has revealed the extraordinary nature and importance of this study. Apart from the Textile Museum in Washington, which is almost exclusively devoted to this branch of study, the greater repositories such as the Metropolitan, Brooklyn, Boston, Cleveland, and Michigan museums have made enormous textile acquisitions, including numerous polychrome samples decorated or inscribed with embroidery. These collections have opened new vistas in a field pregnant with immense possibilities. Medieval glassware is best represented in the Toledo Museum, the Metropolitan, the Brooklyn Museum, and the Steuben glass factory at Corning; and there are various other centers in America and abroad. Some excavations have yielded glass and faience beads which await the scrutiny of the archaeologist and historian of civilization. Venice, of course, played an important part in the development of glass manufacture; Genoa produced velvet, France linen, and Flanders and Lombardy woollens. Ships went eastward loaded with European manufactures, arms and slaves, and returned to their bases laden with fineries and precious cargoes from the East.

MONEY, CREDIT AND BANKING

The spreading use of money in Europe may be justly regarded as symptomatic of the extent of progress in Western civilization. During the early Middle Ages Europe was distinctly divided into East and West, Byzantine and barbarian. While the Byzantine Empire retained most of the traits of Roman greatness and its economy was marked by trade affluence, Western Europe fell into the position of an underdeveloped area depending on provincial agrarian economy, where trade was almost at a standstill. The universal acceptance of the gold "nomisma" minted by the Emperor of Constantinople compared favorably with the primitive system of barter of the countries of Western Europe. The "nomisma" became the "dollar of the Middle Ages," while Merovingian Europe had but few gold coins for its small money circulation, and the Carolingian world depended mainly on silver pennies which Charlemagne tried to force by law on his unwilling subjects. The "nomisma" was therefore the true and right heir to the Roman "solidus" and its memory has outlived its use in the modern science of "numismatics." This Byzantine coin, also called "hyperperon" and "besant" at a latter date, enjoyed a stability of gold quality and weight which commanded general confidence. It was equal to 1⁄72 of the Roman pound weight (327.45 grams), thus amounting to 4.50 grams of gold. Numismatic evidence shows that it actually varied between 3.88 and 4.44 grams. On the other hand, coins became so scarce in the West that settlement of debts in various countries was specified in cash or kind. In Spain in 933 a debt of 600 solidi was settled in vases, caparisons, fine cloths, and coins. In France, as late as 1107, the sum of 20 solidi was paid back with a horse.

While the West was in that state of backwardness, a peer to the elaborate Byzantine civilization appeared in the new Arab Empire. Even in the first century of Islam, the Caliphs, who had first accepted the domination of the "nomisma," soon revolted against it and declared their economic independence by minting their own gold "dinar" and their silver "dirhem." The Umaiyad Caliph ʿAbd-al-Malik ibn Marwān (685–705) inaugurated the new Arab money during the last decade of the seventh century. Religious reasons were advanced for this departure—Muslim rejection of human figures on coins—but economic independence was at the root of this reform. Though the "dinar" did not drive the "nomisma" out of international usage, it acquired immense prestige, not only in the Muslim Empire and the Mediterranean, but also in remote areas and countries, as has been shown by the Arab coins excavated on the Baltic shores and beyond.

It was not really until the age of the Crusades that the

people of the West began to conceive of the importance of money in conducting international transactions. Roger II (1130–54), king of Sicily and duke of Apulia and Calabria, was the first European monarch to strike a gold coin since the more modest attempt by the Carolingians. This was the gold "ducat" minted in 1140 with the famous inscription: "Sit tibi, Christe, datus, quem tu regis, iste Ducatus"—(Let this Duchy, O Christ, which thou rulest, be dedicated to thee). In 1252 Florence adopted the new coin under the name of "ducati gigliati," later identified as the gold "florin" (fiorino d'oro) on account of the Florentine lily sign with which the novel currency was stamped. The turn of Venice came later when the second of the four doges, by the name of Dandolo, decreed in 1283 that the commune should start striking its own Venetian gold ducats. The republic of St. Mark preserved the original old Apulian Latin inscription on the new coin, which, in the course of the sixteenth century, became better known as "zecchini" (sequins) from Zeccha, name of the Venetian mint. The value of the "ducat" * varied from age to age, but originally it weighed 3.5 grams of pure gold, corresponding to the current price of one pound of silver. In modern times, the "ducat" was used extensively by many countries of the continent of Europe until the dawn of the present century. In the Middle Ages, the florin and the ducat were perfectly acceptable as means of exchange in international trade, and their stability was closely guarded until the downfall of Venice and other Italian communes.

Realizing the importance of money in the facilitation of transactions and the enrichment of state budgets, the powerful potentates of Europe began to emulate the economic policies of those who had coined the "nomisma," the "dinar," and the "ducat" in succession. The first monarch of vision to

* Palgrave, Sir Robert Henry Inglis: *Dictionary of Political Economy*, 3 vols., London and N.Y. 1894–1900, estimates the value of the ducat in English money, prior to the date of publication of the work, at 9s. 4½d.

perceive this was Emperor Frederick II, who in 1228 preceded even Venice and Florence by minting his "augustalis," one of the most stable gold coins in medieval Europe. Apart from its perfection as a piece of numismatic art, described as a "chef d'oeuvre" by Pirenne, it was widely sought for the purity of its gold. Unfortunately, the output of the imperial mint was limited, and the scarcity of the "augustalis" prevented its acceptance as a standard currency of international trade. Meanwhile, other monarchs followed Frederick's example. In 1266 St. Louis struck his French "livre," identified as the "gros tournois" (from Tours) and the "gros parisis" (from Paris) for circulation in Europe north of the Alps and west of Germany. He succeeded in rendering it the standard coin of most of Northern Europe for a time, but his heirs failed to keep up this tradition, and its use was interrupted.

Regular coinage can be traced in other countries to varying dates. Alphonso XI of Castile (1312–50) was responsible for the inauguration of a gold currency in Spain. Bohemia was the leading province in the Empire north of the Alps to do the same in 1325. In the Netherlands, famous for its medieval industry and commerce, we find the creation of national coinage by Louis of Nevers prior to 1337, and again by John II (1312–55) in Brabant, by Englebert de la Marche (1345–65) at Liège, William V (1346–89) in Holland, and Renaud III (1343–71) in Guelders. In England, King Edward III minted a gold florin in 1343.

The curse of coinage in medieval Europe lay in the right of all feudal nobility to issue their own local money, which became utterly debased in many instances. In fact, defective coinage and the abuse of this prerogative were reported against numerous monarchs as well as feudal princes. One of the most flagrant examples was the attempt of King John II the Good (1350–64) of the House of Valois to debase the French currency as a means of escape from onerous national debts.

The growing use of money led to an analytical study of its role in commerce, in order to achieve stability and justice. Medieval Europe's first monetary theorist was Nicholas Oresme (d. 1382), rector of Navarre College in the University of Paris and later bishop of Lisieux. He was a theologian, a naturalist, and a student of political science who translated Aristotle's *Politics;* but his real fame rested on a treatise entitled "De mutatione monetarum," in which he examined in a factual way the position of commerce, the difficulties besetting it, and the sources of those difficulties in the monetary system. The fundamental idea behind Oresme's whole argument was that money belonged, not to the monarch or prince who issued the currency, but to the commonwealth of the people who used it, and to whom it represented their labor and material heritage. The prince had no right to make gains out of coinage; tampering with coins was regarded as unethical, unjust, and ruinous to the economic stability and prestige of the whole country. It is interesting to note in passing that fifteenth-century Egypt also witnessed the appearance of treatises on money by such eminent writers as Maqrīzī, Suyūṭī, and the less known Asadī. This literature, however, has not been studied sufficiently and our knowledge of its purport is still obscure, although it might be assumed that its appearance came at a time when the rapacity of the Mamluk sultans was also revealed in currency debasement.

The gold nomisma, dinar, florin, and ducat were not supposed to be reduced below 3.5 grams of gold. In transactions of medieval computation, they should be linked with what is known as ghost or fictitious money, that is, the pound equalling twenty shillings or 240 pennies. Originally the pound or libra represented a pound weight of silver struck into 240 silver pennies.* The gold coins fluctuated in their relation to

* The French system of the livre, sou, and denier was transplanted to England by the Normans after the conquest of 1066. Whereas France changed its monetary system in 1789 during the French Revolution, Eng-

the pound, shilling, and penny, which depended on the gold market in a given area. In the middle of the fourteenth century in Milan, we are told that the gold florin was valued at 1.6 pounds or 32 shillings, the equivalent of 384 pennies. In this range, only the florin and the penny were real units represented by concrete coins and the rest were ghost coins.

Consequent upon the development of international trade and monetary transactions was the establishment of credit and banking. Bills of exchange, already in use among Greeks as well as Jews and Arabs, were introduced by the Christian merchants of the Italian cities in their dealings with one another. Money was deposited in various banking centers to meet these paper transactions. Loans, too, were made, usually at high interest, in defiance of Church orders against all forms of usury. Though adamant in its resistance to any form of interest at the beginning, the Church wavered later on the stringency of the indiscriminate application of the rule which it had laid down. Even leading theologians such as St. Thomas Aquinas argued in favor of participation in profit when the risk (periculum sortis) of a loan or deposit was too great. The Papacy accepted the principle, though the Popes remained adamant in their refusal to legalize all usurious interest.

The Lombard bankers from Venice, Genoa, and Florence, as well as other North Italian cities, began to replace the Jews in this lucrative profession. The money changer in the fair became a small local banking agent. The Venetian bank of St. Mark, the Genoese bank of St. George, the Bardis and Peruzzis in Florence, and numerous other trading and banking organizations were the great novel phenomena of the age.

---

land has retained its "pound sterling," shilling, and pence, philologically derived from the German pfund, schilling, and pfennig, though the signs l.s.d. are taken from the French livre, sou, and denier, or the Latin libra, solidus, and denarius. The silver penny minted by Henry II (1154–89) was the only standard coinage of England until the gold florin was adopted by Edward II in 1343.

At the end of the fourteenth century Florentine money in circulation was computed at two million gold florins. The Peruzzis, for example, had sixteen branches in the European capitals as well as in the mercantile cities of the West, Majorca, the Morea, Cyprus, Rhodes, and Tunis in North Africa. Owing to their international character and the spread of their commanderies all over Europe and the East, the Templars also became one of the chief world banking organizations in the thirteenth century. Kings and feudatories alike used their safe quarters and strong castles for depositing their treasure. A pilgrim could deposit any sum in Paris or London and then obtain cash in Rome or Jerusalem. The enormous fortunes accumulated by the Templars through banking operations invited the covetousness of Philip IV of France, who dissolved the order and confiscated its property in 1312. At a later date the Renaissance Popes, whose medieval predecessors had banned interest, started to abuse the principles of banking. While Pope Sixtus IV (1471–84) prided himself that all he needed to raise any amount of money was writing material, Innocent VIII (1484–92) founded a bank in Rome for the sale of indulgences. Traffic in money became the order of the day toward the end of the Middle Ages.

TRADE SYSTEM

Again the expansion of trade overseas and overland, development in the methods of transactions, the diversified nature of the commodities of exchange, and the intricate laws and customs of the lands where the goods were bought or sold, together with a whole host of other considerations, made it necessary for all the countries involved to establish their own trade systems subject to a written code or to unwritten traditions. Trade became an elaborate business. The fairs of Champagne were run in accordance with a set of regulations imposed by the count and observed by his clients. The cities had their merchant guilds to attend to the organization of internal and external trade relations. Societies of merchants were formed by contract either for one journey and one deal or in permanence. Growing laws and customs were codified for general application.

In the Mediterranean after the outbreak of the Crusade, there arose a series of codes governing maritime procedure and developing some form of international law for the control of commerce. The "Rhodian Code," the "Consulate of the Sea," the "Laws of Oleron," and the "Amalfian Tables" were the chief codes in force in the south of Europe and in the waters of the Adriatic and the Mediterranean. Other codifications in other areas followed for the same purposes. In the North Sea territories, we have the "Black Code of the Admiralty" of England, the "Purple Book of Bruges," the "Sea Laws of Flanders," and the "Maritime Law of the Osterlings." The Hanseatic League developed the "Gotland Sea Laws," the "Wisby Code," and the "Ship Laws of Lübeck." The Baltic sea had two other noteworthy codes—the "Danzig Sea Laws" and the "Sea Laws of the Teutonic Knights."

The dangers with which commerce was perpetually beset necessitated collective action in the form of leagues for self-defense and for meeting the costly business of building lighthouses, docks, and quays, for marking hazardous zones of reef and shoal, and similar functions indispensable for public maritime security. The Hansards had their own licensed pilots, and in the fifteenth century they compiled a "Sea Book" containing a detailed description of the seacoasts, water channels, tides, lighthouses, and harbors frequented by their ships. Marino Sanudo the Elder gives an accurate description of the Egyptian coast and the ports of Alexandria in the fourteenth century, which confirms the Arabic accounts of the city in 1365 and shows the depth of the nautical knowledge of the East.

The international nature of these laws, however, should not

be exaggerated when it comes to their practical application. Their enforcement was essentially a local affair dependent on the good will of the authorities of a given area. But their aims were generally recognized to be the protection of commerce, the safety of cargoes on the high seas, the inspection of vessels for assurance of their seaworthiness, the enforcement of discipline, checking the numbers of the crews to ascertain that ships carried no less than the minimum fixed for them, the status of the foreign trader, the liability of captain and pilot, and many other details.

In Egypt, the control of trade activity became very elaborate, since trade was the chief source of revenue for the sultan. Ships sailing into the harbor of Alexandria had their rudders and sails stripped, and a chain was drawn across the entrances of the harbor at night to prevent ships from stealing away under cover of darkness before payment of customs and dues. Lists of names of visitors and inventories of cargoes on incoming ships were communicated to the central administration in Cairo at once by carrier pigeons, and instructions were immediately issued to the local authorities in the same way. Usually a traveller had to present a letter of introduction from one of the Egyptian agents stationed abroad in numerous European cities to represent Egyptian interests, a kind of medieval consular corps. Each foreigner paid the fee of a gold piece on landing; he was not allowed to wander inside the country at large, especially toward the Red Sea, which the sultans zealously guarded against alien infiltration. Citizens of the same origin stayed at the special fondaco or fonteccho of that nation under the management of a fondicarius, who was instructed to close his gates from sunset to sunrise and at the time of Friday prayers, chiefly as a protective measure. Loading and unloading of ships could be made only at the sea gates which opened into the great city customhouse. Thus all imports and exports were handled and properly taxed before release.

The city was controlled by a high-ranking viceroy (wālī). It had its own finance house (bayt al-māl) and its own arsenal (bayt al-silāḥ), its police and defense forces. Its markets were subject to inspection by an intendant (muḥtasib) whose extensive dutics embraced the supervision of weights and measures, the prohibition and punishment of fraudulent dealings, execution of contracts, and payment of debts. He had the right of summary justice in economic dissensions or breaches of the law, and he thus combined legal, economic, police, and religious responsibilities. "Books of the Intendant" (kutub al-ḥisba) are extant in the contemporary Islamic literature, and they detail the vast area of the intendant's rights and duties. He was also the guardian of public morality in the city and could arrest a wine-bibber or a misbehaving townsman. He had to see that all Muslims attended the Friday religious service. Cruelty to animals as well as to servants and slaves, either by physical torture or by underfeeding or overworking and overburdening, came within the scope of his jurisdiction. He was commissioned to keep the streets in an orderly state of cleanliness and to insure the free passage of merchants and merchandise on all thoroughfares. These details illustrate the meticulous nature of the elaborate trade system in the medieval states of both Europe and the Arab East.

CORPORATIONS AND CAPITALISTS

Discountenanced by the Church and finding no place for itself in the social cadres of an agrarian feudal society, the practice of commerce in the early Middle Ages became confined to the Jews and a very limited number of impecunious Christian adventurers from the lower classes. The Jew was not entitled to own land, and he thus concentrated his capital in commerce, moved from country to country with his goods, worshipped with his coreligionists everywhere, and secured their help in the process of buying and selling. Few examples of Christian traders are encountered in the annals of early commerce. Toward the end of the eleventh-century St. Godric of Finchale in Lincolnshire, who was separated from his peasant parents by dire poverty, wandered over the seashore, where the wreckage of a ship provided him with a peddler's stock. His fortune multiplied, and he eventually formed a company owning ships which sailed around the coasts of the North Sea and managed to accumulate fabulous wealth from international commerce. A certain Werimbold, mentioned in the "Gesta" of the bishops of Cambrai in the early twelfth century, enriched himself in the service of a wealthy merchant, whose daughter he ultimately married, and he gave much property to the Church. In 1174 the founder of the Poor Men of Lyons, who later developed the Waldensian heresy, was a merchant of no mean standing in the south of France. The term "mercator," formerly synonymous with "Judaeus," began to undergo a radical change and gradually became identified with "burgensis." But the real medieval renaissance in commerce was more evident in the cities of southern Europe, where the Christian merchant's enthusiasm was excited by direct contact with the Arab tradesmen from the East, especially after the beginning of the Crusades. The opportunities offered in the field of commerce gave rise to the establishment of "houses" (casa) or "companies" (societates) * of merchants, first in the same family, and later widened to take in more independent capital, where investors paid two-thirds and the active factors paid one-third, and all divided the profits equally in the end.

The Jews had long established a precedent in the Radanite (the Arabic Rā<u>dh</u>āniya) corporations carrying on trade internationally. Their activities had been recorded as early as the ninth century by the Arab geographer and traveller ibn <u>Kh</u>or-

* The "societas" was a partnership financed by people not necessarily linked by blood ties. Originally the word "company" was derived from the Latin "com-panis," that is, "bread-sharer."

dādhbah, who described them in 870 A.D. as merchants who spoke Arabic, Persian, and Greek as well as the languages of the Franks, the Andalusians, and the Slavs. The Radanites seem to have penetrated the Levant, certain regions in Asia, Byzantium, North Africa, Spain, and most European countries. The Cairo Geniza documents have revealed the existence of a flourishing Jewish trade with India and Ceylon in the eleventh century. As early as the tenth century, however, the Arab trader already occupied a prominent place in the business world, side by side with the Jew; but each seemed to specialize in a different class of mercantile operations. Whereas members of the Radanite corporations leaned mainly toward trading in luxuries such as precious stones, pearls, gold and silver objects, silks, precious textiles, and rugs, the Arab merchants responded to the wider human needs for the more indispensable but rather bulky type of articles, such as pepper, spices, salt, sugar, and all manner of natural products and Eastern manufactures. Both organizations, however, indulged freely in the highly remunerative slave trade.

The most outstanding Arab, or rather Muslim, trade corporation was that of the Karimites (the Arabic Kārimiyah merchants), already in existence as a substantial group in the course of the tenth century under the early Fatimids. In this period they are known to have stationed five armed galleys at the port of Aidhab on the Red Sea to defend their merchant ships from the raids of pirates. The Fatimid Caliph al-Ẓāfer granted them a concession to build their own funduq in Cairo in 1154. The Aiyubids and the Mamluks continued the Fatimid policy of the encouragement and protection of the Karimites at least until the beginning of the fifteenth century. They formed an exclusively Muslim corporation, from which Jews were explicitly barred. Their merchant fleets sailed to the Persian Gulf, India, and Ceylon, as well as the shores of East Africa and Somaliland, while their caravans penetrated the Sudan, Central Africa, the Sahara, and North Africa. Their hostelries and depots multiplied rapidly in the great trade emporia inside and outside of Egypt, where none but a Muslim trader could function. They had funduqs not only in Cairo, Alexandria, and Damietta, but also at Qus in Upper Egypt and Aidhab and Aden on both shores of the Red Sea, as well as Mecca and Jadda in the Hijaz. To defend their commerce at key points such as Aden, they interfered with the local politics of Yemen, where one Karimite named Yaḥya ibn Musnad rose to the wazirate of that country in the first decade of the fourteenth century.

Naṣiri Khusru, who visited Egypt in 1046–49, stated that a Karimite merchant had built a college out of one day's transactions. Three Karimites—Burhān al-Dīn al-Maḥallī, Shihāb al-Dīn ibn Muslim, and Nūr al-Dīn ibn al-Kharrūbī—gave Sultan Barqūq in 1396 a loan of one million silver dirhems. The chronicler ibn Ḥajar al-'Asqalānī, commenting on the death of ibn Muslim, the Egyptian Karimite merchant, in the year 1374, said that he had been a miracle of his age owing to the immensity of his wealth, which was beyond all measure. One statement puts his fortune at 10 million gold dinars or approximately $42.5 million. The wealthy Karimites were great patrons of learning. Ibn Muslim spent 16,000 gold dinars, the equivalent of some $76,000, on one school, and Kharrūbi built another school and a religious house (Khāniqāh) bearing his name to accommodate scholars and men of religion in Cairo. Maḥalli spent 50,000 gold mithqāls * on the construction of a vast palace on the Nile, together with another school; and he also repaired the ancient mosque of 'Umar in Old Cairo. The Karimites became the true bourgeoisie of medieval Egypt, and they continued to flourish until the rapacity of

* One "mithqāl" is the equivalent of approximately one and a half "dirhems," in modern weight about 72 grains or 4.66 grams. If the figures mentioned in the text are authentic, then the total weight of the gold mithqāls expended on the occasion must have been 233 kilograms, an exaggeration, of course.

the late Mamluk sultans wrecked their organization in the fifteenth century. Bursbay in 1432 confiscated all their stock of pepper, which he sold at eighty gold dinars the "load" and paid them only fifty.

The ruinous Mamluk policy of trade monopoly and continuous manhandling of the Karimites, who protested in vain, finally turned the latter into mere agents of the administration. Their numbers dwindled and they lost interest in their old activities to the extent that, as ibn Taghri Bardi, the fifteenth-century annalist, recorded, not one Karimite dared or cared to appear in the Egyptian markets in the year 1455. The passing of the Karimites was a prime element in the decline of medieval Egypt and of trade in the Middle Ages.

Europe was more fortunate in the growth of the independent mercantile communes of Venice, Genoa, Florence, Pisa, and other Italian cities, as well as the Hanseatic Leagues in the north. The paramount duty of the states of all those districts was to watch over the interest of every individual merchant or joint company of merchants within their confines. The story of each of these states is chiefly the enumeration of their trade triumphs. Their senates were their boards of trade. Even the reigning dynasties of the Visconti and the Sforza in Milan and the Medici in Florence were predominantly mercantile aristocracies. The tremendous gains which these cities raised from Levantine commerce gave them power. One Venetian galley, carrying iron and timber to Alexandria and returning with a cargo of silk, spices, and pepper, distributed dividends of 1,000 per cent.

It is beyond the limits of this introductory essay to attempt an inventory of the trading and banking houses of these cities, since all their organizations had to do with trade in some way or other. The archives of Venice, Genoa, Florence, and the rest abound in the written testimony of the official document as to the status of trade and traders who rose to the heights of medieval wealth. Even a small and relatively insignificant town such as Prato was the home of Francesco di Marco Datini (1335–1410), a medieval multimillionaire whose trading houses spread beyond his native town to Florence, Pisa, Genoa, Avignon, Spain, and Majorca. The discovery of his archival material almost intact has provided economic and social historians with a unique sample of the records of medieval trade. That material consists of some 150,000 letters, more than 500 ledgers, 300 company deeds, 400 insurance policies, and a few thousand bills of lading, letters of advice, bills of exchange, and checks. At one time France competed with the Italian cities in the Eastern trade. Bonis Frères of Montauban, the Boyssel Frères of St. Antonin in Rouergue, Ponce de Chaparay of Lyons, Raymond Seraller of Narbonne, Jacques Olivier of Bearn, Hugo Teralh of Forcalquiei in Arles, and other noteworthy names are dwarfed by the meteoric career of Jacques Coeur of Bourges, who became one of the greatest capitalists of the Middle Ages.

Born in a merchant family toward the end of the fourteenth century, he was brought up in his father's fur business in the city of Bourges, the seat of French royalty at that point in the Hundred Years' War. He started his career by forming a furniture company with two others and sold to the king. Then he made his first acquaintance with the East when he went to Alexandria to buy spices on a ship from Narbonne in a joint convoy of Venetian, Genoese, Florentine, and Catalan vessels. On the return journey his ship was wrecked and plundered on the coast of Corsica. He lost everything, but gained experience and knowledge. Through his influence with the royal family, and with unflagging labor and ability, he succeeded at last in building his own private fleet of four ships named St. Michel, St. Ouen, St. Jacques, and Madelaine, which he sailed to the Levant. He traded in slaves, spices, silks, carpets, Arabian perfumes, and Chinese porcelain. As his wealth increased to fabulous dimensions, he was able separately to conclude trade treaties with the Mamluk sultans, the grand masters of the Knights of St. John in Rhodes, and the sultans of Turkey. He had hundreds of agents all over the Orient; and in France he had headquarters in Bourges, Lyons, Montpellier, and Marseilles. To the last, he paid annual city taxes amounting to 11,000 gold florins. Instead of just buying the goods he took to the East, he bought off whole industrial concerns for the manufacture of those goods without intermediary. Furthermore, he persuaded the king to grant him mining concessions in the silver, copper, and lead-bearing districts of Beaujolais, Lyonnais, and Chessy against an annuity of 200 livres and one-tenth of the net profit.

A contemporary said once that Jacques Coeur made more money than all the other merchants of the kingdom of France put together. His palace at Bourges is still a standing monument of that extraordinary opulence. He had his own system of carrier pigeons for direct and prompt contact with his distant representatives all over the country. The holes of the pigeons are still to be seen in the attic of his palace; and it is possible that here he copied the example of the Egyptian administration in Alexandria and the Near East. His known wealth was estimated at a million gold écus, and he often subsidized the king and the nobility when they were hard pressed for funds. He financed Charles VII's conquest of Normandy in 1449–50, and paid the king 60,000 gold pieces for the Cherbourg siege in 1450.

In the same year, his immense fortune seems to have precipitated his downfall. Accusations with and without basis were brought against him, which included minting counterfeit currency, selling arms to the Turks while they were menacing the last Byzantine stronghold of Constantinople, returning escaped Christian slaves to the Mamluk sultan, and, what was perhaps more serious in the king's eyes, the assumption that he poisoned the king's mistress, Agnes Sorel, who really died in childbirth and left a will appointing Jacques Coeur as her executor.

The Church and Pope Nicholas V (1447–55) interceded on his behalf with the king in vain. Jacques Coeur was incarcerated for three years on trial, and Charles VII finally pronounced him guilty and sentenced him to death on May 29, 1453, the day of the capture of Constantinople by the Turks. In deference to the Pope, however, the sentence was commuted to imprisonment until he ceded virtually all his property, and then he was sent into perpetual exile. In 1454 he escaped while his property was still on sale and took refuge at the Vatican in Rome, where Nicholas V welcomed him, and the succeeding Pope Calixtus III (1455–58) put him in command of a papal flotilla destined to fight the Turks in the East; but he is said to have died in Chios in the same year.

It is not difficult to draw a parallel between the general policies of Egypt toward the Karimite capitalists and those of the French crown toward Jacques Coeur. To catastrophes like these the merchants of the free communes and leagues were immune. Their decline came as a result of overpowering circumstances of world history rather than clashes of local interests or princely whims and greed.

THE DECLINE

The decline of the Mediterranean trade became evident before the close of the fifteenth century, and it is not difficult to find the causes. Within Egypt, the system of trade monopoly practiced by the later Mamluk sultans, while killing the beneficial Kārimite activity, drove the Western merchants to desperation. The Venetians were almost unable to sell their spices and pepper in Europe at the sultan's prohibitive prices. In the meantime, attempts were continuously being made in that age of discovery by other powers to find other routes for reaching the primary sources of Eastern trade in India. The Portuguese under Vasco da Gama finally rounded the Cape of

Good Hope in 1498, and their fleets appeared in the Indian Ocean and played havoc with the Arab craft. The last of the Mamluk sultans, Qanṣūh al-Ghauri (1500–16), waged an intermittent naval war against them. In 1504 his fleet suffered a severe defeat. He retaliated in 1508 by killing Lorenzo Almeida at sea; but the following year saw the complete discomfiture of the Egyptian maritime power accomplished by Lorenzo's father, Dom Francesco de Almeida (1450–1510), then Portugese governor of Goa. He was replaced by Alfonso Albuquerque (1453–1515), the first European adventurer to enter the Red Sea from the south and attack the key harbor of Aden. Though he failed to occupy it permanently, he was later able to seize Ormuz (1515) and insure Portuguese supremacy over the Indian Ocean. Sultan Qanṣūh was still dreaming of the preparation of another campaign against the new and redoubtable enemies, and he even negotiated naval collaboration with the Venetians against the Portuguese, when suddenly he fell fighting the Turks in 1516, and the whole of his realm passed to Ottoman hands in 1517.

It is interesting to note that, at that time, the Venetians had proposed the digging of a Suez Canal to connect the Red Sea with the Mediterranean. The fulfillment of such a project would have enabled the Venetian galleys to deal more effectively with the Portuguese intruders in the Eastern waters. But the idea remained under consideration until the undecided Qanṣūh was removed altogether from the picture by his Ottoman antagonist Selim I (1512–20).

With the coming of the Turks, Egypt sank to a secondary position in world affairs, while Constantinople became the new pan-Islamic center. The Ottomans formed a new barrier in the face of the Eastern trade. Their aggression against the Christians in Europe and especially Venice, together with the emergence of the Barbary corsairs under Khair al-Dīn Barbarossa in the Mediterranean, virtually brought European commerce with the Levant to a standstill.

Meanwhile the discovery of America in 1492 opened up vistas of immeasurable promise to the powers of the Atlantic seaboard; Spain and Portugal began to replace the declining republics of Venice and Genoa and all the other south Mediterranean trade communes. A new leaf was turned, and the darkness setting on the Middle East gave way to the dawn of modern history in Western Europe.

CHAPTER SIX

Arab Culture and the West in the Middle Ages

BIRTH OF ARAB CULTURE

THE LUMINOUS PERIOD in the development of Arab history is divisible into three main stages. The first is the Age of Conquest, when the Arabs, united for the first time in their long but rather obscure history under the banner of Islam, exploded with dynamic force in every possible direction and subjugated all the surrounding countries to the rule of their new empire. The sons of the desert had already had a measure of contact with their immediate neighbors and possessed some acquaintance with the brilliant and rich civilizations around their sandy wastes. The Arab tribes of the Hira district on the eastern frontier of the Arabian Peninsula knew the Sassanid civilization, which extended its sway from Persia over the green valleys of the Tigris and the Euphrates. To the north, Byzantine civilization was even better known than the Persian, not only to the Christian Arab tribes such as Banu Ghassān, who inhabited the borderland of Syria, but also to numerous nomadic tribes from the interior of Arabia itself.

The Prophet Muḥammad, as a young camel driver, had visited these regions with the trade caravans of Khadījah, the rich old widow of Mecca whom he later espoused. It is said that 'Amr ibn al-'Āṣ had travelled into Egypt as far as Alexandria and that he beheld with wonder and bewilderment the radiance of the city of the Ptolemies and Alexander before leading the Arab hosts to the conquest of that country. The Arabs no doubt coveted those rich areas, and when they waged a holy war (al-Jihād) against both Persian and Byzantine, they fully realized the immensity of the brilliant heritages awaiting them. The two great empires of antiquity had been fighting one another to a standstill for a whole millennium, and both were so exhausted in the seventh century of the Christian era that they succumbed in a short span of time to the virile Arab conqueror.

It is impossible to comprehend the staggering rapidity with which the Arab invasion spread without looking into the inner workings of those nations which were tottering on their past glories. One of the decisive factors in the Byzantine picture was the element of separatism which had set in between the Eastern and Western Christians at the Fifth Ecumenical Council of Chalcedon in 451. After that year the West inaugurated a policy of unremitting persecution toward the Eastern Christians, who accordingly lost all sympathy for their Western brethren. Christianity had become an imperial religion and the historic factors behind the Chalcedonian theological polemics of Monophysitism * versus Diophysitism might be described in a way as the battle of nationalism, combined with a relapse toward primitive Christianity's spirit of democracy in

* From the Greek *monos* = one, and *physis* = nature; signifying the doctrine of the oneness of the indivisible, divine nature of Jesus since the incarnation, as against the double, divine and human nature held to be united by the Orthodox West at Chalcedon (451). Strictly speaking, the variance between East and West was over the degree of unity, and both parties defended their doctrines by relating their arguments to the pronouncements of Cyril I of Alexandria (d. 454).

the East, against the growth of imperial theocracy in the West.

Constantinople was resolved to take the ecumenical lead and become solely endowed with Apostolic authority, hitherto largely associated with both Alexandria and Antioch. The ensuing rift in the ranks of the Universal Church gave rise to the creation of a Melkite * patriarchate with subservient leanings toward the Empire, in defiance of the traditional tendency of independence among the native patriarchates of the East, whether Coptic, Syriac, or Armenian. Justinian's appointment of a single person who combined in his own hands the secular and ecclesiastical authority of both the prefecture of Egypt and the patriarchate of Alexandria only led to the total estrangement of the Egyptian Coptic-Christians from their Byzantine oppressors at the critical moment when the Muslim Arabs attacked the fort of Babylon at the beginning of the summer of 640.**

The outcome of this sordid situation was Egyptian neutrality between the two rivals, and Cyrus, the Melkite patriarch and Byzantine prefect of Egypt, known in Arabic literature as al-Muqauqas, was constrained to surrender Egypt to the Arabs after the downfall of Syria and the invasion of Persia. Within fifty years of the rise of Islam, the Arab Empire had engulfed the vast territories extending from the Indian Ocean to the shores of the Atlantic.

* That is, royal—derived from the Syriac word "melek," meaning "king," and later identified with the Arabic word "malik," though the term predates the Arab conquest.

** The siege of the fortress lasted seven months, and the Arabs finally seized it in April 641. The invasion of Egypt became complete with the fall of Alexandria in the following year. Other landmarks in the Arab westward march are: the Pentapolis or Cyrenaica, taken in 642–43; the conquest of Carthage, completed in 698; Spain invaded in 711; Aquitaine and Southern France raided after 717; the battle of Tours or Poitiers in which the Arab tide was arrested in Europe by Charles Martel in 732; and the eastern invasion of the Byzantine Empire, which was stopped at Constantinople in 717 during the reign of Leo the Isaurian.

The next important stage was the Age of Establishment. Fortified by faith and a sense of justice, combined with high respect for the already existing systems of governance and appreciation for the superiority of native cultures, the Arabs began to settle down quietly and harmoniously with their subjects in their immense acquisitions. A combination of humility and magnanimity marked their behavior toward the peoples among whom they were destined to live for centuries. Their sole contributions during that age were confined to the two realms of language and religion. Coming from an arid desert with no superior culture, the Arabs were extremely proud of their own Arabic tongue and their Islamic religion. The sanctity with which both of these became invested in the Arab mind found its fullest expression in the Holy Qur'ān, a work of divine revelation which embodied the tenets of the new religion in immortal Arabic style. All faithful Muslims were expected to read or at least recite the Book of Allah in its original text. The new Arab legacy to subsequent generations became identified equally with the Arabic tongue and the faith of Islam.

The third of these stages may be described as the Age of Assimilation. After the establishment of the Pax Arabica in their empire, a period followed in which the Arabs began to reap the benefits of the superior civilizations now under their hegemony. Unlike the barbarians who invaded the Roman Empire in Europe, or the Mongols in the Middle East, the Muslim Arab did not barbarize the territories he conquered, but tried to rise to the lofty standards of his subjects in both culture and material refinement. The Arab thus availed himself of the natural resources as well as the intellectual excellence of those nations. When, therefore, we speak of the miracle of Arabic culture, it is essential for us to remember its predominantly synthetic character. This is seen not only in the wider fields of Greek and Persian influence, but equally in regard to the impact of the more localized elements such as Coptic, Syriac, Nestorian, and Indian thought and art. The openness with which the Arabs responded to all those great and ancient civilizations is unmatched in the annals of mankind except perhaps, as the late Professor George Sarton rightly pointed out, in the case of the Japanese assimilation of the methods of Western science and technology during the Meiji era (1867–1912). The analogy, however, is not a perfect one in all details, since the receptivity of the Japanese stopped within Japan, whereas the miraculous achievement of the Arabs proved to be a capital landmark in the universal progress of the human mind and the transmission of ancient wisdom and learning.

The very term "Arab" soon denoted much more than simple ethnic Arabism in its original and purer form, as was the case of the Umaiyad dynasty in Damascus. The movement of Arab culture at its apogee was demonstrable in the reign of the Abbasids of Bagdad, where the outlook was possibly more Persian than Arab; and yet it was here also that the miracle of the Greek mind and of Greek culture was transmitted to future generations. In reality, Arab culture became the meeting place of the two great ancient streams of thought which had been developing quite independently throughout ancient times—the Greek, or, if we go deeper into antiquity, the Egyptian and the Greek on the one side; and the Sumerian, Persian, and Indian on the other. The integration of these widely separated realms of thought became the primary function of the Arab. The birth of Arab culture took place in the amazing synthesis of the intellectual achievements of the older nations.

Yet it would be an error to limit the Arab contribution to the transmission of ancient knowledge. Arab scholars and commentators, as will be seen from the following pages, showed themselves to be creative and attained extraordinary heights of originality, while the later Hellenes relapsed into medieval lethargy. The direct political heirs of the Greeks in the West were the Romans, whose utilitarian outlook on knowledge discredited the nebulous Hellenistic ideal; while the rise of Christianity later in the Empire departed from old pagan thought to a new faith, and from earthly problems to celestial eternities. In a sense, the Arabs became the rightful, though indirect, heirs of the Greeks in the realm of human culture.

AGE OF INTERPRETATION

The beginnings of Arab culture occurred in the form of systematic rendering of philosophic and scientific writings of the great masters of antiquity from Greek into Arabic. The Abbasid Caliphs, with their phenomenal zest for learning, commanded that the good work should be performed at any cost; and the Syrian Jacobite and Nestorian Christians, who were equally proficient in Greek, Syriac, and Arabic, executed the Caliph's orders. Later, al-Ma'mūn founded the "House of Wisdom" (Bayt al-Ḥikmah) at Bagdad in 830, as a home of scholars and scholarship and a great center for the expanding activities in scientific pursuits and interpretation. This was the first real academy of learning in the Muslim capital. Then the Caliphs despatched special commissions to Constantinople to copy important Greek manuscripts for the purpose of translating them into the Arabic language. Cases are noted where the ambassadors of the Caliphate made stipulations in peace treaties with the Byzantines for ceding certain Greek manuscripts to the Arabs.

These diplomatic pressures on the highest level on behalf of the advancement of Arabic learning are almost unique in history. Perhaps the only other similar instance worthy of mention was that ascribed to Ptolemy Philadelphus in the third century B.C. Not content with the importation of Greek manuscripts from the cities of Greece, Ptolemy decreed the search of all ships which dropped anchor in the waters of Alexandria and the confiscation of all written scrolls for the enrichment of the Museon Library.* It may, therefore, be asserted that al-Ma'mūn's academy in Bagdad was the first real revival of the learned atmosphere of the Alexandrine long extinct Museon.

The translation movement, however, began from Persian and not from Greek, when the great Abu Muḥammad ibn al-Muqaffa', a Persian Muslim scholar whose mastery of the Arabic style was extraordinary, rendered the Pahlevi classic, "Kalīlah and Dimnah," into Arabic. Ibn al-Muqaffa' served under 'Isa ibn 'Alī, uncle of al-Saffāḥ (750–54), the first Abbasid Caliph; and the aforementioned text had been transplanted from Buddhist India. He also translated the biographies of Persian kings ("Siyar Mulūk al-'Ajam") from the original "K͟hudai-Nāma," which was used by the immortal Persian poet Firdawsi in the composition of his famous "Shāh-Nāma." The long-lost Arabic text is known only through a number of excerpts preserved by ibn Qutaybah in his annals, " 'Uyūn al-Ak͟hbār." Ibn al-Muqaffa' later became involved in the dangerous game of the politics of his day and was consequently executed in the course of 757–58, during al-Manṣūr's reign (754–75). Though he was a native Persian, his Arabic diction remains one of the most forceful on record.

Hārūn al-Ras͟hīd (786–809) betrayed more pro-Persian tendencies than any of his predecessors; he was especially interested in Persian astronomy and is said to have sponsored the newly founded observatory at Jundishapur, better known in the ninth-century work of Aḥmad al-Nahāwandi, reputed to have been the compiler of the first astronomical "Comprehen-

* The Ptolemaic "Museon" in Alexandria, next to the royal palace, was a combination of a library and research institution under royal patronage—a true ancient academy, often described as a university, though this is somewhat misleading. Our modern term "museum" is, of course, derived from that word in spite of its different connotations.

sive Tables" ("al-Zīj al-Mushtami") drawn from personal observations. It was through his preliminary attempts to study Persian and Indian astronomy and mathematics that the Caliph's appetite was whetted for further work in the field of Greek.

The story had already begun with the Hindu treatise on astronomy known as "Siddhanta," the Arabic "Sindhind" translated by Muḥammad ibn Ibrāhīm al-Fazari (c. 771), who also compiled the Sassanid astronomical tables (al-Zīj, from the Persian Zik) and was the first Arab to build an astrolabe on a Greek model. Owing to the lack of an understanding of mathematical elements among the Arabs, Hārūn al-Rashīd ordered the translation of Claudius Ptolemy's "Syntaxis," known in Arabic as "Almagest," which reviews the fundamentals of astronomic data. Euclid's "Elements" also found their way to Arabic through Hārūn's injunction.

In the end, the Arabs reached Aristotle, probably through the channel of Syriac sources, where the corpus of Aristotelian logic was preserved. Yaḥya or Yūḥannā (John) ibn al-Baṭrīq, cited in the year 815, is associated with this work. In 835, another Christian, ʿAbd al-Masīḥ of Homs, the ancient Emesa, translated the so-called "Theology of Aristotle" from an abridgement of Plotinus. With the foundation of the first hospital in Hārūn's reign, orders were issued for the translation of the medical works of Hippocrates and Galen.

The influential wazir Jaʿafar al-Barmaki shared in the encouragement of the translation by lavish donations to scholars. The Caliphs al-'Amīn (809–13) and al-Ma'mūn (813–33) continued with enthusiasm and devotion their father's patronage of Greek science. Al-Ma'mūn actually maintained a formidable retinue of scholars, whom he housed in "Bayt al-Hikmah," which was becoming increasingly a manuscript repository.

Paper had been manufactured in Bagdad since 794, and its use began to supplant the scarce and costly parchment as well as the tender and destructible Egyptian papyrus. This signalled a revolution in the history of writing materials and the facilitation of the copyists' task.

Nestorian physicians who had studied Greek medicine were honored at the Caliph's court. Yūḥannā ibn Māsawayh (777–857), author of the earliest work on ophthalmology, entitled "The Ten Treatises on the Eye ("Al-'Ashr Maqālāt fi al-'Ayn"), and Jibrīl ibn Bakhtīshu (d. c. 830) both enjoyed the highest regard in the highest circles of their time. Al-Ma'mūn went further to organize what may be described as the beginnings of field work when he commanded the measurement of the geographical degree in the Syrian desert by a team of seventy scholars including the famous al-Khuwārizmi, author of the lost but not unknown "Image of the Earth."

The pride of the Age of Interpreters was the Nestorian Ḥunayn ibn Isḥāq (809–73). The son of a Christian druggist from Hira, he learned Arabic, attended ibn Māsawayh's lectures, and was expelled from his classes for being too inquisitive. Then he went to Greece, where he studied Greek to perfection. Afterward he settled in Basrah and resumed Arabic under Khālid ibn Aḥmad, until 826, the year in which he moved to Bagdad and became the protégé of the state physician, Jibrīl, for whom he translated Galen's medicine into both Syriac and Arabic. Ḥunayn, the most illustrious of all translators, ultimately settled down in the "House of Wisdom," and around him grew a new school of other scholars, including his own son Isḥāq (d. c. 911), his nephew Ḥubaysh ibn al-Ḥasan, and 'Isa ibn Yaḥya ibn Ibrāhīm, who labored steadily in the translation of numerous Greek sources. One hundred works are attributed to Ḥunayn alone, though only a few of them have survived. Besides Hippocrates' medicine, Ḥunayn translated Dioscorides' "Book of Simples" or "Materia Medica," often reproduced with magnificent miniatures and illustrations in Arabic manuscripts. This important book was translated first into Syriac by Stephanos ibn Basilos, another of Ḥunayn's pupils, and then into Arabic by either Ḥunayn, his son, or Ḥubaysh, his nephew.

Other translators included Yūsuf al-Khūri al-Qiss, a priest who rendered Archimedes' "Triangles" into Arabic from a Syriac version about 908, later revised by Thābit ibn Qurra. His contemporary, Qusṭa ibn Lūqā of Ba'albeck, translated "Hypsicles," which was revised by the Arab philosopher al-Kindi; Theodosius' "Sphaerica," revised by ibn Qurra; Heron's "Mechanics"; Theophrastus' "Meterora"; John Philiponus on "Aristotle's Physics"; a revised version of "Euclid"; and several other texts. Aristotle's "Poetica" was translated by Abu Bishr Matta ibn Yūnus al-Gamā'i (d. 940), and Ammonius' "Prolegomena" as well as Porphyry's "Isagoge" by the Monophysite Abu Zakariya Yaḥya ibn 'Adi al-Manṭiqi, the logician (d. 974).

A school similar to Ḥunayn's arose at Harran in Mesopotamia, under the leadership of Thabit ibn Qurra (825–901), a Sabian star-worshipper whose fame rests on his great ability both as a translator and as an astronomer. Bar Hebraeus (ibn al-'Ibri), writing in the early thirteenth century, states that Thābit was master of Greek, Syriac, Arabic, and that he composed in Arabic about 150 books on logic, mathematics, astronomy, and medicine, as well as fifteen other works in Syriac. His translations and revisions included works by Apollonius, Archimedes, Euclid, Ptolemy, Theodosius, and other ancient writers.

Thus enriched with a solid groundwork of the philosophic and scientific heritage of the Greeks, as well as the astronomical and mathematical knowledge of the Indians and Persians, Arab culture moved with confidence toward the fulfillment of its ultimate goals in creative thought. It was no longer a mere vehicle for the transmission of the wisdom of the ancients, but attained sufficient maturity to be able to leave behind it independent monuments of the mind in many spheres. In the course of approximately five centuries, the miracle of the Arab mind reached incredible heights, at first through interpretation. This might be described as the silver age, occupying roughly the latter decades of the eighth, the whole of the ninth, and the beginning decades of the tenth century. The golden age overlapped the silver toward the end of the tenth century and included the eleventh and most of the twelfth century. During that period we can sense two apogees of Islamic culture, in the East at Bagdad and in the West at Cordova. It will be illuminating to outline the main aspects of this brilliant picture and its impact on world progress in the various departments of the humanities, of the exact sciences, of astronomy, medicine, art, and architecture.

PHILOSOPHY AND THEOLOGY

The Islamic school of philosophers was inaugurated on the basis of Aristotelian philosophy by a pure Arab, Abu Yūsuf Ya'qūb ibn Isḥāq al-Kindi (d. post 873), whom Caliph al-Ma'mūn appointed as tutor to his son and successor, al-Mu'taṣim (833–42). Al-Kindi may be considered as the founder of Arab Aristotelianism with its Mu'tazilite * or liberal school of theologians, who accepted Aristotle's philosophical doctrines even if they were in conflict with the text of the Qur'ān, which would then be regarded as merely figurative or allegorical. The sponsorship of this rationalist attitude toward philosophy by al-Ma'mūn and his immediate successors caused a great uproar among the conservative Arabs who were persecuted by the authorities. One of the four Sunnite imams of

* That is, Secessionists or Seceders, an unorthodox group of thinkers who digressed from the general way to the secluded path and refused to accept the doctrine of predestination as opposed to free will, contrary to the traditional viewpoint of conservative Muslims.

Islam,* ibn Ḥanbal, perished (855) in the inquisition held by the Caliphs for the trial of orthodox thinkers and leaders.

In spite of conservative resistance, Aristotelian philosophy survived in all its strength and found numerous supporters among Arab writers, of whom al-Fārābi, the Latin Alfarabius, was the next great representative. Abu Naṣr Muḥammad al-Fārābi (d. 950), a member of the court of a highly lettered prince, Sayf-al-Daulah, at Aleppo, earned the title of "second teacher" after Aristotle for his prodigious works in the realm of philosophy. His vast commentaries on Aristotle and Plato became standard for centuries. At the outset of his career he turned agnostic, then later became mystic, and was eventually reconciled to orthodoxy and godhead. His system of philosophy, however, bore the impressions of a syncretism of Plato and Aristotle as well as the Islamic mystical philosophers. Of the thirty-nine works written by him, the "Encyclopedia of Science" ("Iḥṣā' al-'Ulūm") sums up all the knowledge of his time. In the treatise entitled "The Virtuous City" ("Al-Madīnah al-Fāḍilah"), a kind of Utopia inspired by Plato's "Republic" and Aristotle's "Politics," he viewed natural law in the light of the perpetual strife of every organism against all others. At the end of his discussion of political science, he arrived at the conclusion that an enlightened monarchical regime based on strong moral and religious feeling was man's best opportunity for saving the world from the law of the jungle. Al-Fārābī is also known as a physician of no mean merit, a mathematician, and possibly the greatest Arab musicologist ** under the Caliphate.

* The other three imams are ibn Mālik, Abu Ḥanīfah, and al-Shāfe'i. Every Sunnite or orthodox Muslim usually follows the creed of one of these four imams, who are in agreement on the essentials of Muslim theology, although they vary in regard to the particulars and the stringency of certain Muslim observances.

** Al-Fārābī actually wrote a considerable tome on musical theory ("Kitāb al-Musiqā al-Kabīr"), translated into French in the monumental work of R. d'Erlanger: *La Musique Arabe,* 6 vols., Paris 1930–59. See also

Abu 'Ali al-Ḥusayn ibn 'Abdallah ibn Sīnā (980–1037), al-Fārābī's greatest disciple, better known in the West as Avicenna, was another gifted author in the fields of medicine and philosophy. A native of Bukhara in Central Asia, he ultimately became so famous in distant Spain that Raymond, archbishop of Toledo, ordered his deacon, Dominic Gundisalvus, and a converted Jewish scholar by the name of Juan Avendeath of Seville, to collaborate in the translation of Avicenna's work into Latin during the years 1130–50. Avicenna labored to save religion and the existence of God without marring the doctrines of philosophy, thus laying the foundations on which Averroes (ibn Rushd) built his system later during the following century in Muslim Spain. In fact, his influence was perceptible in many other European centers of learning. His logic of procedure from the known to the unknown was adopted by the great scholastic, Albertus Magnus; and his metaphysics and discussion of the nature of God and the creation gave rise to considerable speculation in Western humanism.

One of the greatest Arab thinkers, whose authority in philosophy and influence on European learning almost equalled Avicenna's, was Abu Ḥāmid al-Ghazzāli (1058–1109), known in medieval Latin literature as Algazel. He taught at Nishapur and in the Bagdad Academy, where his intellectual adventures in Aristotelianism rendered him a prey to skepticism, which temporarily ruined his peace of mind. So he discarded his position at the Academy and retired from public life to contemplative seclusion. In the end he became a mystic and set out to study the various systems of philosophy in a different light. His analytical studies on logic, physics, and metaphysics became the subject of Latin renderings in the twelfth century at Toledo. Raymond Martin's "Pugio Fidei" embodied many of

H. G. Farmer: *The Sources of Arabian Music,* Bearsden, Scotland, 1940; and "Oriental Influences on Occidental Military Music," *Islamic Culture,* XV-1941, 235–42. Al-Fārābī was an excellent musician himself.

Algazel's arguments in his treatise "Tahāfut al-Falāsifa" (Incoherence of Philosophers). His system evidently suited the philosophical and theological thought of medieval Christendom.

It is noteworthy that al-Ghazzāli himself, during his early mental struggle, fell under the influence of a group of philosophical thinkers of Basra known as "The Brothers of Purity" (Ikhwān al-Ṣafā). Their philosophy had flourished in the second half of the tenth century, although they were condemned in Bagdad as a heretical Shi'ite sect. Their fifty-two epistles ("Rasā'il Ikhwān al-Ṣafā") were planned to incorporate all contemporary knowledge as a unified system comprising mathematics, astronomy, geography, music, ethics, science, and philosophy.

Arab philosophy reached its apogee in Spain in the course of the twelfth century, in the immortal work of Abu-l-Walīd ibn Rushd (1126–98), the famous Averroes of European scholasticism. A native of Cordova, he spent part of his time in Spain and part in Morocco, where he ended his later years. His philosophy presented a curious paradox in its impact on East and West. While Averroism struck root in medieval European thought and remained in force until the rise of experimental science, the authority of its author never commanded general applause or acceptance among Muslims. On the contrary, we find Averroes subjected to bitter criticism, and he was often accused of apostasy by Arab theologians. Yet he was recognized by the Western humanists as the greatest commentator on Aristotle in history; and his works on psychology, theology, logic, and jurisprudence must be regarded as outstanding contributions to general medieval culture.

The impact of Averroes on the principal thesis of St. Thomas Aquinas (1225–74), in his immortal "Summa Theologica," seems clear from his discussion on the place of revelation between faith and reason. Though St. Thomas deliberately criticized the Muslim thinker and belittled his system, he unwittingly fell under the spell of the very Averroism which he labored to undo. Averroes' theme that faith and reason were not incompatible, and that philosophical doctrines could be implemented in support of faith, was precisely the basic approach advanced by the great Christian saint and medieval theologian. The parallelism in the details of the two arguments are too numerous to be attributed to mere chance. Averroism must have reached Aquinas directly through the Latin translations of Michael Scot, made in Toledo a few years before the saint's birth, and indirectly through the Latin versions of the works of the great Jewish philosopher, Moses Maimonides (1135–1204) —Mūsā ibn Maimūn—, who had also written his original texts in Arabic. It is worthy of note that the Averroist philosophical interpretations, although condemned by the ecclesiastical authorities, were openly commended for student use by the professors of the University of Paris.

Students of Arab philosophy continued to multiply in Europe, more particularly from the eleventh to the thirteenth centuries. These included some of the most famous names of the age, such as Gerbert of Spain, who became Pope Sylvester II (999–1003), Adhemar of Bath, Hermann of Dalmatia, Michael Scot, Daniel Morley, Robertus Anglicus, and Peter the Venerable. The last two were the first known medieval writers to attempt a Latin version of the Qur'ān. The School of Toledo in the twelfth century, sponsored by Archbishop Raymond of that city, was reminiscent of Caliph al-Ma'mūn's ninth-century Academy (House of Wisdom) at Bagdad. In the meantime, Alfonso X the Wise, king of Castile and Leon (1252–84), gave his royal patronage to learned men of all confessions and encouraged the movement of rendering Arab philosophy and learning into Western languages. Gerard of Cremona translated sixty-one texts which provided the reader with a global encyclopedia of contemporary thought.

Arab literature was translated in the first instance into a

Romance vernacular in Spain with the help of the Mudejars * or Arabs left in Christian lands behind the advancing curtain of the Reconquista, the Mozarabs ** or Arabicized Christians, and the Hebrew scholars who moved freely between the Arabs and their European neighbors. It was from these vernacular renderings that the Latin versions were accomplished. The words philosophy and Arabic became synonymous. Roger Bacon (1215–91), who was greatly influenced by Arabic philosophy, wrote that "Philosophia ab Arabico deducta est." Europe owed the rediscovery of Aristotle and the Greek philosophers to the Arabs long before the original Greek texts were revealed during the Renaissance and after the downfall of Constantinople to the Ottomans in 1453. It is rather strange to note that some of the Latinized texts were translated into Greek by papal order, and thus the cycle became complete, from Greek to Greek by way of Arabic and Latin.

Arab philosophy, which reached its zenith in the twelfth century, appears to have come to a standstill after Algazel (al-Ghazzāli) in the East and Averroes (ibn Rushd) in the West. This is one of the strangest phenomena in the history of culture, and it is hard to offer any conclusive causes for the sudden petrification of the Arab mind. Could the state of insecurity and impoverishment arising from the Mongol invasions of the Middle East and the Christian Reconquista of Spain be at the root of this? There is no doubt that the Mongol hordes thoroughly barbarized the lands of the Eastern Caliphate; but what of Spain under the enlightened rule of such men as Alfonso the Wise? Is it possible to reckon that the triumph of orthodoxy over philosophic heterodoxy resulted in the establishment of intellectual conformity to the pedestrian standards of the docile theologian? Or was it the disappearance of the

* From the Arabic term Muta'kh khir, literally meaning "the retarded" or those lagging behind.

** From the Arabic term Musta'rib, that is, a non-Arab who adopts Arab culture.

burcaucratic sponsorship of the great centers of learning by the state and the Church—al-Ma'mūn's "House of Wisdom" at Bagdad, al-Ḥākim's "House of Science" in Cairo, the Alfonsine court in Christian Spain, and the School of Toledo, which flourished through the offices of Archbishop Raymond? Is it true that the Arab mind at a given moment became so saturated that its creative power was arrested and decline was ushered in as a natural corollary? Or is it due to all these and other reasons that the death of Arab philosophy and culture came to pass? All these are questions still to be answered.

Although this problem is still open to consideration, the fact remains that the later Middle Ages saw a sharp flagging in the fever of Arab thought, except perhaps in the solitary case of the meteoric personality of ibn Khaldūn (d. 1406), the great philosopher of history and the father of social studies. His towering figure on the deserted horizon of Arab culture, however, passed unnoticed by both his Muslim and his Christian contemporaries. His "Universal History" ("Kitāb al-'Ibar") in seven large tomes is dwarfed by the "Prolegomena" of the work. In this introduction, ibn Khaldūn outlines his philosophy of history and his pragmatic sociology. He examines the factors, geographical and climatic, physical and spiritual, governing the rise and fall of empires. He formulates the laws at work in the genesis of events, with comprehensiveness and profound insight such as no other social or philosophical historian demonstrates throughout the Middle Ages. He is also sometimes described as the first sociologist, founder of the modern science of sociology. But he arrived too late to have any impact on Western thought through Latin translation, and the Muslims were unable to understand or even accept his theories. It was not until the first modern translation of his "Prolegomena" into French in the nineteenth century that ibn Khaldūn became known to the world of scholarship, and through him a last lingering ray of light from Islamic culture shone for the human mind.

SCIENCE AND MATHEMATICS

Arab inspiration in the field of the exact sciences was stimulated by the translation of the great Greek masters of antiquity —Euclid, Ptolemy, Hippocrates, Hero or Heron, and others. Their knowledge was, moreover, soon reinforced by a totally fresh stock of a different nature from the East. We must assume that by the end of the tenth century the Arabs had become familiar with Brahmagupta's Hindu arithmetic and algebra as well as with the use of the zero and the decimal system, which revolutionized the world of mathematics. The very words algebra, alchemy, algorism, and cypher are of purely Arabic origin. The Arabs laid the foundations of analytical geometry and of plane and spherical trigonometry, so little known to Greek mathematicians.

As early as 825 the great al-Khuwārizmi * published his monumental work on algebra, which he called "Book of Calculation of Restoration and Reduction," ** and in the composition of which he used the Greek works from the West as well as Babylonian and Hindu sources from the East. He dedicated it to his enlightened patron, Caliph al-Ma'mūn, and pointed out in the introduction that it would facilitate computation of inheritance, legacies, partition, lawsuits, trade accounts, measurement of lands, plans for the digging of canals, geometrical processes, and other operations. His famous treatise on arithmetic, based on decimal notation and a new system of numerals, was translated into Latin by Gerard of Cremona as early as the twelfth century and had a tremendous influence on mathematics in Europe. It was responsible for the introduction of Arabic numerals, the cypher, and fractions in Western

* Muhammad ibn Mūsa of Khwarizm or Khiva east of the Caspian Sea. He died between 835 and 844. Al-Khwārizmi's name is said to have been corrupted in Latin into the term algorism or algorithm, although some writers doubt this.

** The Arabic "Kitāb Ḥisāb al-Jabr (algebra) wal-Muqābalah."

arithmetic. His mathematical tables, revised and improved by al-Majrīṭī (d. 1007), were put into Latin by Adelard of Bath in 1126.

It would be idle to attempt a survey of all the developments of Arab mathematics after al-Khuwārizmi. One name, however, seems to stand out in the general picture. This is 'Umar al-Khaiyām (1038–1123), a Persian from Nishapur, better known in the West as the poet who composed the "Ruba'iyāt" (quatrains) immortalized by Fitzgerald in English poetry, although his real title to fame rests on his mathematical genius and contributions to the advancement of science. He reformed the ancient Persian calendar and made substantial improvements on the algebra of al-Khuwārizmi and the mathematics of the Greeks. While solving cubic equations by geometrical constructions, he conjectured the impossibility of finding two cubes whose sum should be a cube, a problem which Pierre de Fermat (1601–65) generalized several centuries later. His algebra was put into French in 1857.

In physics, the Arabs did not just reproduce the Greek theorems lucidly, but also added to them their own discoveries. Ibn al-Haytham (c. 965–1039), the Latin Alhazen, a native of Basra who moved at a later date to Fatimid patronage in Cairo during the reign of al-Ḥākim, was the greatest of all Arab physicists. In his significant work "On Optics" he opposed Euclid and Ptolemy in their erroneous conception that visual rays were emitted from the interior of the eye to outside objects. Thus he reversed the Greek theory about the function of the "camera obscura." He studied refraction of light and, in mechanical science, he knew the principle of inertia which Isaac Newton formulated much later in his First Law of Motion. Alhazen's "Opticae Thesaurus" became the basis of most of the medieval optical treatises, notably the thirteenth-century work of Roger Bacon. During the Renaissance, it influenced Leonardo da Vinci (1452–1519) and Johann Kepler (1571–1630).

Another Arab of Persian extraction, and a contemporary of Alhazen (ibn al-Haytham), was al-Bīrūnī * (973–1048). Geographer, historian, astronomer, and physicist, he travelled widely in India and learned Sanskrit, which enabled him to translate Indian scientific writing into Arabic. He made outstanding contributions to the principles of hydrostatics, which he investigated in the artesian wells of India. His works on the "Chronology of Nations" and on the "History of India" are well known. In mathematics, he finalized Arabic knowledge and the use of the Hindu numerals, and solved many problems connected with angles, conics, and cubic equations. In physics, he employed the displacement method in calculating the specific weight or gravity of eighteen different precious and semi-precious stones. He also experimented on some minerals and arrived at results of a high degree of accuracy.**

The true successor of al-Bīrūnī as a physicist was al-K͟hāzini (Abul-Fatḥ 'Abd-al-Raḥmān al-Manṣūr), who wrote on the subject about 1118 A.D. He calculated the more difficult specific gravity of liquids such as water, oil, milk, and human blood; and in the case of water, he differentiated between soft and sea water, cold and hot water, with an imperceptible margin of error when compared with modern figures. Al-K͟hāzini was also aware of the force of gravitation toward the center of the earth and is said to have discovered the formula of acceleration in the case of falling bodies.

It would, however, be a mistake to exaggerate the Arab contribution to experimental sciences as a whole. In chemistry, they were inspired by the Persian, Chinese, and Alexandrian sources, which were rather primitive. Recognizing the

* Abu Rayḥān Muḥammad al-Bīrūnī, known in Arabic as 'al-Ustād͟h', that is, the Master.

** Al-Bīrūnī's estimate of the specific gravity of gold ranged from 19.05 to 19.26, of mercury 13.59 to 13.74, of copper 8.83 to 8.92, and of bronze 8.58 to 8.67. Later al-K͟hāzini revised these figures to 19.05, 13.56, 8.66, and 8.57 respectively. Compare these with the modern estimates of 19.26, 13.56, 8.85, and 8.40.

old Greek principle that all metals were derived from the same fundamental matter, which varied only in degree and proportion, they wasted a great deal of time and energy in trying to solve the problem of the transmutation of "base" into "noble" metals, in order to change lead into gold. Together with the secret of transmutation, they also sought the Philosopher's Stone as well as the Elixir of Life to cure all diseases of the human being and lengthen human life. In these attempts, however, they became acquainted with a series of important chemical processes, such as melting and distillation, evaporation and filtration, sublimation and crystallization—all of which were known to the remarkable eighth-ninth-century alchemist of Kūfa, Jābir ibn Ḥaiyān. He is further said to have devised both calcination and reduction and to have prepared numerous oxides.

The Arabs knew alcohol and alkalis, both words being of Arabic derivation. They used the alembic, another Arabic term. They became acquainted with the aqua regia, sulphide of mercury, saltpeter, alum, pure vitriols, and numerous other chemical combinations. They separated antimony and arsenic from their sulphides, described the preparation of steel, the dyeing of cloth and leather, the use of manganese dioxide in glass manufacture, and the distillation of acetic acid from vinegar. Yet somehow they strangely continued to believe in the old Greek theory of the four basic elements in nature, that is, earth, air, water, and fire. That theory was first announced in the fifth century B.C. by Empedocles, and it was quoted with approval by Aristotle in the following century.

Al-Rāzī (865–925), the Latin Rhazes,* an Arabicized Muslim Persian physician, identified numerous substances and described new chemical and scientific processes known to Roger Bacon. Ibn Sīnā (980–1037), better known in the realm

* Abu Bakr Muḥammad ibn Zakariya al-Rāzī, better known for his monumental contributions to medical science, will be treated at greater length under Medicine.

of philosophy and theology, also wrote a memorable treatise on natural science in which he described the formation of mountains, stones, and minerals, and discussed the phenomena of earthquakes, wind, water, temperature, sedimentation, desiccation, and causes of solidification.

ASTRONOMY

Astronomical tradition is very ancient in the Near and Middle East, and the Arabs had their full share of it. During their peregrinations through the pathless desert they had to depend on the stars to direct them toward their destination. Their interest in the sky was maintained and even nurtured by the Caliphs, under whose rule we begin to hear of the establishment of several observatories. The Umaiyads started one in Damascus at an early date, and the Abbasids added a second in Bagdad. Caliph al-Ma'mūn equipped the new observatory at the Shammasiyah Gate of the Abbasid capital with every astronomical instrument of his time, affiliated it with his academy or "House of Wisdom," and entrusted its directorship to Sind ibn 'Ali, a converted Jew, and Yaḥya ibn Abi Manṣūr, both of great competence in astronomy during the first decades of the ninth century. The Abbasids further set up a third observatory at Jundishapur in Iran, a city hitherto known as a great center of learning especially in medical science. Nestorian scholars came there after the fifth century, following the closing of the historic school of Edessa by the Byzantines in their struggle for orthodoxy; and the Greeks subsequently found their way there when Justinian suppressed the School of Athens in 525. Jundishapur was favorably situated to become a focal point for Western influences and Hindu and Persian contacts.

In Egypt at the turn of the tenth century, Caliph al-Ḥākim instituted a fourth observatory on the Muquattam Hills just outside Cairo. Even after the downfall of the Caliphate and the seizure of Bagdad by the Mongols, Hulagu Khān was led by his superstitious belief in astrology to devote considerable attention to the foundation of the great Maragha observatory near Lake Urmia in Azerbaijan during the thirteenth century, which became known for its monumental instruments. The Il-Khān appointed his private astrologer, Nāṣir al-Dīn al-Ṭūsi (d. 1274), as its director and appended a good library to the observatory. Al-Ṭūsi was an astronomer of no mean stature. He compiled the "Il-Khanian Tables" ("Al-Zīj al-Ilkhāni"), dedicated to his master, and comprising Arabic, Persian, Greek, and Chinese chronologies. He also recorded the planetary movements from observation by means of his formidable instruments, which included a mural quadrant, armillary sphere, solstitial and equinoctial armils, and an alidade.* He compiled earlier observations by Greeks such as Hipparchos and Ptolemy, and by Arabs, who were legion in this field of study from the earliest times. The Mongols also sponsored another observatory at Samarqand, their capital. Both the Maragha and Samarqand observatories were short-lived, since they depended for support on the pleasure of ephemeral potentates.

It is evident that the study of astronomy on a scientific basis received its first really great impetus in the Arab period from al-Ma'mūn. Most scholars and philosophers of the age, in their quest for complete knowledge, tried their hand at all branches of science including astronomy, with varying degrees of accomplishment. Muslim worthies in astronomy are too numerous for a complete survey. But names such as those of al-Farghāni (c. 860), Abu Ma'shar (d. 886) of Balkh in Khurasan, al-Baṭṭāni (877–918), ibn Yūnus (d. 1009), al-Bīrūni (973–1048), al-Zarqali (1029–87), and al-Biṭrūji

* The Arabic "al-'iḍāda," defined in the *Encyclopaedia of Islam* (II, 445) as "the line of vision (diopter) marked on the reverse of the astrolabe, turning round the axis or pivot, with the aid of which various observations can be made, particularly the taking of the altitude of a star."

(d. c. 1204) are far too prominent to be overlooked even in a brief outline.

The "Astronomical Compendium" of al-Farghāni (Alfaraganus) was translated into Latin by Gerard of Cremona and "Johannes Hispalensis" before 1187, and was published at Nuremberg in 1537 by the famous Melanchthon of the German Reformation. Abu Ma'shar's treatise on astronomy was put into Latin by Adelard of Bath in collaboration with the same Johannes under the title of "De conjunctionibus et annorum revolutionibus." The astronomical tables of al-Baṭṭāni (Albategnius) superseded the Greek material and were widely diffused throughout medieval Europe. His work was continued by Abul-Wafā (940–98) some sixty years later, although the latter's reputation rested on his contributions to trigonometry, extensively used by Copernicus in his "Opus palatinum de triangulis." Al-Bīrūni, among other things, established the relativity of astronomical hypotheses. 'Ali ibn Yūnus, al-Ḥākim's astronomer royal, compiled his tables (al-Zīj) in the Muqattam observatory.

Further west at Toledo in Spain, Abū Isḥāq Ibrāhīm ibn Yaḥyā al-Zarqali (Arzachel) composed the "Tables of Toledo" from personal observation, determining planetary positions, and made a new astrolabe which King Alfonso the Wise used in his thirteenth-century delineation of longitudes. Copernicus benefited from this astrolabe treatise together with the work of Abū Isḥāq al-Biṭrūji * (Alpetragius), known in Latin under the title "De revolutionibus orbium coelestium." A Spanish Arab, al-Bitrūji, revived interest in some Aristotelian works on astronomy, physics, and meteorology which were the last to be rendered into Latin from Arabic.

The Arabs preserved the idea of the sphericity of the globe throughout the dark ages of Europe until it was brought out

* Nūr al-Dīn abū Isḥāq, author of "Kitāb al-Hay'ah," translated into Latin by Michael Scot in 1217 and into Hebrew in 1259. Cf. P. Hitti: *History of the Arabs,* London 1958, 572, n. 5.

in 1410 by Pierre d'Ailly in his map of the "Imago Mundi," used by Christopher Columbus with immense consequences. Aḥmad ibn Mājid, the fifteenth-century Arab mariner who showed Vasco da Gama the route to India, is credited with the transmission of the mariner's compass to European sailors, one of the revolutionary features of the dawn of modern history.

GEOGRAPHY

The geographical lore of the Arabs, unlike most of the other branches of the humanities, cannot be traced back to Greek influence. Though they were not unaware of the contributions of Ptolemy, Eratosthenes, and Strabo from classical antiquity, the Arabs depended for the regeneration of their general and local geography on their own travels and direct observations. Their voyages covered the map of the world of their time from the first Hijra century to the end of the Middle Ages. While al-Khuwārizmi (830) and Sulaiman, the merchant of Siraf (850), are known to have reached India and China respectively in the course of the Christian ninth century, ibn Baṭṭūṭa (c. 1353), in his mid-fourteenth-century peregrinations, travelled over North Africa, Egypt, Syria, the Byzantine Empire, Arabia, Persia, some central Asiatic territories, India, Ceylon, and the Maldives. Between al-Khuwārizmi and ibn Baṭṭūṭa, we have a whole galaxy of Arab travellers, geographers, cartographers, and compilers of gazetteers and immense geographical dictionaries. These are represented essentially in the contents of the *Bibliotheca Geographorum Arabicorum*.*

The "ḥajj" or pilgrimage to Mecca, an obligation binding on all the faithful who could undertake it, brought Muslims

* This is analyzed in Atiya: *Hist. and Bibl.*, Monumental Collections, section VII.

of the East and the West together in a holy pursuit and for the exchange of commerce and of ideas and information. Most travellers describing kingdoms (mamālik) or roads (masālik) began their itineraries with their faces toward Mecca. The earliest ninth-century descriptive writers were ibn Khurdādhbah (c. 870), al-Ya'qūbi (c. 890), ibn al-Faqīh (c. 903) and ibn Rusta (c. 910).

But the first real geography of the Islamic world appeared during the tenth century in the work of Abu Zayd al-Balkhi (d. 934) of the Samanid * court of Khurasan in Transoxonia, Though his work is lost, his school has been well represented in the other tenth-century geographies of al-Iṣṭakhri (c. 950), ibn Ḥauqal (c. 975), al-Maqdisi (c. 985) and al-Mas'ūdi (c. 956), in spite of the fact that the last two did not come under al-Balkhi's direct influence. Western Arab geographers and travellers began to emerge on the scene in the eleventh century. The Hispano-Arab al-Bakri (c. 1067) left a monumental work of which only a fragment on North Africa has been published.

It was al-Idrīsi who left his mark on the development of geographical literature both Eastern and Western. Born at Ceuta in 1100, he completed his studies at Cordova, and was subsequently invited by King Roger II (1101–54) of Sicily to his court at Palermo. The Norman monarch commissioned the Arab scholar to compile a comprehensive work on world geography. The result was one of the greatest achievements in medieval geographical writing and map-making. In his work, dedicated to the king and called after him "Roger's Book" ("Al-Kitāb al-Raujari"), al-Idrīsi divided the earth into seven climatic zones with ten parts to each zone. The seventy sections were illustrated by seventy sectional maps which could be construed together in one continuous unit representing the entire world. The whole accomplishment was un-

* Founded by Naṣr ibn Aḥmad (874–92), a great grandson of a Zoroastrian noble called Sāmān, who gave his name to that dynasty.

precedented and unparalleled in its magnitude, fullness, and precision. Unlike ibn Ḥauqal's map (c. 975) which is circular, al-Idrīsi's is an oblong rectangle with some similarity to the earlier Alexandrian pattern of Ptolemy. It is more explicit for the area of the Mediterranean, with which he had a better acquaintance.

Other Spaniards, such as ibn Jubayr (c. 1192), recorded their geographical impressions. Yāqūt (c. 1228) and al-Qazwīni (c. 1275) compiled their geographical dictionaries alphabetically from the vast Arabic geographical heritage at their disposal. It would seem, however, that the contribution of the Arabs in this field had no great influence on the development of geographical knowledge in Europe, which remained backward until the Renaissance.

Nevertheless, the Arab impact on the opening of the trade routes between Europe and Asia enlivened the progress of international commerce with immeasurable consequences in world history. As mentioned above, the Arabs had known Cathay in the ninth century, when the Nestorian Christian missionary as well as the Muslim merchant and preacher penetrated the Far East about four hundred years before the first Europeans could find their way to China in the later Middle Ages.

MEDICINE

The Arabs were great pioneers in the field of medicine and their contribution to its progress staggers the imagination. The interest of the early Caliphs, notably Hārūn al-Rashīd and his son al-Ma'mūn, was displayed in the orders issued for the translation of the classical medical works of the Greek physicians. In the meantime, we hear of the existence of hospitals where medical men made clinical observations while treating their patients. It is said that by 850 A.D. thirty-four hospitals were in existence in the Arab world, some of which were heavily endowed by the Caliphs. In 978 the hospital (bīmāristān) of Damascus housed twenty-four resident practitioners. Mention is made of separate hospitals for women and of regular dispensaries for prescriptions.

Attached to the hospitals, there arose schools of medicine where training in clinical treatment of all kinds of diseases were offered, as well as surgical practice. Students attended lectures and retired to the rich medical libraries for recapitulation. Examinations were held and diplomas ('ijāzah) were granted to those who were allowed to practice the medical profession. Physicians were highly respected at court and in society, and some of them were able to amass enormous fortunes. The Nestorian physician Jibrīl ibn Bakhtīshū (d. c. 830) is said to have accumulated 88,800,000 dirhems * in the reign of the Abbasid al-Ma'mūn. It is very possible that, later in the course of the Crusades, the Europeans learned more about the "bīmāristāns" of the East and that the Orders of the Hospitallers and Templars, dedicated to hospital service on the Crusading battlefields, were based on older Arab models.

The golden age of Arab medicine was marked by the career of Abu Bakr Muḥammad ibn Zakariya al-Rāzi (865–925), the Latin Rhazes, an Arabicized Muslim Persian from al-Rayy near Tehran, who became acquainted with Greek, Persian, and Indian medicine, studied alchemy and science, and ultimately became one of the most prolific writers of the age, completing no less than 200 books, half of which dealt with medicine. One of his most famous original contributions is his treatise on smallpox and measles, where he provides an accurate diagnosis of both diseases and warns against their contagion. He appears to have prescribed a form of vaccination for treatment. This treatise was rendered into Latin at an early date and was put into other languages with many edi-

* The equivalent of approximately $7,104,000 in modern funds.

tions after the invention of printing. His greater work on general clinical medicine, in twenty volumes, the Arabic "Al-Ḥāwi" or "Comprehensive Book," was translated into Latin by Gerard of Cremona and remained the standard text in European medical colleges until the seventeenth century. Rhazes makes systematic reference to Greek, Syriac, Persian, Indian, and Arabic medical writers, then presents his own observations and opinions. His erudition was colossal and his insight was profound.

Al-Rāzi's greatest successor in the field of medicine was the philosopher and physician ibn Sīnā (Avicenna, 980–1037), a native of Bukhara who became attached to the court of the Samanid sultan Nūḥ ibn Manṣūr. He was a voracious reader and a prolific writer. His list of known works includes ninety-nine items on medicine, astronomy, geometry, philosophy, theology, and philology. He assimilated the fruit of both the Greek and Arabic universal and medical scholarship in two works of reference: "Kitāb al-Shifā" (Book of Healing) and "al-Qānūn fī al-Ṭibb" (Canon in Medicine). Both are monumental in size and importance. The first, in eighteen volumes, is a veritable encyclopedia comprising all the knowledge necessary for "healing the spirit," from the exact sciences to the humanities, and even economics and music. The "Canon in Medicine," which was translated into Latin by Gerard of Cremona in the twelfth century, consisted of no less than a million words and superseded all previous works on medicine, al-Rāzi's included. A comprehensive encyclopedia of the medical profession, it embodied the fullest exposition of anatomy, physiology, pathology, hygiene, therapeutics, and pharmacology of the day. His listed drugs number at least 760, and his pharmacopoeia remained the standard authority until the dawn of experimental science in modern history. He described pleurisy and tuberculosis, showing the latter to be contagious. He explained the way in which certain diseases might be transmitted by contamination through soil or water.

Arab physicians warned against spread of the plague through contact with infected clothing and food utensils. They diagnosed stomach cancer, prescribed antidotes for cases of poisoning, used cauterization, and treated eye diseases. They practised anesthesia by inhalation and prescribed soporific drugs to be taken by mouth, conducive to profound sleep or stupor, in preparation for the performance of surgical operations. They performed the earliest Caesarian section in the Middle Ages and used animal gut for sutures. The name of Abul Qāsim al-Zahrāwi of Cordova, the caliphal physician of Abd-al-Raḥmān III (912–61), was known in Latin medical literature as Abulcasis. He was recognized as a miracle of his age in surgery, and his book entitled "Al-Taṣrīf" was an authoritative work of reference on surgery, the finest of the kind in the field for centuries.

In ophthalmology, perhaps the most reputable Arab oculist was ʻAli ibn ʻIsa, the Jesu Haly of Latin literature, presumably a Christian from Bagdad in the first decades of the twelfth century. His work, "Tadhkirat al-Kaḥḥālīn" (Memorandum for the Oculists), was used in medieval Europe from an early date. There is hardly any doubt that, on the whole, the Arabs produced the most astute physicians of the medieval world in both East and West.

ART AND ARCHITECTURE

In keeping with the policy laid down by the Muslims from the earliest times, the Arabs did not seek to obliterate already existing civilizations. On the contrary, they aspired to become part of the new amalgam. Their synthetic influence, together with such modifications as befitted the tenets of the new religion, produced in the end a composite style of art and architecture which became identified as Islamic. They availed themselves of the forms, materials, and technical resources of the varied countries under their sway; and they employed

Syrian, Armenian, Egyptian, Byzantine, Iranian, and Indian architects and artists, irrespective of religious differences, in the accomplishment of what by right of conquest they could have done alone. The result was a staggering achievement in the rise of magnificent cities, palaces, citadels, mosques, mausolea, bridges, aqueducts, and all manner of works of art and technology spreading out from Spain to India, and paradoxically bearing the marks of unity and diversity at one and the same time. The cities of Bagdad, Samarra (the Arabic Surra man Ra'ā, that is, "pleasing to him who gazes on it"), and Fustat (i.e., Pavilion); the innumerable palaces and buildings from the Alhambra in Andalusia to the Taj Mahal in India; and the hundreds of mosques throughout the empire from the Blue Mosque in Cordova to the mosque of Sīdi 'Uqba in Qairawan, the Great Mosque of Tunis, the mosques of ibn Ṭūlūn and al-Azhar in Cairo, the Dome of the Rock in Jerusalem, the Umaiyad mosque at Damascus, the Great Mosques of Mecca and Medina, and the mosques of Bagdad, Samarra, Meshhed, Shiraz, Nishapur, and elsewhere—all emerged as works of great beauty, united by characteristics of Islamic distinction, yet each displaying a splendid magnificence of its own and representing the fountainhead of the native art from which it derived its attractive personality.

Islamic artists and architects were prone to observe certain criteria from the outset. Foremost among these was the adamant objection of Islam to complete human and animal representations in sculpture and painting, which were generally disparaged by religious doctrine and the Prophet's disapproval. On the one hand, these were held to be vestiges of ancient heathen idolatry; and on the other, good Muslims considered such works blasphemous since they were attempts by man to make himself a peer of the Almighty, the Creator of living beings. This prohibition, however, was not always maintained by the Caliphs, especially in the decoration of their palatial abodes, where paintings and mosaics of hunting scenes, bathing girls, and other themes of great archaeological interest can be seen in the remains. The Fatimid dynasty (909–1171) in Egypt, except in religious architecture, almost completely disregarded this rule. Islamic decorative art, however, found an outlet in non-representational forms of a geometrical character of floral and plant motifs, with the most felicitous results, now known as arabesque style. This appears in all manner of structures from stone mouldings to manuscript ornamentation, often enriched by the decorative Arabic script, Kufic and non-Kufic, which lent itself harmoniously to that motif.

It is beyond the limitations of this short essay to delve into the details of Islamic architecture, which are intricate and lengthy. What matters here is to survey the salient features which in some way or other influenced Western art and architecture. We have referred to the impact of Eastern military architecture on the evolution of the Western castle when we reviewed the results of the Crusade—notably the concentric systems and such new features as machicolation, crooked entrances, and the keep. It might be added here that the pointed arch, which became a distinctive feature of Gothic architecture in medieval Europe, had been known to Egyptian architects for centuries. It had furnished the pattern of the arcades of the ancient mosque of ibn Ṭūlūn, begun in Cairo in the year 876. Then it recurred in 970 in the al-Azhar Mosque and University, built under the sponsorship of the Fatimid Caliphate.

Traceried windows and towers, multifoil or cusped arches and doorways, ribbed vaulting, friezes of arabesque decorative motifs, and church campaniles strewn all over the cities of medieval Europe have their ancestral parallels in the mosques, citadels, colleges (madrassahs), hospitals (bīmāristāns), mausolea, and minarets of a much earlier age in the Islamic countries of the Eastern and Western Mediterranean. The glory of Muslim art found vent in stone moulding and reliefs, certainly accomplished in the main by the Christian sculptors of Syria, worthy sons of the generations that produced the miracle of Ba'albek in Roman times, St. Simeon's monastic settlement, and the "Dead Cities" of northern Syria in the early centuries of our era. It is impossible to quote all the instances of excellent friezes and decorative reliefs which abound in Muslim medieval structures. One of the earliest artistic miracles of stone carving has survived in a wall fragment of a palace built by the Umaiyad Caliph al-Walīd about 743 in the Syrian desert, an unfinished royal winter resort (mshatta or mashta) containing some of the most exquisite arabesques in existence. The whole structure was discovered by German archaeologists, who deemed it worthy of being transferred piece by piece to be reconstructed in the Berlin Museum in 1904. The wall representations of winding vine branches, of fruits, flowers, birds, animals, mythical griffins, rosettes, triangles, and friezes of geometrical designs formed an ensemble of sculptured relief which was comparable to the daintiest lace work.

In the realm of the minor arts, Arab civilization proved to be a wonderful bridge between the excellence of workmanship in antiquity and the accomplishments of the medieval artisan. Spain, Sicily, and Palestine provided three points of contact between the craftsmen of Europe and the Arab Empire. In fact, the countries of the Near and Middle East had attained a very high level of perfection in the minor arts at the time of Arab expansion. The Arabs treasured and nurtured this legacy in the East, while Europe was sliding into comparative backwardness. In the Middle Ages, the marts of Cairo, Damascus, and Bagdad overflowed with objects of art of all description. Jewelry, gold and silver work with repoussé and inlay, ceramics with and without metallic luster, colored glazes, fine pottery, all sorts of vases, glasswork, rock crystal, embossed leather craft, embroidered and woven monochrome and polychrome textiles—these and many more art objects were continuously on display at the Oriental bazaars. They proved to be the vehicles by which the arts were transmitted to Europe in the course of the later Middle Ages.

Still more important was the transplantation of the art of paper making. The invention of paper, which replaced parchment and papyrus, marked a milestone as a civilizing factor. Its introduction in the Middle East can be traced back to 712, year of the Arab invasion of Samarqand, where linen was beaten into a paste and spread out in the form of rag writing paper. The establishment of the first paper factory then took place at Bagdad in 794. Egypt followed suit before 900, and paper appeared in Morocco in 1100, spreading from there to Spain and Sicily. In Europe, however, the use of paper was not general until the Crusaders returned from the East in the later Middle Ages with the exact technique of its manufacture.

The production of glass by the commune of Venice found its inception in a contract dated June 1, 1277 between Bohemond IV, prince of Antioch, and the doge, Contarini, whereby the secret and techniques of the industry brought from Syria were sold to Venice. The work began under the supervision of Saracen artisans with materials imported from the Holy Land, and the glass monopoly was preserved by Venice until the seventeenth century, when its secret was divulged to France through the intermediary of Colbert. Palermo in Sicily, owing to its direct relations with the Arabs, had manufactured glass and even made mirrors as early as the twelfth century. But the crystal industry seems to have been the monopoly of Cordova, where a Moor, ibn Fīnās, was able to perfect the process of its manufacture during the last decades of the ninth century. In the Middle East, only rock crystal was used, and the Fatimid Caliphs possessed a thousand vases of this precious material, such as the tenth-century ewer in the treasury of St. Mark's in Venice, a miracle of workmanship. Rock crystal reliquaries can still be seen in many cathedrals in Europe, and they must have been brought by the Crusaders and medieval pilgrims from the East. The ceramic industry, so elaborate in Persia, Syria, and Egypt, was introduced by the Eastern Muslim potters into Italy and France, probably in the course of the twelfth century.

The weaving of fabrics by Eastern looms was one of those achievements which bewildered the Western imagination. The Copts in Egypt were able to produce some of the finest linen material ever known before the advent of the Arabs. The textile exports from the Eastern emporia to Europe continued to flourish throughout the Middle Ages. Specimens of medieval royal robes and episcopal vestments with embroidered Arabic inscriptions can still be found in museums and the vestiaries of medieval cathedrals. Again, it was Roger II of Sicily who copied the Eastern "ṭirāz" factories by setting up a palace workshop at Palermo for the weaving of embroidered robes of honor, which he presented to the potentates of Europe.

The art of leather work and fine embossed leather binding, long known in the East, made its first appearance in the West during the fourteenth century on a very limited scale, and spread more widely in the fifteenth century. Copper work with gold and silver inlay and enamel, wood carving, and numerous other artistic achievements were copied from the Eastern artisan. The influence of the Arabic motif penetrated even medieval and Renaissance iconography, where Arabic Kufic lettering decorated the borders of robes in many religious paintings, for example the central scene in Fra Lippo Lippi's "Coronation of the Virgin."

PHILOLOGY

Word building and the exchange of terms between two languages can indicate a great deal of history, for culture undoubtedly lies behind the spoken word. Arabic has left its impression on Western languages in many fields in which the contribution of the Arabs were felt. Although a fair amount of work has been done to indicate the degree of infiltration of Arab terminology, the opportunity still presents itself for further inquiries into this interesting field. Perhaps the only contribution of any real magnitude in the area of the Romance languages is the formidable list compiled by Professor Arnold Steiger of the University of Zurich in Switzerland. Similar volumes are equally needed for other Western languages, although we have to assume that they will necessarily be less voluminous as we move further away from the Arab world. A variety of short word lists occurs in the *Legacy of Islam;** though inadequate, it is representative.

For purposes of illustration, we have compiled a selection of words to indicate the extent, nature, and variety of Arabic words which have made their influence felt on the English language. The fields of astronomy, science, music, maritime life, textiles, colors, vegetables and fruits, flowers, commerce, and place names could each be documented at length; but a few examples must suffice. The Arab impression on astronomy is particularly great.

algebra (al-jabr)
alchemy and chemistry (al-kimiā')
almanac (al-manākh)
zero or cypher (ṣifr)
jar (jarrah)
monsoon (mausim)
amber ('anbar)
guitar (qūthāra)
tambourine (ṭambour, ṭablah)
admiral (amīr al-baḥr)
cotton (quṭn)
lemon (līmūn)
sugar (sukkar)
syrup and sherbert (sharbāt)
coffee (qahwah)
jasmine (yasmīne)
traffic (tafrīq)
tariff (tar'īf)
check (ṣakk)
Trafalgar (ṭaraf al-ghār, i.e., cape of the cave or of the laurels)

* Edited by T. Arnold and A. Guillaume, Oxford 1952.

arsenal (dār al-Sinā'a)
damask, from Damascus (Dimashq)
Algeciras (al-jazīra, i.e., the island)

Hundreds of place names in both Spanish and Portuguese can be traced to Arabic origins and are too numerous to be presented here. Common words in the spoken language, too, may be found in Spanish, such as "adobi" from "ṭūb" or brick, now adopted in America to signify the unburnt brick from the days of the early Spanish settlers. Some other examples are:

alfiate (al-khayyāt, tailor)
safara (saḥra, desert or waste place)
almacen (al-makhzan, warehouse)
almahada (al-makhadda, pillow)
alcalde (al-qādi, judge or mayor)
alcoba (al-qubba, dome, meaning bedroom)
mosque (masjid)
mangonel (manganīq)
chess (shaṭarang, from Persian via Arabic)
el Cid (al-sayyid, sir)
alfandega (al-funduq, hostel or custom-house)
alfaca (al-khass, lettuce)
alacena (al-khizāna, depot or safe)
fulano (fulān, somebody)
hasta (hatta, until)
camel (jamal)
gazelle (ghazāl)
minaret (manāra)
mattress (maṭraḥ, place or locale)
divan (diwān, Persian devan, Italian dogana, French douane)
usted ('ustādh, master)

LITERATURE

We have seen that the impact of Arab thought and culture on the progress of European civilization was by no means slight, especially in the fields of philosophy, theology, science, and medicine. There is, however, another area with which we have not dealt and which came into existence only after the outbreak of the Crusades. The whole range of the "Chanson" literary output, from the "Chanson de Roland," depicting Charlemagne's Spanish adventure (eighth century), to the "Chanson des Chétifs" (1130) and the "Chanson d'Antioche" (1180) emerged as literary saga rather than history, and it was these that Tasso used in the composition of his heroic epic, "Gerusalemme Liberata," in the sixteenth century. In this manner, we see how Charlemagne and King Arthur in the "Morte d'Arthur" became Crusaders. The songs of the troubadours in Spain, of the Provençal poets in Southern France, and of the minnesingers in Germany bear signs of Arab influence. The old French romance "Floire et Blanchefleur," with its Oriental setting, and the parallel tale of "Aucassin et Nicolette" draw somewhat from the Hispano-Arabic tale of Abul-Qāsim.

How far Arab rhymed lyrical verse affected European poetry and vice versa, is the subject of a special study still to be made. But there is no doubt that in Spain and Sicily some interaction must have taken place independently of the Crusades. In fact, two literary streams from Arab sources left their impression on Western romance in medieval and modern times. The "Arabian Nights," known in Arabic as the "Thousand and One Nights" ("Alf Laila wa-Laila"), are said to have given rise to some of Chaucer's *Tales* and parts of Boccacio's *Decameron;* though it remains to find the channels through which they reached Europe at those early dates. In recent years, *Robinson Crusoe* and *Gulliver's Travels* were conceived from episodes in the same work. Moreover, the influence of the Crusades also continued from the Middle Ages to modern times and gave birth to no small part of the historical poetry and fiction of Milton and Sir Walter Scott, to be followed by a multitude of still more recent historical novels of varying value.

The new theory which gave rise to a vast polemic over the

extent of the infiltration of Arab thought and even legend in Western letters was formulated by the great Spanish Arabist and Christian theologian, Miguel Asin Palacios, in his work *La Escatología Musulmana en la Divina Commedia,* first published in 1919 and rendered into an abridged English version in 1926. Asin Palacios' life was mainly devoted to the study of Arabic philology and culture, and his immense erudition in the field of medieval scholasticism and theology enabled him to speak with great authority on the influence of Averroes (ibn Rushd) on St. Thomas Aquinas. He further clarified the debt of a great Catalonian philosopher, Raymond Lull, to the writings of a Spanish Muslim mystic, ibn 'Arabi (1165–1240), and he demonstrated beyond doubt the effects of the work of the "Brothers of Sincerity" (Ikhwān al-Ṣafā) of Abbasid fame on Anselmo de Turmeda's thought.

But Asin Palacios' daring argument about the Islamic origins of Dante's *La Divina Commedia* came as a much greater shock than anything he had written in the past. The immortal philosopher-poet of the Rennaissance, hitherto considered by critics and historians to have been an Aristotelian and a Thomist, appeared to Asin Palacios to have been under more remote influences. The ascension of Dante and Beatrice to the spheres of Paradise, he concluded, had its counterfoil in the ancient Arabic legend of the ascension of the Prophet Muḥammad with the Archangel Gabriel to heaven, a legend elaborated in the thirteenth century by the aforementioned Hispano-Arabian mystic, ibn 'Arabi of Murcia, who happened to die only twenty-five years before the birth of the great Florentine poet. The origins of the story go back to the days of early Islam, and its elements became embedded in the works of Muslim theology under two headings representing two cycles: first, the "Isrā'," or the miraculous nocturnal journey of the Prophet to Jerusalem; and second, the "Mi'rāj," or ascension of Muḥammad from the holy city of Jerusalem to the throne of Allah.

The originality of Dante's creative genius remained uncontested as long as scholars found nothing in Christian literature which might have had an impact on his thesis. Then the discovery of a prototype in Arabic literature by Asin Palacios came as a revelation and called for a revision of the sources which must have inspired the prince of poets of the Renaissance. The new inquiry into the parallelism of the "Divine Comedy" and the Muslim legend yielded striking results. It became obvious that Dante owed a share of the very texture of his immortal poem to Islamic mysticism, legend, and letters.*

EDUCATION

This great array of achievements in the world of scholarship among the medieval Arabs was not a mere game of chance. It implied prolonged intellectual labor, a genuine interest in culture by the rulers and the ruled, and the existence of a highly developed system of public education, with extensive library services and resources. Mention has been made of the "House of Wisdom" in Bagdad, and its counterfoil, the "Abode of Science," in Cairo; but these were academies of learning rather than regular schools, and it may be assumed that they performed the function of postgraduate institutions. They were the medieval equivalents of the Institute for Advanced Study at Princeton and Dumbarton Oaks in Washington in our time. They were, above all other considerations, intended for the promotion of research and the advancement of learning.

The first real center for public education in the technical sense of the word was apparently the mosque-university of al-Azhar, originally created under Fatimid auspices in 970 as an instrument for the propagation and defense of Shī'ite theology,

* See Appendix: Dante's Sources and Muslim Legend.

though eventually it survived as the stronghold of orthodoxy. After the extermination of Fatimid rule from Egypt in 1171, Saladin and his Aiyubid successors immediately turned it into a Sunnite college under their full patronage. Subsequent dynasties and sultans held it in great esteem and enriched it with considerable endowments (waqfs). One of its greatest benefactors was the Burji Mamluk sultan, Qaitbay (1468–95), who made extensive additions to its buildings. It became the symbol of Islamic spiritual leadership and religious education; and the sanctity of the whole establishment was universally accepted by all Muslims, many of whom sought refuge within its precincts. The comprehensive history of that great Islamic institution with its vast documentary evidence, published and unpublished, remains to be done.* The role it played as a beacon of Muslim learning in the Middle Ages should not be eclipsed by the present critical mood toward its antiquated system. The long and checkered life of the oldest medieval university in existence passed through a period of frustration under Turkish rule. The period extending from Selim I's conquest of Egypt in 1517 to the French Expedition of 1798 was the darkest in Egyptian history, and the rude awakening which followed the first contacts with Europe in the nineteenth century was partly associated with al-Azhar and its faculty of 'ulemas (professors).

Throughout the Middle Ages, however, al-Azhar was frequented by thousands of students from every corner of the Islamic world. Of the students who resided within the mosque, each group lived and learned together under the "riwāq" system,** so similar to the organization of the student body into

* A fine short account has recently been published by Bayard Dodge: *Al-Azhar—A Millenium of Muslim Learning*, Princeton, N.J., 1961. The sources of al-Azhar history in print are still meager, however, and this is the first step toward a fully documented account of an ancient institution.

** Riwāq or ḥārat means loggia or emplacement allotted to a group of scholars of the same place of origin.

"nations" in the medieval European university. Students from the outside were also admitted, and they lived in the neighborhood of the mosque. Unlike the "five nations" in the University of Paris, al-Azhar is known to have comprised twenty-six riwāqs or loggias, each associated with a geographical unit, and each occupying a given space in an alley between a fixed number of the 375 pillars of the great mosque.

Both professors and students were supported by voluntary contributions. Every professor became identified with a pillar at which he squatted, and the students gathered around him in a circle where they studied the "transmitted knowledge" ('ulūm naqliyah), that is, theology, jurisprudence, tradition, and mysticism; or the "rational sciences" ('ulūm 'aqliyah), that is, philology, meter, rhetoric, logic, and astronomy. Other studies included belles-lettres, history, geography, physical science, mathematics, and other branches of the humanities. On the whole, teaching at al-Azhar was rather a way for the transmission of the wisdom of earlier generations than an attempt to conduct research in novel fields. It was arduous and the lecture went on for hours depending on the pleasure of the professor, who wandered freely from one sphere of learning to another without control. Memory work was essential and it was begun by learning the whole text of the Qur'ān by heart. That system, which produced many famous names, became petrified in the long run, together with the core of Islamic culture as a whole.*

Other schools multiplied in the Islamic world with the passing decades. It would be difficult to provide any accurate or even semi-accurate census of those educational foundations.

* An attempt is at present being made by the United Arab Republic to modernize al-Azhar and turn it into a regular university with all the traditional colleges or faculties (medicine, engineering, science, arts, etc.) rather than an institution for the study of Islamic theology and Arabic language and letters. This revolution in the constitution of al-Azhar is still in progress and it is difficult as yet to assess its extent and impact.

We find references in the contemporary sources to innumerable institutions of varying caliber, not only in the greater cities, but also in very obscure villages. From medieval Arab travellers and writers, such as ibn Jubayr in the twelfth century, ibn Baṭṭūṭa in the fourteenth, and al-Maqrīzi in the fifteenth, it may be deduced that at least 74 colleges were in existence in Cairo, 73 in Damascus, 41 in Jerusalem, 40 in Bagdad, 14 in Aleppo, 13 at Tripoli in Syria, 9 at Moṣul, and a great many in Alexandria.* But these were by no means exclusive. Arab Spain teemed with schools and teachers, and illiteracy was almost non-existent under the Western Caliphate, if not in the East, which had its rather special circumstances.

As time went on, the fashion grew among the leading people of wealth in most countries of the Arab commonwealth of nations to found schools (madrassahs) and mosques (jāmi'ṣ or masjids, i.e., places of kneeling or worship) bearing the names of the founders. As a rule, schools were generally but not exclusively created within the mosques. In Islam, the mosque had a much wider usage than the church in Christendom. It was the place of worship, a political and social center, the seat of state and civil administration in the early history of the Islamic Empire, a court of justice, and, moreover, an educational institution. The very origin of the word university (jāmi'a) in Arabic is the mosque (jāmi'). In some cases, the school (madrassah) was appended to a mausoleum or to a Muslim monastery (ribāṭ or khāniqāh). A Persian traveller, Nāṣiri Khusru, provides an interesting picture of the old mosque of 'Amru in old Cairo or Fustat, and states that it was frequented daily by 5,000 persons including a considerable percentage of students and professors, who held open classes within its walls.

* The traveller ibn Jubayr quotes a curious estimate of the mosques and "ribāṭs" of Alexandria in the twelfth century—between eight and twelve thousand. Cf. Khalil A. Totah: *The Contributions of the Arabs to Education*, N.Y. 1926, 31.

Higher education, however, was mainly centralized in Cairo and Bagdad. The University of al-Azhar found two great rivals in the Niẓāmiyah and the Mustanṣiriyah schools in Bagdad. The first was founded in 1050 by Niẓām al-Mulk, the famous wazir of the Saljuq sultan Alp Arslan, and the intimate friend of the Persian mathematician and poet 'Umar al-Khaiyām. Al-Ghazzāli (Algazel), the great Arab philosopher, lectured there from 1091 to 1095. The enlightened wazir was a staunch believer in education, and he created other smaller colleges bearing the same name as the Niẓāmiyah—at Nisabur, Balkh, Herat, Isfahan, Marw, Basrah, and Mosul. An estimate is given of the annual expenditure on all these institutions as the equivalent of one and a half million dollars. Apart from granting comfortable stipends to professors, the wazir gave the students special allowances (ma'ālim). The Niẓāmiyah of Bagdad continued to function until the later decades of the fourteenth century, when it was merged with the Mustanṣiriyah after the second Mongol invasion of the city by Timurlane in 1393.

The Mustanṣiriyah was founded by the Abbasid Caliph al-Mustanṣir in 1234. Originally it was meant to be a theological seminary and a school of Islamic law (sharī'ah) for the four Sunnite or orthodox sects, with a professor at the head of each department of seventy-five scholars. As in the Niẓāmiyah, both master and pupil received an adequate stipend, daily food, and free writing utensils and material. It was a kind of boarding school furnished with dormitories, kitchen, a cistern for cooling the drinking water, a bath (ḥammām), and a hospital (bīmāristān) with a physician on duty for attending the sick. A clock, probably of the clepsydra type, stood in the great hall for announcing the hours of prayer. Lamps and oil were provided to the students who frequented the library quarters and studied through the night. The school survived the devastations of the Mongol Hulagu when he seized Bagdad in 1258, and of Timurlane in 1393, until it merged with the Niẓāmiyah. Both schools were housed in buildings of singular beauty, and Caliph al-Mustanṣir caused a private garden to be laid out with a belvedere (manẓarah) overlooking the college for his own use, as he was accustomed to spend some time there sitting at a veiled window to watch the scholars' activities and attend lectures unnoticed.

Appended to every school or institution was a reference library, enriched by manuscript donations and acquisitions. Furthermore, scholars spent a great deal of time copying books, which ultimately found their way to school or mosque libraries. The rapid growth and spread of libraries in practically every city of the Islamic world was made possible by the introduction of paper from China to the Middle East in the course of the eighth century. Paper mills were established at Samarqand, Bagdad, Tripoli in Syria, and many other centers in Egypt and Andalusia to cope with the increasing demand for paper by scribes. Tremendous accumulations of manuscripts filled the palace libraries of the Caliphs as well as all the famous learned institutions. Most large libraries had their own binderies for the restoration and mending of the codices.

It is difficult to give any accurate estimate of the contents of any of these reference libraries beyond the statement that they were beyond inventory. Only occasionally do we find concrete numbers. The Maragha observatory library housed 400,000 manuscripts. When the Mustanṣiriyah was founded, the Caliph started its reference library with an initial donation of 160 camel loads of books. Saladin is said to have destroyed two million books of Shi'ite origin or influence from the palaces of the Fatimid Caliphs. This, however, appears to be an exaggeration, though the most conservative estimate of 120,000 is equally inacceptable. Even in some of the smallest towns, we often hear of the existence of surprisingly large libraries. Al-Rayy, a relatively obscure village town in Upper Iran, not far from the Caspian Sea (Baḥr al-Khazar), had a library which contained 400 camel loads of manuscripts with a catalogue in ten volumes. At the storming of Bagdad by Hulagu Khān in 1258, his Mongol hordes cast into the Tigris river such incalculable quantities of manuscripts that a kind of solid bridge was formed over which both pedestrian and horseman, it was contended by contemporaries, could safely cross from one bank to another. The water of the river changed in color as a result of the dissolution of the manuscript ink in the current. Even with so much ruination and vandalism, and if we allow for considerable exaggeration, much has actually survived of a brilliant civilization which we have been able to comprehend only in part.

Epilogue

THE STORY OF RELATIONS between the Middle East and the West has been long and tortuous; many of its chapters have told of violence, some of peaceful and wholesome contributions to the progressive march of mankind. A tremendous drama, beginning in remote antiquity, has unrolled with increasing vigor throughout the medieval and modern periods of history. Although the central action has shifted over the centuries, and the causes of dispute have changed in outward appearance, the fundamentals betray unmistakable signs of continuity. The racial and cultural clash between ancient Greece and Persia, the hegemony of Roman imperialism over the whole of East and West, the rise of the Islamic Caliphate and its expansion around the Mediterranean, the Crusading thrust from Europe into the Muslim East, the Counter-Crusade, and the Turkish sultanate with its Pan-Islamic predispositions are all chapters which lead to the threshold of modern history. As we reach the nineteenth century, we turn a new leaf in this unfinished story and enter a period of new implications for the crucial areas of the Near and Middle East.

Ottoman ascendancy over Eastern Europe, Western Asia, and

Mamluk Egypt at the close of the Middle Ages and the dawn of modern history ushered in a period of darkness for most of the subjugated provinces. The Turkish Counter-Crusade, launched in the first instance against European Christians, soon was destined to be an unremitting war of conquest of Muslim territories in the sixteenth century; and the Arab world sank into servitude under the Ottoman yoke. Bagdad and Cairo, which had been seats of a superior civilization and culture, began to lose their ancient glamor and ultimately fell into complete decay. The deflection of Eastern trade from the marts of Egypt and Syria led to the impoverishment of these hitherto affluent countries. Ignorance, disease, and poverty prevailed; and the way of progress was blocked by misgovernment and disregard of human rights. For centuries the natives of the Middle East grew more and more forgetful of the glory of their forebears and stagnated into political lethargy.

Then came a rude awakening with the advent of the short-lived French Expedition of 1798 * to Egypt. Suddenly an isolated people found themselves confronted by new influences from the civilized West; while Europe became conscious of the opportunites offered by the countries of the Middle East. With the establishment of French dominion over Egypt, Napoleon Bonaparte envisioned possibilities of wresting both India and the Eastern trade from the hands of the English. In those days Turkey was represented as a dying old man, and the European Powers were incessantly engaged in contention about the division of the Turkish Empire. In the tumult of their arguing, and especially in the tug of war between England and France, we witness the birth of modern colonialism and imperialism, with immeasurable consequences on East-West relations.

* The French withdrew from Egypt in 1801 after their contingents became isolated as a result of a decisive naval defeat by the English fleet at Canopus, the modern Abu Qir.

This opens up a new and unfinished chapter in the area of contemporary history, which is essentially foreign to the theme of the present work. Nevertheless, it is not unfitting to try to present the modern reader with a brief enumeration of the prominent phases wherein older movements became transmuted into new ones in our day.

Imperialistic colonialism was a logical if remote successor to the Crusade, just as nationalism was the natural counteraction to Western incursions. Though parallelism in history is never complete in its minute details, there is sufficient evidence to prove that violence usually begets violence. Just as the Crusade from Western Europe precipitated the Counter-Crusade from the Islamic East, so modern colonialism has given rise to nationalism in the same areas. In Egypt this is clearly exemplified by the revolutionary upheavals of 1864, 1919, and 1952.

Outside Egypt, the Arab Revolt of 1916 originated in support of the Allies during the First World War, in the hope of attaining independence from the Turks, but only led to the paradox of a mandatory regime whereby England and France attempted to resuscitate the moribund cause of colonialism in another form. Once again extensive territories of the Arab Middle East were subdivided into zones of influence between two great colonialist powers under the aegis of the League of Nations. This unnatural system was foredoomed; it gave way to the rise of a series of new states. Amid the ensuing confusion, the emergence of the state of Israel in 1948 and the Suez warfare of 1956 must be viewed against the background of relations between the Middle East, seeking dignity and self-realization, and the West, where England and France searched for ways and means of arresting the steady awakening of a menacing giant.

The complicated problems of the relations of East and West assume a new complexion in our lifetime, reflecting the rival ideologies of Communism and Democracy, occasionally referred to by onlookers in the depressed areas as the new imperialisms. We begin to perceive treaty formations of a most formidable character. While the Communist camp behind the Iron Curtain has engulfed the whole of Eastern and East Central Europe, together with continental China, the democratic powers under the younger leadership of the United States have been trying to foil Russian maneuvers by such military alliances as NATO, the Bagdad Pact, and SEATO. Entrenched between these gigantic conglomerations, the uncommitted nations have tended to lean toward a fresh though not entirely new doctrine of positive neutralism. The pioneers of this movement have been India, Egypt, and Yugoslavia. Meanwhile Black Africa is a slowly awakening giant; its peoples, whose sympathies are now divided among the three existing power blocs, may in time introduce a new and powerful element in the shaping of international affairs.

At the same time one may perceive the birth of fresh forces making for regional alignments. Though incomplete, certain approaches in the interest of economic and even of political survival are perceptible among neighboring groups of nations. The Pan-American constellation is already well established. The short-lived merger of Egypt and Syria in the United Arab Republic, and the equally transitory Arab Federation of Iraq and Jordan, should be studied within the framework of the greater Arab bloc in the Arab League, aspiring strongly but as yet ineffectively toward Arab unity. In Europe a number of Western states have been constrained by the overwhelming superiority of their American ally, as well as by their redoubtable Soviet foe, to take certain steps toward a local bloc of their own. The notion of a European community, possibly including Great Britain, and designed to buttress the economic well-being of member states without impairing their individual sovereignty, is gradually taking shape. Some writers have advanced daring prospects of extending the economic alliance into the military and even the political sphere. Optimists have had the utopian dream of integrating Western sovereignties into a confederation or "United States of Europe," with a common parliament and a common executive, but this revolutionary step is not yet within sight.

A penetrating report submitted by Sir Oliver Franks,* former British ambassador to the United States, advances a novel and bold thesis: that the "East-West" problem is gradually being superseded by what he terms the "North-South" problem. The crucial confrontation in world affairs, as he sees it, is increasingly one of the rich industrialized nations of the North in relation to the underdeveloped nations of the South. In his opinion, the North-South problem is destined to be the decisive factor in the fate of East-West relations. The hope for a settlement of world difficulties hinges on the ability of the countries of Europe and North America to collaborate in raising the economic and democratic standards of life among the emerging peoples of Asia, Africa, and Latin America.

Amid all this, we witness a novel dimension of tremendous potential in the United Nations Organization, whose historic Character affirms human rights and dignity, justice, treaty obligations, international law, and collective maintenance of peace and security, thereby expressing today's hopes for tomorrow's peace, and a sense of world oneness if not unity.

In the world of tomorrow, the present must integrate with the past, and it is not likely that the identities of centuries will be lost. The vitality of the classic Greek plays has not diminished because modern stage production differs so much from that of the ancients. In similar fashion, although the stage is expanding and new dramatis personae are being

* Now chairman of Lloyds Bank in London, Franks left this memorandum in the hands of the former Secretary of State, Christian A. Herter, before he retired from diplomacy. This was reported in the *New York Times* of Tuesday, December 8, 1959.

added to the cast, the forces of Crusade and Counter-Crusade persist under other guises.

Persian, Greek, and Roman soldiers, warriors of Islam, Frankish knights, Ottoman conquerors, the soldiers of Bonaparte, and those of two world wars have all moved across the Mediterranean world, in turn succeeding and in turn subsiding beneath the counterthrusts of opponents. Today the arena has broadened, and the contestant powers are led by the U.S.S.R. and the U.S.A., both with devasting arms and ideologies. But the East of the Crusade and the Counter-Crusade still remains as a powerful factor in the assessment of world power or the sharing of any spoils.

APPENDIX

Dante's Sources and Muslim Legend

DANTE, the immortal philosopher-poet of the Renaissance, was long considered by scholars to have been an Aristotelian and a Thomist. Then, in Madrid in 1919, the Spanish Arabist and Christian theologian, Miguel Asin Palacios, published *La Escatología Musulmana en la Divina Commedia.** Asin Palacios questioned the originality of Dante's thesis and proceeded to demonstrate a striking parallelism between the "Divine Comedy" and Muslim legend, an agreement both in essentials of plan and in numerous particulars. Action, allegorical purpose, the concept of an astronomical architecture of heaven and the spheres, the didactic moral, and many literary devices were revealed to be almost identical in Dante and in Muslim legend.

The story was twice recounted in Arabic: first by the illustrious blind skeptic of the ninth and tenth centuries, Abul-'Alā' al-Ma'arri (973–1057), often described as the "philosopher of poets and the poet of philosophers." In his "Treatise on Pardon" ("Risālat al-Ghufrān") he skillfully and elo-

* An abridged English translation was rendered by H. Sunderland: *Islam and the Divine Comedy,* London 1926.

quently reviewed Muḥammad's celestial journey with a touch of irony, and he stressed the elements of God's great mercy as opposed to traditional moralist austerity. Nearly two centuries afterward, the story was retold in a totally different spirit and at much greater length by ibn 'Arabi, the illuministic (iṣhrāqi) mystic (ṣūfi), or psuedo-Empedoclean and Neo-Platonist pupil of the Cordoban school of ibn Masarrah (883–931). This he accomplished in two books, the one unpublished and the other published. "The Book of the Nocturnal Journey toward the Majesty of the Most Magnanimous" ("Kitāb al-Isrā ila Maqām al-Asra"), still in manuscript, must be read in conjunction with "The Book of the Meccan Conquests" ("Kitāb al-Futūḥāt al-Makkiyah"), which is in print.

The analogy of the episodes of both ibn 'Arabi and Dante may be elucidated by quoting some concrete examples. Throughout the two texts, both Muḥammad and Dante are made to narrate their eschatological experiences in the world beyond. Both begin the journey at night. In the Muslim version, a lion and a wolf bar the road to hell; and in Dante's poem, a leopard, a lion, and a she-wolf impede his progress. Khayṭūr, the patriarch of the genii addressing the Prophet, is replaced by Virgil, the patriarch of the classicists, who accompanied Dante. The warning of the approach to hell is the same in both writers—confused noises and bursts of flames. The architecture of the Inferno is the same in the two accounts—an inverted cone or funnel consisting of a series of levels for the various classes of sinners.

After passing the Mount of Purgatory, we find the Muslim and Christian heavens identical. Beatrice leaves Dante, and Gabriel leaves Muḥammad, as they approach the Divine Presence. The Muslim gigantic angel in the form of a cock suggests Dante's heavenly eagle. Dante beholds Saturn with a golden ladder leading to the last sphere, and Muḥammad ascends a ladder rising from Jerusalem to the highest heaven. The apotheosis in both ascensions is the same. Both describe the Beatific Vision as a focus of intense light surrounded by nine concentric circles of myriads of angelic spirits shedding wondrous radiance, with the cherubim in the center. The reactions of the two pilgrims to the great vision are alike. Both, dazzled by indescribable brilliance, believe that they have gone blind. Gradually they gather strength and are able to gaze steadfastly upon the miraculous spectacle, and then they fall into ecstasy.

The question now in need of an answer is how to tie together these two rather independent channels of thought, one Eastern and the other Western, the one in Arabic and the other in the Florentine vernacular. The problem is not as insoluble as it looks, thanks to Asin Palacios' research in the medieval Hispano-Arabic sources and in Christian theology. One document of the Mozaribic literature of the ninth century is worthy of close scrutiny. The Latin "Historia Arabum," by Archbishop Rodrigo Jiménez de Rada of Toledo, contains a life of Muḥammad in which the author incorporates the literal translation of the "Miʿrāj" legend from an authentic source of Islamic traditions (Ḥadīth). That account is almost identical with the text in the famous old work of al-Bukhāri, the first great Muslim jurisconsult (faqīh). The story thus recorded in the "Historia Arabum" passed to the "Crónica General" or "Estoria d'España," compiled between 1260 and 1268 by King Alfonso X the Wise, with minor additions from other original sources.

Later in the same century, another work entitled "Impunación de la seta de Mohomah" was written by St. Peter Paschal, bishop of Jaen and friar of the new Order of Mercy, during his captivity at Granada between 1297 and 1300, the year of his martyrdom at the hands of the Moors. His career shows that he was a man of high standing and profound learning. He was tutor of the heir to the throne of Aragon. While on a visit to Rome, he commanded Pope Nicholas IV's admiration as a theologian, and he lectured at the

University of Paris on his return journey. In his work he quotes the Qur'ān as well as "alhadiz," i.e., "al-Ḥadīth" or tradition, in connection with Muslim eschatology. The value of his quotations is enhanced by specific reference to a book called "Miragi," "Elmiregi," or "Elmerigi," which is doubtless the "Mi'rāj" or ascension of Muḥammad to heaven. He uses one of the elaborate cycles of the text, with striking resemblance to Dante's conception. He speaks not only of heaven and hell, but also of the "ṣirāṭ," which is a thin line or straight path constituting the bridge between hell and heaven on which the soul must balance during its passage. This is the Muslim equivalent of Dante's purgatory. By the end of the thirteenth century, the whole story was widely established in the literary circles of Spain and probably also in the West, including Italy.

Not withstanding this genealogical exposition, the meticulous scholar might judge the whole thesis to be an interesting hypothetical conjecture, unless supported by other concrete data, a requirement which Asin Palacios again fulfills with dexterity. He reminds us that Dante received his literary training from a Florentine encyclopedist named Brunetto Latini, who rose to the highest offices in the administration of the commune. Dante as a young poet enjoyed Brunetto's patronage and followed his counsel. The spiritual ties which bound master and pupil become evident in their discussions when they meet later in hell. The commentators on the "Divine Comedy" are agreed on this and even establish Brunetto's allegorical poem "Tesoretto" as one of Dante's sources of inspiration. What must be taken into consideration is that Brunetto himself had a taste of Arab culture when he was Florentine ambassador to the court of Alfonso the Wise in 1260. He also visited Toledo and Seville, where intense activity in the translation of Arab sources was afoot. His two main works, the "Tesoretto" and the "Tesoro," composed immediately after his return from Spain, reveal a strong Arabic influence. That Brunetto imparted to his disciple a high regard for the superior Arab culture seems to be a foregone conclusion. Many of Dante's statements in the "Divine Comedy" support this assumption, and it will be difficult to argue against that theory in the face of the textual similarity to ibn 'Arabi's "Mi'rāj."

Asin Palacios has made it obvious that the literary father of the Renaissance owed a share of the very texture of his immortal poem to Islamic mysticism, legend, and letters.

Bibliography

THIS bibliography is designed to suggest major avenues for research on the subjects covered in this volume: Crusade, Commerce, and Culture. Significant bibliographical works are listed, along with major encyclopedias and large reference works. Source collections of a monumental nature are indicated. A brief selection of secondary studies is provided.

The reader is urged to consult these works for further bibliographical information, because a wealth of material exists in past and current periodical literature, in the languages of almost all countries.

Finally, the reader is reminded that a companion volume by the author—*The Crusade: Historiography and Bibliography*—provides a more complete and partly annotated list of materials. One may find there a detailed topical analysis of the bibliography of the Crusades and the Crusade movement, sources both Eastern and Western, and secondary literature; and an Index topically designed to cover the contents (*e.g.*, The Art of War, The Military Orders of Religion, Romance Literature, The Counter-Crusade, Mongols and Missions, Geography, Travel and Atlases).

I. BIBLIOGRAPHICAL WORKS

American Historical Association: *Guide to Historical Literature,* ed. by G. F. Howe, G. C. Bryce, T. R. S. Broughton, H. F. Cline, S. B. Fay, M. Kraus, E. H. Pritchard, and B. C. Shafer, N.Y. 1961. (Replaces 1931 *Guide to Historical Literature.*)

Brockelmann, C.: *Geschichte der arabischen Litteratur,* 2 vols., Weimar 1898–1902; 2nd ed., Leiden 1943–49; Supp., 3 vols., Leiden 1937–42. (Register of Arabic works.)

Chevalier, C. U. J.: *Répertoire des sources historiques du moyen âge.* (a) Bio-bibliographie, 2 vols., Paris 1877–88; 2nd ed., 1905–07. (b) Topo-bibliographie, 2 vols., Paris 1894–1903.

Ettinghausen, R. (ed.) : *A Selected and Annotated Bibliography of Books and Periodicals in Western Languages dealing with the Near and Middle East,* 2nd ed. with Supp., Washington, D.C., 1954.

Golubovich, R. P. G.: *Biblioteca Bio-Bibliografica della Terra Santa e dell' Oriente Francescano,* 5 vols., Florence 1906–27. (A tremendous archival collection.)

Malclès, L.-N.: *Les Sources du Travail—Bibliographies Spécialisées,* 2 vols., Geneva and Lille, 1952. (Major guide to encyclopedias, dictionaries, reference works, manuals, histories, periodicals, and source collections.)

Mayer, H. E.: *Bibliographie zur Geschichte der Kreuzzüge,* Munich 1960. (Current and excellent.)

Molinier A.: *Les Sources de l'histoire de France des origines aux guerres d'Italie (1494)*, 6 vols., Paris 1901–06.

Paetow, A. C.: *Guide to the Study of Medieval History* (Medieval Academy of America), rev. ed., N.Y. 1931.

Pearson, J. D.: *Index Islamicus 1906–1955* (School of Oriental and African Studies, University of London), Cambridge 1958. (A catalogue of articles in periodicals and other collective publications. Current and excellent.)

Potthast, A.: *Bibliotheca Historica Medii Aevi (375–1500* A.D.), 2 vols., Berlin 1896.

Sarkīs, Yūsuf Eliās: *Mu'jam al-Kutub al-'Arabiyah wa-l-Mu'arrabah* (Dictionary of Arabic and Arabicized Books), Cairo 1928. (Lists all printed books in Arabic to 1919, with Supp. for publications after that date.)

Walford, A. J. *Guide to Reference Material,* London 1959. (A librarian's guide to reference works.)

II. LARGER REFERENCE WORKS

Cambridge Mediaeval History, ed. by J. B. Bury, 8 vols., Cambridge 1911–36.

The Catholic Encyclopedia, ed. by C. G. Herbermann *et al.,* 12 vols., illus., with Supp. and yearbook, N.Y. 1951 ff.

The Encyclopaedia of Islam, ed. by Th. Houtsma *et al.,* 4 vols., Leiden 1913, with Supp., 1933; 2nd ed. in progress, ed. by J. H. Kramers, H. A. R. Gibb, and E. Lévi-Provençal, Leiden and London 1945 ff.

Migne, abbé (ed.): *Dictionnaire historique, géographique et biographique des croisades (Nouvelle Encyclopédie Théologique,* XVIII), Paris 1852. (Old but still valuable.)

Roolvink, R., Roelof, *et al.; Historical Atlas of the Muslim Peoples,* Amsterdam 1957.

Shepherd, W. R.: *Historical Atlas,* 8th rev. ed., N.Y. 1956.

III. SOURCE COLLECTIONS

Bibliotheca Geographorum Arabicorum, 8 vols., Leiden 1870–94. (Basic starting point in study of Arab geography and contributions of Arab geographers. See Atiya: *Hist. and Bibl.,* Monumental Collections, section VII.)

Exuviae Sacrae Constantinopolitanae, 3 vols., Geneva 1877–78, and Paris 1904. (4th Crusade. See Atiya, *Hist. and Bibl.,* Monumental Collections, section IV.)

Histoire Littéraire de la France, 36 vols., new ed., Paris 1865–1949. (Attempt to publish entire range of sources, Oriental as well as Western. Work continued by Michaud: *Histoire des Croisades* and *Bibliothèque des Croisades* [see below]; and in *the Recueil des Historiens des Croisades* [see below]. Also consult Atiya: *Hist. and Bibl.,* Crusade Historiography.)

Michaud, J. F.: *Bibliothèque des Croisades,* 4 vols., Paris 1829. (Extracts from chronicles of France, England, Italy, Germany, northern Europe, Greece, Turkey, Armenia, Austria, Bohemia, Hungary, and from Arabic chroniclers. See Atiya: *Hist. and Bibl.,* Monumental Collections, section V.)

Palestine Pilgrims' Text Society Library, 13 vols., London 1890–97. (Pilgram source materials. See Atiya: *Hist. and Bibl.,* Monumental Collections, section II.)

Records of Civilization (Columbia University), N.Y. 1915 to date. (Includes such source translations as Ambroise: *The Crusade of Richard Lion Heart;* Pierre Dubois: *The Recovery of the Holy Land;* Helmold: *The Chronicle of the Slavs;* John of Salisbury: *De expugnatione Lyxbonensis;* Odo de Deuil: *De profectione Ludovici VII in Orientes;* Otto of Freising: *The Two Cities;* Otto of Freising: *The Deeds of Frederick Barbarossa;* Philip of Novara: *The Wars of Frederick II;* Robert de Cléry: *The Conquest of Constantinople;* Usāmah ibn Munqidh: *An Arab-Syrian Gentleman and Warrior in the Period of the Crusades;* J. F. Venette: *The Chronicle of Jean de Venette;* William of Tyre: *A History of Deeds Done Beyond the Sea.* See Atiya: *Hist. and Bibl.,* Monumental Collections, section VI.)

Recueil des Historiens des Croisades, Paris 1841–1906. *Historiens Occidentaux,* 5 vols. *Lois,* 2 vols. *Historiens Orientaux,* 5 vols. *Historiens Grecs,* 2 vols. *Documents Arméniens,* 2 vols. (See Atiya: *Hist. and Bibl.,* Monumental Collections, section I.)

Société de l'Orient Latin: *Archives de l'Orient Latin,* 2 vols.,

Paris 1881–84. (Inventory and description of varied source materials. See Atiya: *Hist. and Bibl.*, Monumental Collections, section II.)

———: *Série Géographique,* 5 vols., Geneva 1879–89. (Unpublished itineraries of pilgrims and travellers to the Holy Land.)

———: *Série Historique,* 5 vols., Geneva 1877–87. (Chronicles, correspondence, charters, and other historical documents.)

IV. SELECTED STUDIES

1. CRUSADE

Atiya, A. S.: *The Crusade in the Later Middle Ages,* London 1938.

Baldwin, M. W. (ed.): *The First Hundred Years* (Pennsylvania *History of the Crusades,* I), Philadelphia 1955.

Brockelmann, Carl: *Geschichte der islamischen Volker und Staaten,* Munich and Berlin 1939; trans: *History of the Islamic Peoples,* London 1949.

Cahen, C.: *La Syrie du nord à l'époque des croisades,* Paris 1940.

Grousset, R.: *L'Empire du Levant—Histoire de la Question d'Orient au moyen âge,* Paris 1946.

———: *Histoire des croisades et du royaume franc de Jérusalem,* 3 vols., Paris 1934–36. (Standard view that the Crusade movement ended with the 13th century.)

LaMonte, J. L.: "Crusade and Jihad," in *The Arab Heritage,* ed. by N. A. Faris, Princeton, N.J., 1944, 159–98.

———: *Feudal Monarchy in the Latin Kingdom of Jerusalem* (Medieval Academy of America), Cambridge, Mass., 1932.

Lane-Poole, S.: *History of Egypt in the Middle Ages,* new ed., London 1952.

Munro, D. C.: *The Kingdom of the Crusaders,* N.Y. 1935.

Ostrogorsky, G.: *Geschichte des byzantinischen Staates,* Munich 1940; English trans. by Joan Hussey: *History of the Byzantine State,* Oxford 1956.

Paetow, L. J. (ed.): *The Crusades and Other Historical Essays, Presented to Dana C. Munro,* N.Y. 1928.

Röhricht, R.: *Geschichte des Königreichs Jerusalem (1100–1291)*, Innsbruck 1898. (Monumental erudition.)

Runciman, S.: *A History of the Crusades,* 3 vols., Cambridge 1951–54.

Stevenson, W. B.: *The Crusaders in the East,* Cambridge 1907.

Vasiliev, A.: *History of the Byzantine Empire,* in 1 vol., Madison, Wisc., 1952.

Wolff, R. W., and H. R. Hazard (eds.): *The Later Crusades* (Pennsylvania *History of the Crusades,* II), Philadelphia 1961.

2. COMMERCE

Heyd, W.: *Geschichte des Levantehandels im Mittelalter,* 2 vols., Stuttgart 1879; standard French trans. by Furcy Reinaud and author: *Histoire du commerce du Levant au moyen âge,* 2 vols., Paris 1885–86; 11th ed., Leipzig 1936, reprinted 1959.

Lopez, R. S., and I. A. Raymond: *Medieval Trade in the Mediterranean—Illustrative Documents, trans. with Introduction and Notes (Records of Civilization)*, N.Y. 1955.

Pirenne, H.: *Economic and Social History of Medieval Europe,* 5th ed., N.Y. 1937.

Sapori, A.: *Le Marchand italien au moyen âge,* Paris 1952.

3. CULTURE

Arnold, T., and A. Guillaume: *The Legacy of Islam,* Oxford 1931. (Selected essays: e.g., geography, astronomy, science, minor arts, painting, architecture.)

Asin Palacios, Miguel: *La Escatología Musulmana en la Divina Commedia,* Madrid 1919; abridged English trans. by H. Sunderland: *Islam and the Divine Comedy,* London 1926.

Boer, T. de: *Geschichte der Philosophie im Islam,* Stuttgart 1901; English trans. by E. Jones: *The History of Philosophy in Islam,* London 1903.

Carra de Vaux, B.: *Penseurs de l'Islam,* 5 vols., Paris 1921–28.

Dodge, Bayard: *Al-Azhar—A Milennium of Muslim Learning,* Princeton, N.J., 1961.

Erlanger, R. d': *La Musique Arabe,* 6 vols., Paris 1930–59.

Farrukh, O. A.: *The Arab Genius in Science and Philosophy,* trans. by J. B. Hardie, Washington, D.C., 1954.

Gabriele, F.: *La Poesía araba e la poesía occidentale,* Rome 1943; new ed. (*Storia e Civita musulmana*), Rome 1947.

Gibb, H. A. R.: *Arabic Literature, An Introduction,* Oxford 1926.

Grünebaum, Gustave E. von: *Islam: Essays in the Nature and Growth of a Cultural Tradition,* Menasha, Wisc., 1955.

———: *Medieval Islam, A Study in Cultural Orientation,* 2nd ed., Chicago 1953. (Predominantly literary and religious.)

———: *Unity and Variety in Muslim Civilization,* Chicago 1955. (An evaluation of the important relations between the universal Muslim culture pattern and the diverse local traditions of Islamic countries.)

Haskins, C. N.: *Studies in the History of Medieval Science,* Cambridge, Mass., 1934.

Hell, J.: *Die Kultur der Araber,* new ed., Leipzig 1919; English trans. by S. Khuda Bukhsh, Cambridge 1926.

Huyghe, R. (ed.): *L'Art et l'Homme,* 2 vols., Paris 1957–58; see Vol. II: G. Wiet, "L'Islam et l'art musulman," 148 ff.

Khān, Mu'īd: "The Muslim Theories of Education during the Middle Ages," *Islamic Culture,* XVIII-1944, 418–33.

Leclerc, L.: *Histoire de la médicine arabe,* 2 vols., Paris 1876.

Lévi-Provençal, Évariste: *Islam d'Occident: études d'histoire médiévale,* Paris 1948. (Annotated edition of selected lectures and papers on cultural aspects of Islam in Spain and North Africa.)

Marçais, G.: *L'Art de l'Islam,* Paris 1946.

Neuberger, M.: *Geschichte der Medizin,* 2 vols., Stuttgart 1906–11; English trans. by E. Playfair: *History of Medicine,* 2 vols., Oxford 1910–25.

Nicholson, R. A.: *Eastern Poetry and Prose,* Cambridge 1922.

———: *A Literary History of the Arabs,* 2nd ed., London 1930.

———: *Studies in Islamic Mysticism,* Cambridge 1921.

———: *Studies in Islamic Poetry,* 2nd ed., London 1930.

O'Leary, De Lacy: *Arabic Thought and Its Place in History,* London 1954.

Sarton, George: *Introduction to the History of Science,* 3 vols. in 5, Baltimore, Md., 1927–48.

Schirmer, O.: *Studien zur Astronomie der Araber,* Erlangen 1926.

Thorndike, L.: *History of Magic and Experimental Science,* 6 vols., Cambridge, Mass., 1927–41.

Totah, Khalil A.: *The Contributions of the Arabs to Education,* N.Y. 1926.

Index

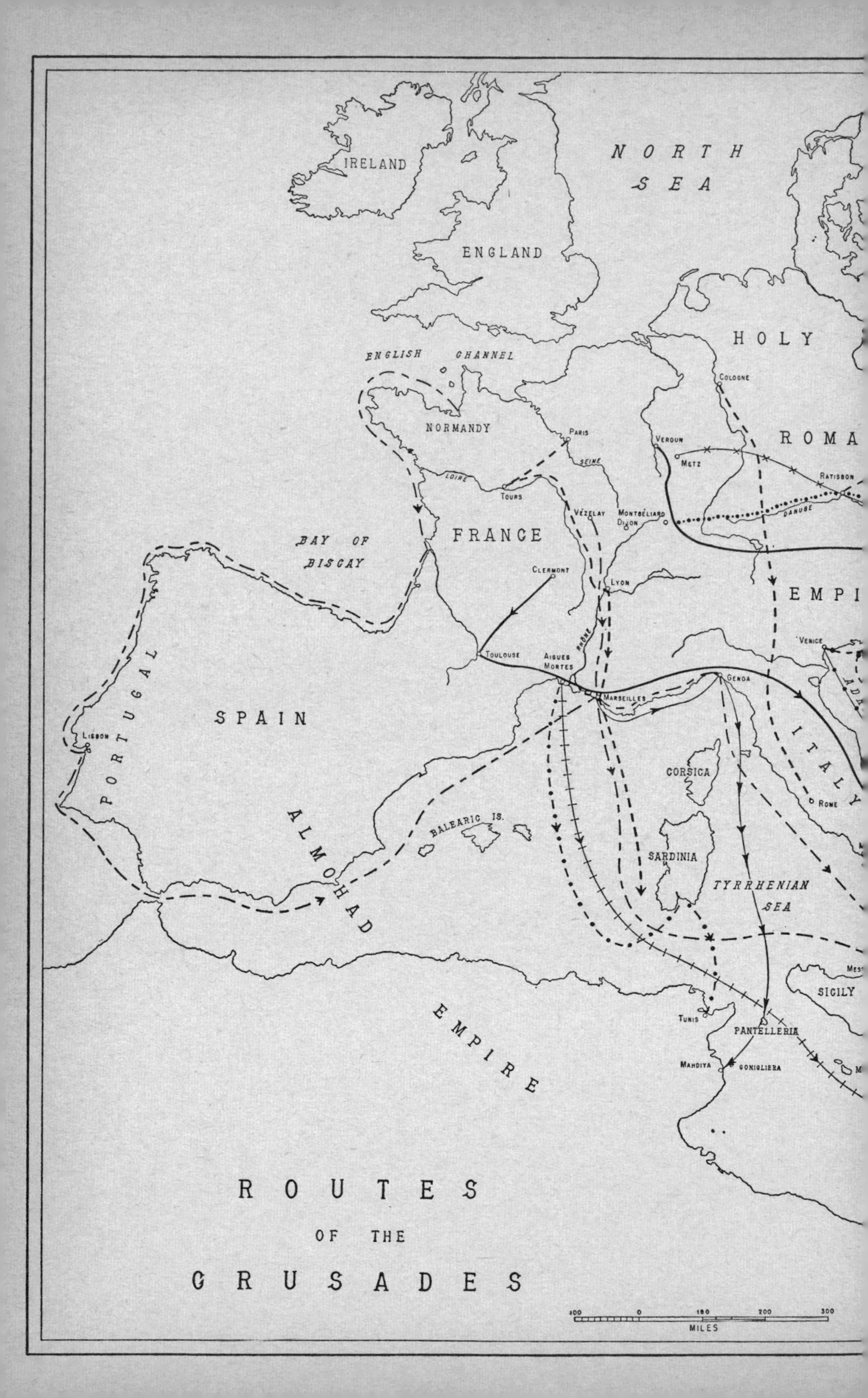

NORTH SEA
IRELAND
ENGLAND
HOLY
ROMA
EMPI
ENGLISH CHANNEL
NORMANDY
PARIS
SEINE
LOIRE
TOURS
VÉZELAY
MONTBÉLIARD
DIJON
VERDUN
METZ
COLOGNE
RATISBON
DANUBE
FRANCE
BAY OF BISCAY
CLERMONT
LYON
RHÔNE
TOULOUSE
AIGUES MORTES
MARSEILLES
GENOA
VENICE
ITALY
ROME
CORSICA
SARDINIA
TYRRHENIAN SEA
SICILY
SPAIN
PORTUGAL
LISBON
ALMOHAD EMPIRE
BALEARIC IS.
TUNIS
PANTELLERIA
MAHDIYA
GONIGLIERA
ROUTES OF THE CRUSADES
100 0 100 200 300
MILES

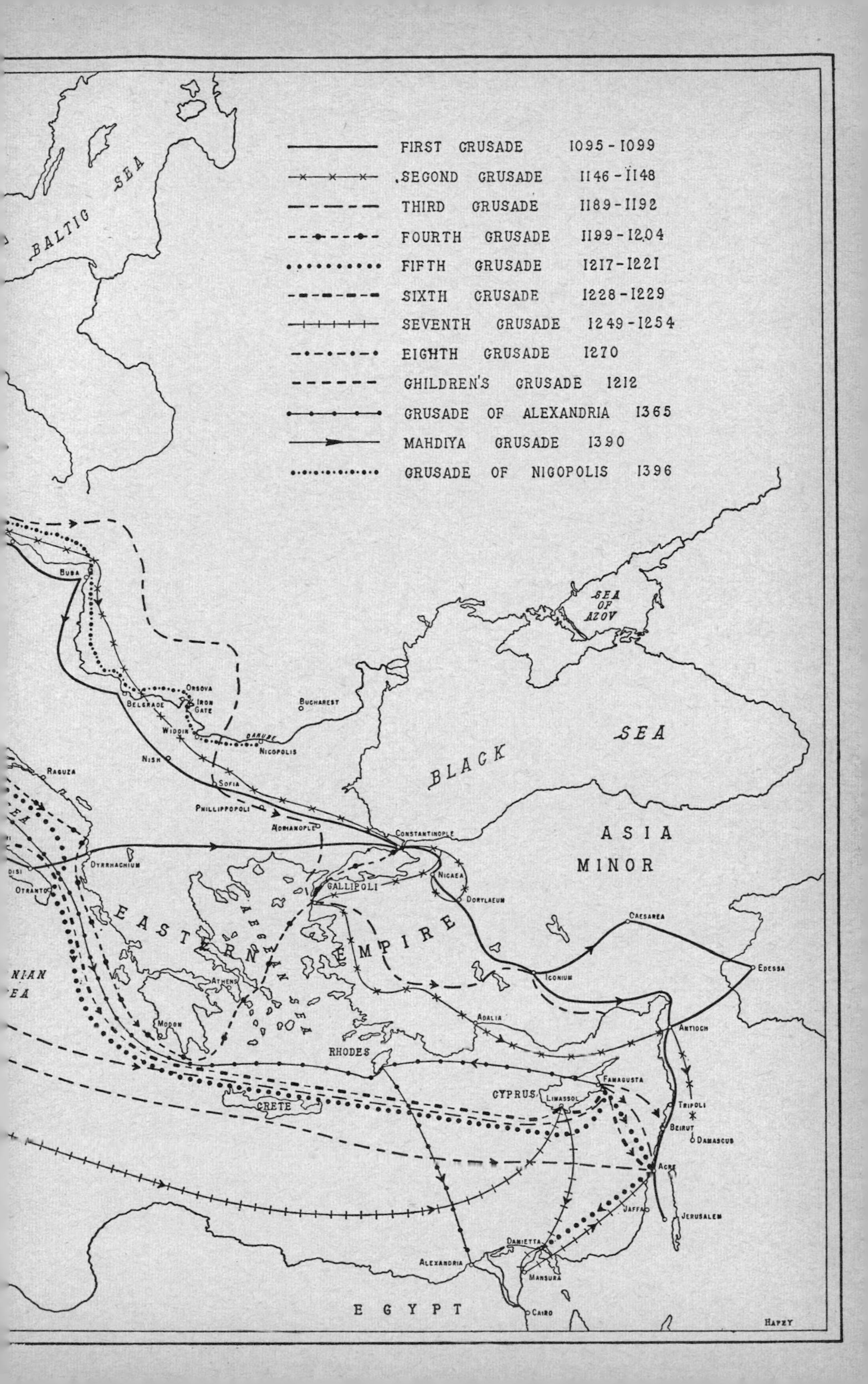

FIRST CRUSADE 1095-1099
SECOND CRUSADE 1146-1148
THIRD CRUSADE 1189-1192
FOURTH CRUSADE 1199-1204
FIFTH CRUSADE 1217-1221
SIXTH CRUSADE 1228-1229
SEVENTH CRUSADE 1249-1254
EIGHTH CRUSADE 1270
CHILDREN'S CRUSADE 1212
CRUSADE OF ALEXANDRIA 1365
MAHDIYA CRUSADE 1390
CRUSADE OF NICOPOLIS 1396
BALTIC SEA
SEA OF AZOV
BLACK SEA
ASIA MINOR
BUDA
ORSOVA
IRON GATE
BELGRADE
BUCHAREST
WIDDIN
DANUBE
NICOPOLIS
NISH
SOFIA
RAGUZA
PHILLIPPOPOLI
ADRIANOPLE
CONSTANTINOPLE
DYRRHACHIUM
OTRANTO
GALLIPOLI
NICAEA
DORYLAEUM
EASTERN EMPIRE
AEGEAN SEA
CAESAREA
EDESSA
ICONIUM
ATHENS
MODON
ADALIA
ANTIOCH
RHODES
CYPRUS
LIMASSOL
FAMAGUSTA
TRIPOLI
BEIRUT
DAMASCUS
CRETE
ACRE
JAFFA
JERUSALEM
DAMIETTA
ALEXANDRIA
MANSURA
EGYPT
CAIRO
HAPZY